COLORING THE NATION

Race and Ethnicity in the Dominican Republic

David Howard

Signal Books

Oxford

LYNNE
RIENNER
PUBLISHERS

Boulder

First published in 2001 by

Signal Books Limited
9 Park End Street, Oxford OX1 1HH, United Kingdom
www.signalbooks.co.uk

First published in North America by
Lynne Rienner Publishers,Inc.
1800 30th Street, Boulder, Colorado 80301, United States
www.rienner.com

A catalogue record for this book is available from the British Library.
Signal Books ISBN 1-902669-10-X Cloth
Signal Books ISBN 1-902669-11-8 Paperback

Library of Congress Cataloguing-in-Publication data
Howard, David, 1969-
        Coloring the nation: race and ethnicity in the Dominican Republic/ by David Howard.
p.cm.
        Includes bibliographical references and index.
        ISBN 1-55587-973-X (alk.paper) — ISBN 1-55587-998-5 (pbk.: alk. paper)
        1. Dominican Republic—Race relations. 2. Racism—Dominican Republic. 3. Race
awareness—Dominican Republic. 4. Ethnicity--Dominican Republic. 5. Dominican
Republic—Relations—Haiti. 6. Haiti—Relations—Dominican Republic. 7.Social classes—
Dominican Republic. I.Title.
     F1941.AS1 H69 2001
305.8'0097293—de21

                                                                          2001019097

Design and typesetting: WorldView Publishing Services
Cover image: Roger La Brucherie
∞ The paper used in this publication meets the minimum requirements of the
American National Standard for Information Science—Permanence of Paper for
Printed Library Materials, ANSI Z39.48-1984 and ISO 9706.
Printed in the United Kingdom by Biddles Ltd.

Contents

Preface

Coloring the Nation, David Howard's remarkable exploration of the role race and ethnicity have played in the formation of national identity in the Dominican Republic, makes several important contributions to the study of blackness in the modern world. The book brings current theories of race and class to bear meaningfully on the historically specific and culturally discrete Dominican case. Howard draws appropriate parallels that connect race matters among Dominicans to comparable experiences of race in the rest of the hemisphere, thus introducing regional context that has often eluded the works of those colleagues who have viewed the Dominican case as outright exceptional. Also, in *Coloring the Nation* Howard has admirably surveyed the existing bibliography while using to advantage the data collected through interviews in three well-chosen sites. On the whole, he has done the estimable job of bringing into scholarly visibility the Dominican story and has thereby revealed an empirical reality that might help other scholars expand their understanding of the tribulations of blackness and racial identity in the modern world.

The scholars who currently have risen to intellectual stardom by speaking about race and blackness, with the advent of cultural studies and post-colonial theory, do not exhibit any knowledge of the Dominican Republic, a country whose intercourse with blackness and African roots would seem incontestably to qualify it as an ideal candidate for induction into the watery corridors of the 'transcultural, international formation' that Paul Gilroy has called 'the black Atlantic'. The specialists in social dynamics of Latin America and the Caribbean, writing primarily in English in the United States and England, would do well to become acquainted with Dominican society. The titles of some of their most recent books include: *Race and Ethnicity in Latin America* (1997) by Peter Wade, *The Idea of Race in Latin America, 1870-1940,* edited by Richard Graham (1990), *African Presence in the Americas (1995)*, co-edited by Carlos Moore, Tanyia R. Sanders, and Shawna Moore, and the two-volume collection *Blackness in the Americas: Social Dynamics and Cultural Transformation* (1998), compiled by Arlene Torres and Norman E. Whitten. These fail to include Dominican society in their panoramic vistas of race in the hemisphere. Nor do Dominicans attain any particular prominence in *Africana: The Encyclopedia of the African and African American Experience* (1999), the compendium of knowledge on black people of the world gathered by Kwame Anthony Appiah and Henry Louis Gates, Jr.

Only with Peter Winn's *Americas: The Changing Face of Latin America and the Caribbean* (1999) do Dominicans attain center stage in the hemispheric discussion of blackness and racial identity. However, the 1992 PBS documentary on which the book is based offers a representation of Dominicans that borders on caricature. The program highlights the oddity of an African-descended people unable to come to terms with its own blackness. Clearly an astonishing occurrence for an audience socialized to view race as a biological fact, the reticence of Dominicans to privilege the African aspect of their heritage in their self-definition appears in Winn's documentary devoid of historical context. *Americas* does no better a job in that respect than *Wonders of the African World* (1999), the PBS documentary hosted by Henry Louis Gates, Jr. There the Harvard scholar regales the audience with a learned elder from the island of Lamu, just off the coast of Kenya in East Africa, who, despite his discernibly Negroid features, categorically defines his ancestry as Arabic rather than African. Similarly, another 'black looking' interviewee on the neighboring island of Zanzibar describes his heritage as exclusively Persian. The two documentaries, in failing to contextualize Dominican and East African racial discourses within discrete historical experiences, end up inviting perceptions that construe the interviewees' understanding of their self-identity as delusional. They do not study; they indict, in keeping with the attitude discernible in *The African Experience in Spanish America* (1976) by Leslie B. Rout Jr., who describes the Dominican Republic as an 'ailing' mulatto nation whose reticence to 'accept its racial image' indicates a state of collective self-deception.

The recent literature on blackness in the Americas has dealt with the Dominican case, then, in either of two ways: omission or trivialization. This might seem a strange lot indeed for a people whose land I have elsewhere had reason to call 'the cradle of blackness in the Americas'. Hispaniola received the first blacks ever to arrive in the Western Hemisphere. It inaugurated both the colonial plantation and New World African slavery, the twin institutions that gave blackness its modern significance. On this island in 1503, black maroons first raised their subversive heads, and there too the hemisphere's first black slave insurrection took place on December 27, 1522. The island eventually bifurcated into two contiguous colonial sites, a Spanish domain in the east and a French one in the west. The Dominican Republic, which came into being as an independent nation-state in 1844 by delinking from Haiti, which had unified the island under its rule 22 years earlier, broke the pattern of the typical independence movements in the region. Unlike those which usually achieved independence by separating from European colonial powers, the Dominican Republic attained selfhood by dissolving its ties to a former colony, a nation founded by ex-slaves.

The Dominican case broke with the normal regional pattern in other ways as well. Black Dominicans interrogated the ideology of the independence movement and succeeded in shaping the way the 'founding fathers' imagined the nation. Juan Pablo Duarte, the intellectual architect of the new republic, distinguished himself from the creole elites that championed independence projects in nineteenth-century Latin America in forging a nation-building doctrine that was devoid of racist formulations. He posited the vision of a multiracial society united by a common purpose: 'white, black/copper-skinned, cross-bred/Marching together/ United and daring/let us flaunt to the world/Our brotherhood/And save the fatherland/ From hideous tyrants.' On the surface these lines point to a racial ideology akin to the pluralism favored by the celebrants of Latin American *mestizaje*, a good many of whom managed to pay lip service to diversity while adhering to white supremacist social practices. However, Duarte went beyond the conundrum of *mestizaje*. He radically proclaimed an end to the 'aristocracy of blood'. He also avoided racial othering when articulating the need for separation from Haitian rule. The fact that once independence had been declared the nascent government quickly passed a resolution to reassure Haitians who wished to stay in the Dominican side of the island that no plans existed to expel anyone and that their 'physical safety and prosperity' would be protected may have emanated from Duarte's anti-racist legacy.

If the foregoing did not suffice to stress the richness of the Dominican field for any exploration of the tribulations of blackness in the modern world, the way the country wrestled with slavery and emancipation, culminating in anti-slavery policies of unprecedented radicalism, would most certainly help make the case. First in 1801 the liberator Toussaint Louverture came from Saint Domingue in western Hispaniola to Spanish Santo Domingo in the east and, having unified the island under the French banner he still represented, proceeded to abolish the 'peculiar institution'. Then in 1802, during the French invasion sent by Napoleon, the French commander who took over the

Spanish-speaking side of the island immediately reinstated it. Slavery would remain in effect—a couple of anti-slavery uprisings having failed—until 1822, when Haitian President Jean Pierre Boyer, effectuating another unification of the island, abolished it again.

With the birth of the new country, the independence movement having triumphed in 1844, the black and mulatto population pressured to have their freedom guaranteed. As a result, on March 1, 1844—two days after the founding of the nation—the newly formed government agreed to declare that slavery had disappeared 'forever' from the land. When the resolution was ratified as a law on July 17, 1844, it carried an article that penalized the slave traffic with capital punishment. Another stated emphatically that slaves coming from abroad would become automatically free upon setting foot on Dominican soil. This law becomes more radical if one remembers that slavery still existed in all of the Caribbean and most of Latin America. Since Spain still held on to slave-based economics in the neighboring colonies of Puerto Rico (until 1878) and Cuba (until 1886), enacting that law constituted a provocation to Spanish imperial authority in the region. For it created a lure that attracted runway slaves whose masters had no hope of reclaiming them once they entered Dominican territory. Black slaves escaped regularly from Puerto Rico to Santo Domingo from 1822 through 1878. In declaring the immediate change of status of the servile population from abject slavery to unqualified freedom, the policy surpassed any other emancipation declaration in the region in its adoption of human rights logic.

Needless to say, then, the Dominican case is one that merits attention by anyone seriously interested in exploring the complexity of race relations and the black experience in the modern world. Speculation on why scholars have so strongly ignored it may yield ground for discussing the geopolitical contexts that allow certain sites to emerge as exemplars of the human experience while others do not, regardless of epistemic value. But perhaps this panorama will change. And when it does, it will be due to important interventions like David Howard's *Coloring the Nation*, which has invested great intellectual energy in discerning crucial aspects of the story of blackness in the place where modern blackness—concurrently with modern world—actually began.

Silvio Torres-Saillant
Syracuse University, New York
January 2001

Acknowledgements

Firstly, I owe an enormous debt of gratitude to Colin Clarke for his friendship, scholarship and patience while guiding my stumbling steps through the course of postgraduate studies and research. Tutorials as an undergraduate with Colin during 1990 sparked off an interest in Caribbean societies, which I have been lucky enough to continue in subsequent years. This book arose from research undertaken for a D.Phil. thesis submitted to the University of Oxford in 1997.

I would also like to acknowledge the help and the inspiration that the late David Nicholls offered to me as a budding Caribbeanist. I have been fortunate to have had such enthusiastic mentors.

Although not mentioned individually, I would like thank friends and colleagues in various parts of the Dominican Republic, Europe, and the United States who have helped along the way. Harry Hoetink has offered invaluable support, criticism and hospitality during the course of my research. Sincere thanks to Ciudad Alternativa and EndaCaribe for their assistance in Santo Domingo; especially to Ada, Tití and Altagracia for their help during field work. I would also like to thank the three hundred Dominicans who made time for my interviews— I have learnt more from our conversations than I would ever be able to write down in a book. Names of interviewees in the text have been changed to maintain anonymity.

Thanks also to the following bodies for their generous financial support at various stages during the period of my research: Jesus College, Oxford; the School of Geography, Oxford; the Inter-faculty Committee for Latin American Studies, Oxford; the Dudley Stamp Memorial Trust; the John Brooks Travel Awards; the Cyril Foster Fund; the Sir George Labouchere Fund; and the Family Welfare Association. A semester at the Dominican Studies Institute at the City College of New York, funded by the Rockefeller Foundation, proved to be one of the many stimulating and enlightening periods that this research has offered. Many thanks to Silvio Torres-Saillant and Sarah Aponte for their immense help and friendship.

James Ferguson has been a great editor, while Abs and Tabs have provided large doses of help and fun at home. Final thanks are saved for my Mum, whose sacrifices have been far greater than her son could ever have so willingly endured, and for Dad, who'd be proud.

David Howard
Edinburgh, February 2001

Principal Research Sites

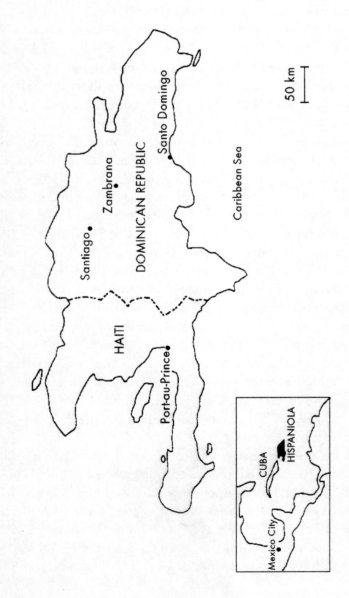

Santiago

Zambrana

HAITI

DOMINICAN REPUBLIC

Santo Domingo

Port-au-Prince

Caribbean Sea

50 km

Mexico City

CUBA

HISPANIOLA

1.
Introduction

'Dominican society is the cradle of blackness in the Americas'
—Torres-Saillant (1995, 110)

The Dominican Republic holds an important position in the context of today's Caribbean. Increasingly coupled with the United States via the transnational flows of people, capital and culture, Dominican society faces many challenges ahead: adaptation to the changing demands of external cultural, economic and political relations, and recognition of the internal tensions produced by a fraught civil history and contested social identities. The following chapters focus on the importance of race for the understanding of nation and ethnicity in the Dominican Republic, a situation in which racial ancestry and spatial proximity to Haiti are paramount.

Firstly, racial legacies are of primary importance among a Dominican population where cultural, linguistic and religious differences are limited. Racial differences are manipulated through the unequal standing and significance given to European, African and indigenous ancestries. European and indigenous heritages in the Dominican Republic have been celebrated at the expense of an African past. Secondly, Dominican identity is constructed *vis-à-vis* Haiti, most notably with respect to race and nation, and through the ancillary variables of religion and language. The importance of the Dominican Republic's shared insularity and shared history with Haiti is stressed, though a racially-constructed fault-line has arisen from this territorial and historical association.

The issue of race is fundamental to the discussion of nationalism in the Dominican Republic. The nation is a collective noun to represent a population, delimited by a territory, whether real or imaginary, which attaches that population to a place. Dominican nationalism has been colored by a pervasive racism, centered on a rejection of African ancestry and blackness. This exclusion of an African past and the manipulation of a European colonial legacy and indigenous heritage underpin the current analysis of Dominican society. *Negritud* is associated in popular Dominican opinion with the Haitian population. *Dominicanidad*, on the other hand, represents a celebration of whiteness, Hispanic heritage and Catholicism. The analysis of secondary material is contextualized throughout the book by in-depth interviews undertaken in three study sites: a low-income neighborhood and an affluent suburb in the capital, Santo Domingo, and a rural community in the central lowlands.

The Dominican Republic is part of the former Spanish Caribbean. Contrary to Commonwealth Caribbean beliefs, the Spanish colonial legacy is demographically and by land area the most significant in the region (Table 1). For almost two centuries after 1492, the entire Caribbean region was part of the Spanish colonial empire. The Hispanic Caribbean constitutes two-thirds of the regional population, and accounts for three-quarters of the land surface area.

Table 1. Caribbean Populations and Land Area

Region	Population	Land Area (000s kms)
Spanish-speaking Caribbean	22.6 million	175
(Cuba	11.0 million	1115)
(Dominican Republic	7.1 million	49)
(Puerto Rico	3.5 million	9)
Haiti	6.7 million	28
English-speaking Caribbean	5.0 million	25
French Caribbean	1.0 million	3
Dutch Caribbean	0.2 million	1
Total Caribbean	**35.5 million**	**230**

Sources: Population Reference Bureau (1998); Rayner (1996)

Race, racism and identity

Ethnicity is an umbrella term under which to group shared identities and the commonalities of race, nation, religion, aesthetics, language and kinship. Race, as a component of ethnicity, is created by attaching social and cultural significance to physical features or color, and then by grouping individuals according to phenotype. The quantitative and qualitative aspects of the Dominican Republic's demographic composition pose great problems of accuracy and applicability, given the ambiguities involved in the definition and ascription of race. Strict racial categories become meaningless, confusing or blatantly inaccurate depending on the viewpoint of the observer or statistician. A census in 1940 declared that *mulatos/as* made up 77 percent of the population, *negros/as* 12 percent and *blancos/as* 11 percent (Alvarez Perelló 1973, 68). In 1960, the enumerators of the national census were instructed to avoid registering Dominicans as *negro/a* where feasible, thus classifying less than a tenth of the population as such.

Results from the 1993 census have been published sporadically amid significant concerns of accuracy and authenticity. The Dominican Republic experienced two presidential elections in 1994 and 1996, during which the analysis and publication of complete census details was given marginal priority. Accusations of fraud surrounded the results of the 1994 election, and it is likely that it became politically expedient for the government to withhold accurate details of the electorate's size. Census material concerning race is therefore either unavailable or unreliable.

In general terms, social geographers would describe the Dominican population as *mulato/a*. Some authors divide the population up into various proportions—65 percent *mulato/a*, 15 percent *blanco/a* and 15 percent *negro/a* are commonly quoted figures, the remaining five percent of the population being made up of other ethnic groups, such as Chinese or Lebanese.[1] However, these figures are fairly meaningless. One author suggests that 96 percent of the Dominican population could be represented as *jabao*, describing a 'multiplicity of colors' (Corcino 1988, 18). Firstly, the continuum of skin color and phenotype does not fall into neat groups. Secondly, and more importantly, what to one person may be *mulato*, will be *negro* to another. Racial terms are highly specific to person and place. Thirdly, Dominicans describe race with a plethora of color-coded terms, ranging from coffee, chocolate, cinnamon and wheat, to the adoption of *indio/a*, a device which avoids using *mulato/a* or *negro/a*. The term *indio/a* is a key component of Dominican racial perception. It translates as 'indian', a much-used reference to the island's indigenous inhabitants before the arrival of Columbus in 1492.

Vega suggests that the refusal to acknowledge African ancestry was common thirty years ago, but that this perception has changed a great deal since then:

'With the possible exception of Brazil, we have the greatest racial mix. Our culture is, essentially, a half-caste one. There are no reliable statistics on this, but it is probably right to say that two thirds of our population are half-caste and the other third is divided into fifteen percent of genuine blacks and fifteen percent genuine whites. The mix is not just racially apparent. It comes out in all sorts of other ways too—in music, for example... We are the only country in the whole of Latin America not to have claimed our independence from Spain. We claimed ours from Haiti. And although that was halfway through the last century, there is still the idea that we have to look for a way of separating ourselves from the country which conquered us for more than twenty years, hence the temptation to seek in Spain something that will distinguish us from the other part of the island. It's a quest which has really lost its *raison d'être*. What we are looking for now is a way of maintaining our identity in relation to North America, not Haiti.' (interview, David 1992, 14-15)

Vega makes a salient comment regarding the importance of North American cultural influence with respect to Dominican society, but his words are otherwise heavily loaded with the conservative terminology and racist essentialism which, he argues, is redundant. He conceives race as a biochemistry of 'genuine' elements and 'half-caste' compounds. Race under these terms conflates biology, social experience and ethnicity, since it suggests that cultural traits are determined by genetic make-up. Musical ability thus becomes an outcome of the 'racial mix.'

Definitions of race and racism have filled many tomes of academic debate, frequently providing textual examples of the pervasive lack of action against racism. Racism remains a harsh fact based on theoretical fiction. Is the term 'race', as Montagu (1974) implies, so weighed down with false meaning that the use of the word is now untenable, provocative and dangerous? Or is there still room enough to use such a highly inflated and false theoretical concept by redirecting the evident potency of its use back upon itself? Williams (1983) argues that we cannot divorce words and concepts from the social context of their use. The discussion of race and ethnicity in Dominican society, whilst acknowledging etymological changes within racial discourse, is placed in the context of the everyday language of race.

Can we legitimately use the term 'race'? Race, as a biological category, does not exist. The range of human gene frequencies provides a correspondingly infinite kaleidoscope of body forms and colors. Grouping humans into biological categories of gene types has been recognized as a fatuous exercise, although terms such as Caucasian still appear in the popular media. Biological definitions linked to socio-cultural traits have long been refuted, and the arbitrary choice of gene-type frequencies to label 'race' groups has been shown to be worthless, leaving social scientists to delve into the social-psychological concept of race as a social construction. People recognize and endorse the hollowness of race, yet continue to believe in it, organizing their social relations accordingly. Race is therefore subjectively real, or as real as people want or believe it to be (Cashmore 1995, 268).

Identities are both inclusive and exclusive. This notion of inclusion and exclusion is again manifest in the well-worked ruminations concerning Self and Other. The concept of the Other errs towards the acceptance of strict dichotomies, the either/or rigidity that pigeonholes West and East, Black and White, Right and Wrong into binary, non-porous categories. Such dualism creates false structures biased towards established philosophies and reductionist analytical frameworks. Responses to the question, 'What does it mean to be Dominican?' frequently provoke the reaction, 'not Haitian.' The Other would appear to have significant potency in the construction of identity—not rich, not black, not gay, not from there—yet changes in near schizophrenic leaps depending upon the context of the situation. Schizophrenia splits the mind, incorporating contradictions and self-denials that are evident in the widespread Dominican negation of African ancestry and antagonism towards Haitians. The Other is invariably perceived as black, heathen and alien to white, Spanish *dominicanidad* or 'Dominicanness.' Haiti in popular prejudice, stands for all that is allegedly not Dominican: *négritude*, Africa and non-Christian beliefs.

A recent psychological study has emphasized the importance of the stigmatized Other in the construction of racial and ethnic prejudice (Westhoff 1993). In the Dominican Republic, popular belief about

Haitians provides the false stereotypes from which to construct an out-group, a coherent focus amid a confusion of racial visibility and explanation. An alternative interpretation of the contrasting medley of ethnic identities within and between Caribbean societies seeks order through the theory of chaos. Benítez-Rojo (1992) uncovers the confusion of syncretic cultures, and recounts their ordered repetition throughout the Caribbean islands, most notably via the framework of plantation society. The plantation, he argues, is the commonality from which to explore the region's ethnicities.

Identities hold a negotiated status, an amalgam of subjective and objective impulses negotiated by the researcher and the researched. Given the subjectivity of identity and its analysis, Geertz (1975, 20) outlines a best-guess policy:

> Cultural analysis is (or should be) guessing at meanings, assessing the guesses, and drawing conclusions from the better guesses, not discovering the Continent of meaning and mapping out its bodiless landscape.

Of course, the researcher will not know for sure which are the better guesses, but that remains the dilemma of research. The consideration of ethnicity and identity in the Dominican Republic can only be an interpretation of what the researcher perceives the situation to be, producing an analysis consisting of, one hopes, the better guesses. The following stanza was written at the beginning of the nineteenth century, and illustrates the transitional nature of identity through the changes in sovereignty experienced by the Dominican people:

> Yesterday I was born Spanish,
> In the afternoon I was French,
> By the evening I was Ethiopian,
> Today they say I am English.
> I do not know what I will be![2]

Within a shorter time scale, identity may be evoked instantaneously. A family member may not consciously register an ethnic identity whilst in the household, but only when confronted by forms of prejudice in the wider Dominican society. Identity only becomes a reality to the individual when certain responses are stimulated from a reservoir of identities capable of being summoned in differing contexts. This is fundamental to the analysis of identity as a transitory and situational reaction. The stimulation of racial identities will occur in a context where race is believed to be salient to the form of social interaction. Racism is often the basis for this identification.

Hall makes a distinction between overt and inferential racism. Inferential racism describes apparently naturalized or allegedly neutral representations of race based on the premise of unquestioned assumptions (Hall 1990, 12-13). Immigration, for example, is often opposed on the grounds that nationalism is a natural human response, rather than an exclusionary, racist reaction. Overt racism is the elaboration of an openly racist argument. Racist discourse tends to be polarized around issues of inferiority or superiority, subordination or domination, or expressed through a false history of naturalness. Inferential racism expressed in the literature and history of the Dominican Republic is well encapsulated by Hall's statement: 'The 'white eye' is always outside the frame—but sees and positions everything within it.' (Hall 1990, 14) This white bias in Caribbean social relations, the reification of the white aesthetic, is well documented. However, the eye does not have to be 'white' to cast a racist glare. Racial prejudice operates between and among all members of society.

Dominican society is, of course, not only subject to racial stratification, but divided by class relations. How does race relate to class in the Dominican Republic? Race is not reducible to class even when they become mutually entangled and enmeshed in societal structure. In Caribbean societies, neither race nor class may be dismissed. Hall (1980) adopts a useful approach to relations of race and class. He argues that social divisions can be explained largely by economic processes—race is the 'modality' through which class relations are experienced. Race is not reducible to class, but, in Hall's terms, social struggles may be 'articulated' through race. Race relations always operate within the framework of a class-based society.

The Dominican Republic has a specific history and physical location, which heavily influence the perception of race today. The population of eight million contains people of diverse origins, although Peréz Cabral (1967, 11) described the Republic as the only true *mulato* country in the world. However, the term *mulato/a* has seldom been used by Dominicans to describe their ethnicity. Historically, the Dominican elite emphasized strong European heredity and 'purity of blood'. Three groups formed the demographic basis for colonial society in the Dominican Republic—the indigenous population, Spanish settlers and African slaves. By the middle of the sixteenth century only a minute fraction of the indigenous population remained, although the notion of *indio/a* has become very much a part of contemporary Dominican identity. Lizardo (1979), in an analysis of African culture in the Dominican Republic, has attempted to incorporate *indio/a* into a racial classification of the population. Another survey stressed the importance of *indio/a* as an ethnic group rather than a mere notation of skin color (Alcántara Almánzar 1979). History has been re-negotiated, re-signified and reinvented to create a sense of the past appropriate to the social and political present.

Three statues outside the *Museo del Hombre Dominicano* in Santo Domingo tell a similar story. The statues, erected in the early 1980s, represent the figures of the indigenous leader Enriquillo, the African slave Lemba, and the Spanish priest Bartolomé de Las Casas. The inclusion of Lemba created some opposition to its position outside the national museum of Dominican culture. Lemba was the leader of an important slave rebellion against the Spanish colonists. African heritage is deemed unsuitable not only at the individual level, but also in institutional terms.

Aesthetics are a key aspect of Dominican race. In advertisements which ask for employees of 'good presence' there is an implied bias towards whiteness or *la blancura*. In Dominican banks, for example, color prejudice is most clearly seen at the cash desks. It is still rare for a major bank to be staffed in the public space by dark-skinned cashiers. The aesthetics of racism are illustrated in a study of university students who were asked if they would marry a darker-skinned partner. Fifty-five percent replied that they would not, frequently expressing their concern for the 'corruption' of physical appearance through 'race mixing' (Menéndez Alarcón 1987, 52). Subsequent writing by the same author outlines a basis of racist logic in the Dominican Republic, which is often portrayed as harmless, or disguised by a traditional rivalry with Haiti. Common sayings or popular folklore frequently incorporate racial or ethnic prejudice.[3]

African ancestry in Dominican society is largely ignored or denied. By downgrading African-Caribbean identity, aspirations for a lighter aesthetic automatically rise on the other side of the scale of perception. Hoetink writes that 'few Dominicans have not judged the period of Haitian domination as a black page in the history of a people that would have liked to be white' (Hoetink 1970, 117). Does this represent a clear aspiration to be *blanco/a*, or simply the wish not to be perceived as African-Caribbean? Many Dominicans are more concerned to disassociate themselves from Haiti than to claim 'white lineage.' A plethora of terms is used to avoid the implication of African ancestry. *Trigueño/a, rosadito/a, desteñido/a, rubio/a* and *cenizo/a* respectively refer to skin color as wheat-colored, rosy, faded, blond or fair, and dark or ashen. These terms are regularly applied to the slightest variation of color and tend to be wholly inconsistent and variable in their usage. The latter two, *rubio/a* and *cenizo/a*, are located at opposite ends of the color spectrum, but differentiation may be slight according to the context of their usage.

The aesthetic matters. Racial description frequently focuses on perceptions of ugliness and beauty. During an interview, Elena Garcia, conscious of her light skin color, combined her confusion of the racial complex with that of physical attraction: '*Prietos* (dark) *haitianos*, they're ugly. There are some *negritos dominicanos finos*. Not all are rough looking. Being *prieto* is the same as *azulito*... *Blancos*? They're too white... they've all been washed in milk!' Haitians, she says, are dark-skinned and ugly, and *blancos/as* are too pale. Some *negros* Dominicans may be good-looking, but not if their skin color is so dark as to appear blue (*azul*). The regular correlation of 'bad hair' and 'ordinary' features, and their juxtaposition *vis-à-vis* the desired traits of 'straight' hair and 'fine' features, manifests itself through a bias for European, and now North American, identity in terms of aesthetics and culture. The white bias, especially in elite circles, stems from a history of antagonism with Haiti.

Rafael Leónidas Trujillo, dictator of the Dominican Republic from 1930 to 1961, actively castigated Haitian and African ancestry. His grandparents were either *negro/a* or *mulato/a*, so he resorted to lightening his skin with cosmetic powders. Trujillo was acutely aware of his ethnic and socio-economic origins, having been born outside the traditional elite. Commissioned biographies stated that he was descended from a Spanish officer and a French *marquis*, and his parents were officially declared 'pure' French and Spanish.

Spain, the former colonial power, has frequently been celebrated in elite circles as *la Madre Patria*, and Europe was conceived as the source of Dominican culture and civility. In 1896, a Dominican writer constructed a 'mental photograph' of himself in a national newspaper, which illustrated his European aspirations (Hoetink 1982, 162). His musical and literary tastes were exclusively European, and his desired residence was Paris. None of the twenty statements, which he made about himself, included any reference to Dominican society. Whilst this bias has been substituted for a dependency on the United States in many aspects of Dominican life, the bias towards a light aesthetic remains fundamental to any consideration of contemporary social relations.

The location of research

Between 1992 and 1995, I lived in the Dominican Republic for a total of two years, conducting a series of interviews which form the basis for much of the subsequent discussion. Semi-informal interviewing of three hundred residents in three study sites focused on the issues of anti-Haitian sentiment and race in Dominican society. Two survey sites were urban neighborhoods in the capital city of Santo Domingo, and the other was an area of rural settlement around Zambrana. One hundred residents were interviewed in each site, and the duration of interviews ranged from thirty minutes to two hours.

The majority of interviews were carried out following the presidential elections in May 1994. The elections were of great significance, since the elderly, white President Balaguer was opposed, principally, by the late Dr Peña Gómez, a black politician of Haitian parentage. Given the long-standing and pervasive antagonism between Haiti and the Dominican Republic, and the evident racism in many aspects of Dominican society, the presidential elections became a bitter forum for thinly disguised racial politics. A second research visit to Santo Domingo during the summer of 1995 allowed further discussion and informal interviews to be carried out, this time during the run-up to the 1996 presidential elections, which were again characterized by a racialized political agenda. Whilst the survey results cannot claim to represent the views of an entire population of over eight million people, they nevertheless provide informative insights into the issues of race and ethnicity in the Dominican Republic.

The survey sites were chosen to provide a sample with a varied range of incomes and urban or rural experiences. Santo Domingo has a population of over 2 million people and is the capital of the Dominican Republic. Sixty percent of the Dominican population are classified as urban dwellers, with just under half of this urban population living in Santo Domingo itself. The national economy, however, is less marked by the urban primacy of Santo Domingo. The agricultural region of the Cibao in the north has always rivaled the capital's economy, and has traditionally been perceived by many as the cultural heartland of the country. During the last decade, with the expansion of export production zones and the tourist industry, secondary urban centers have experienced rates of growth above that of Santo Domingo. The economy on the whole is one of the poorest in the western hemisphere, heavily reliant on tourism, ferronickel extraction, telecommunications, migrant remittances and sugar production. Low labor costs have encouraged the growth of foreign-owned export manufacturing, located in free trade zones throughout the country.

The two neighborhoods in Santo Domingo chosen for interview work exhibited markedly different socio-economic profiles. The first site, Gazcue, is predominantly a middle and upper-middle-class neighborhood. Following the re-building of the city after severe hurricane damage in 1930, Gazcue established itself as an elite residential area. Today the neighborhood is still perceived as a well-to-do residential zone, although the upper classes began to move out to the more modern and affluent suburbs in the west of the city during the 1960s. The architecture of Gazcue is a mixture of modern apartment blocks and single-story nineteenth- and twentieth-century town houses. The Presidential Palace is located in the north-east corner of Gazcue, and ambitious redevelopment during the 1970s led to the construction of the *Plaza de la Cultura* in the northern half of the neighborhood, which houses the national theater, art gallery and museums. Several companies have set up offices in the area, combined with a number of successful small businesses, restaurants and hotels. Despite this affluence, a few areas of the neighborhood have become visibly run-down as the local property market stagnated during the 1980s. There have been recent calls for the government to recognize Gazcue as a national heritage site in an attempt to maintain the neighborhood's traditional 'character.'[4]

The second urban survey site, Los Guandules, is a low-income neighborhood, situated north of the city center, partly on marshland near the river. Los Guandules, the northern half of the district of Domingo Savio, originated during the late 1950s as a result of the relocation of city center residents by the government, and more importantly, due to the increasing influx of rural migrants to the capital. The population of Santo Domingo doubled to over 300,000 between 1950 and 1960, largely because of rural-urban migration. Many of these migrants settled to the north of the city center, establishing the area as one of working-class housing and squatter settlements, particularly along the banks of the River Ozama. These *barrios obreros* have been a traditional location for political militancy and civil unrest since the April Revolution of 1965, and continue to give rise to popular protests. The initial settlement of Los Guandules was consolidated during the 1960s with the construction of a primary school, church and surgery. However, an element of residential uncertainty remains. The area has been targeted for urban renewal by the government during the last five years to provide a site for a new wharf development. It is unlikely that such plans will come to fruition in the foreseeable future, but the threat of relocation and forceful government intervention remains.

Los Guandules can be divided into two sections: the upper part of consolidated, single-story concrete housing, and the lower, poorer section of shanty dwellings on the edge of the river. The latter area is frequently affected by flooding, yet the installation of basic drainage could improve the living conditions and health environment for the whole neighborhood. Over three-quarters of residents have no direct source of potable water, and, although the majority have access to electricity (especially in the upper section), the supply is usually tapped illegally making it irregular and dangerous.

The third study site is Zambrana, the name given to a dispersed collection of rural settlements in an area of mixed and subsistence farming in the center of the country. Several foreign-owned banana and pineapple plantations provide agricultural labor opportunities, although the majority of holdings are less than five hectares. Incomes in this rural region are low, generally much lower than those found in poor urban areas, and many households exist at the subsistence level. An agro-forestry initiative, begun in 1984 by the non-governmental agency Enda-Caribe, has developed a program of multiple cropping, diversifying local production from the traditional crops of coffee and cacao. Outside agriculture, the local economy and environment is dominated by the Falconbridge ferronickel mine and the gold mine of La Rosario Dominicana. The former Canadian company was handed over to Dominican management in 1986, although mining operations were curtailed dramatically in the 1990s due to falling profitability. The main river running through Zambrana has been contaminated by out-wash from the mine, and several residents were recently relocated by the mining company away from highly polluted sites.

Despite its position on a main road, Zambrana is a relatively remote location. There are no telephone lines, electricity mains or piped water supply. Lighting and the occasional television set are run off car batteries, and water is drawn from a series of wells located away from the contaminated groundwater near the mine. There are two primary schools, although secondary education requires a half-hour road trip to the regional urban center of Cotuí. A surgery, four small Catholic and two Protestant chapels are visited on a weekly or monthly basis by the doctor and priests who live in Cotuí.

Interviews in Los Guandules and Zambrana were undertaken with the assistance of two local organizations, Ciudad Alternativa and Enda-Caribe, respectively. Members of these organizations provided valuable introductions to influential community leaders and helped to establish recognition and acceptance for interviewing in the area. As a resident in Gazcue for much of the research period, the researcher's introduction to an interview sample in this location posed fewer problems of access. The timing and topic of the survey work were controversial, following the international denunciation of fraudulent presidential elections in the Dominican Republic, in which the losing candidate also endured a long-running series of racist attacks as a result of his Haitian ancestry. National strikes and brief incidents of civil protest hindered research work at times, but overall the salience of the topic made respondents more ready to express their opinions and offer comments, since the very same issues were topics of popular conversation at that time.

Socio-economic differences between the survey sites are obvious even to the casual observer. A walk through the paved streets of Gazcue might be accompanied by the sound of classical music playing on an expensive stereo system, or by the crowd noise from a World Cup soccer match being broadcast live by cable television. In contrast, the dirt tracks of

Zambrana linked remote clusters of houses, where the quiet of the landscape was occasionally broken by the *bachata* or *merengue* blaring out from the bass-bereft loudspeakers of a village store or *colmado*. The densely packed neighborhood of Los Guandules resonated more frequently to the frenetic tunes of the *merengueros*, but it was also the site of regular typhoid outbreaks. In order to illustrate concern over conditions of urban poverty, a national newspaper published a front-page photograph of three children in Los Guandules playing in the highly polluted waters of the Ozama river.[5]

The definition of race in the Dominican Republic is related very closely to aesthetics—people have 'fine' or 'bad' hair, a 'clear' or 'burnt' complexion. An investigation carried out by a Dominican researcher in the 1970s attempted to define and categorize Dominican racial characteristics, by analyzing skin color, hair color and type, as well as eye color among forty-eight interviewees in the city of Santiago. The study tried to classify people into five racial categories based on physical appearance, but used implicitly derogatory labels such as 'bad' and 'good' hair, and 'fine' and 'ordinary' features. By definition, *negros/as* and *mulatos/as* had 'bad' hair.

Social prejudice is frequently phrased in aesthetic terms, and being *blanco/a* remains a social and aesthetic ideal for many. The subjectivity of race is shown by the discrepancy in the usage of the term *mulato/a*. In parts of the former British Caribbean, the term mulatto incorporates the notion of a lighter aesthetic, having been associated during colonial times with the legal category of freepersons. Whereas many outsiders may view the Dominican population as *mulato/a*, within the country itself, the term is seldom used since it projects the negatively perceived image of African ancestry. This negation of African descent is the key to an understanding of race in the Dominican Republic.

Racial subjectivity is clear when the researcher's ascriptions are compared with the self-descriptions of interviewees. From the author's perspective, over two-thirds of the sample population could be described as *mulato/a*. The vast majority of those interviewees described as *blanco/a* were from the Gazcue sample, with *negros/as* concentrated in Los Guandules and Zambrana. The author's ascriptions differed markedly from the self-descriptions of race among interviewees. For the sample more respondents described themselves as *blanco/a* than would have been apparent at first sight. With respect to *mulato/a* and *negro/a*, the differences are more marked—only 5.3 percent and 6.0 percent respectively of interviewees used these terms. In addition, *negro/a* was used predominantly in the more affluent neighborhood of Gazcue, rather than in the lower income areas of Los Guandules and Zambrana. *Indio/a* was employed by over half of all interviewees to describe their race. This symbolic reference to an indigenous past is crucial for an explanation of the Dominican racial complex. *Mestizo/a* is used to a limited extent, largely due to the popularity of *indio/a*. *Moreno/a*, again seldom used as a term of racial self-description, may be translated as 'brown.'

Dominican identity incorporates a racism that is more often insidious than overt. Manuel Comas, resident in Gazcue, described himself carefully as *trigueño* and outlined the problems of dark skin color: 'Socially, to be *blanco* is an advantage. It's never mentioned openly, but inwardly there is a real sentiment that says *'that negro.'* *Trigueño/a* is a term used by Dominicans to stress their generally lighter skin color that refers to the color of wheat. Ignacio Brito, living in Los Guandules, agreed that racism exists, although it is usually expressed in a covert manner or in terms that are popularly accepted as derogatory: 'There's racism. Nothing's happened to me, but if two people are arguing, and one is slightly lighter than the other, he'll call the other *negro*.' The interviewee described himself as *negro*, but said that he too would use the same term as a mark of disparagement, but in a different tone.

Issues of race, nation and ethnicity are discussed in a variety of contexts. The underlying prejudice against African ancestry, its 'common sense' expression through anti-Haitian sentiment, and the ensuing practices of discrimination are the foci on which the discussion is structured. The first two chapters outline the nature of the research, then introduce the historical basis of race in the Dominican Republic, examined in the context of relations with Haiti. The development of Dominican society from the colonial period is presented, and the influence of anti-Haitian sentiment and the use of *indio/a* as an ambiguous racial term discussed with reference to contemporary opinion.

The third chapter opens up the analysis of social differentiation in the Dominican Republic by considering the role of class and its implication for racial identification. I then address the role of race in popular culture, with a specific focus on the household. Racial terminology is frequently used in combination with the presuppositions inherent in a patriarchal culture. Women's roles are reviewed with particular reference to household structure, occupation and the gendered nature of race under patriarchal norms. The domestic or private sphere is a key site for the expression of patriarchy, but it is also the location for the practice of Afro-syncretic religious beliefs, which themselves are racialized and gendered. Aspects of race in everyday lives, thus, are inherently gendered, domesticated and sanctified.

Chapter five expands the analysis of race to include the influence of international migration on Dominican racial identification. The Dominican Republic is a transnational society that relies on migrant remittances and commerce, in particular from the migration of Dominicans to the United States. International migration has dramatically shaped Dominican society over the last three decades. The last two substantive chapters focus upon the specific aspects of race and nation as revealed through contemporary Dominican literature and politics. The first reviews the importance of *negritud* in contemporary literature, and argues that many modern writers maintain idealized and misleading perceptions of the racial reality. The second concentrates on the impact of race during the Dominican elections in 1994 and 1996. Overt racial prejudice marked the campaigns of leading political parties, and the alleged Haitian 'threat' to Dominican sovereignty became a dominant item on the election agenda. Finally, the concluding chapter outlines existing theories of race and ethnicity, analyzing their applicability to the Dominican situation and suggesting alternative viewpoints in the light of the current research. It is suggested that the promotion of a popular ideology of multiculturalism could provide the basis for effective anti-racist policy in the Dominican Republic.

2.

La Raza Dominicana and Haiti

'Few Dominicans have not judged the period of Haitian domination as a black page in the history of a people that would have liked to be white.'
—Hoetink (1970, 117)

La raza dominicana, traditionally, represents whiteness, Catholicism and a Hispanic heritage. It clashes dramatically with the popular Dominican image of Haiti—one of *negritud* or blackness, *vodú* and African ancestry. Bluntly, *la raza dominicana* defines an alleged difference between the civilized and the savage—a sentiment that is regularly expressed in everyday language, in the newspapers and in contemporary literature. The manner in which race and ethnicity have been constructed in relation to Haiti has colored, or perhaps more accurately bleached, the image of the Dominican nation.

Historical notions of *la raza dominicana* have combined overt racism and nationalism. Rather than be translated directly as race, *la raza*, in this context, refers more openly to race and nation. When Dominicans talk of *la raza* it may include color, phenotype, nationality or cultural traits. Whilst interviewing residents in Gazcue, Juana Peña Richardo outlined her views on the racial make-up of Dominican society, 'Most people here are *negros. La raza blanca* is a mixture—Jews, *blancos*, Arabs, Chinese... But I'm *blanca*, my family is Spanish. My husband, well, he's pure European. His parents are Italian and Spanish.' She clearly illustrates the importance placed on a light aesthetic and European heritage, particularly among the affluent classes. Her comments are typical of many Dominicans who are able to claim direct familial links with Europe to confirm their racial ancestry. *La raza blanca* translates literally as 'the white race', but *la raza* is more readily interpreted here as ethnicity, where it acts as an umbrella term to incorporate notions of race and nation. *La etnia* or *la etnicidad* are seldom-used terms in Dominican vocabulary.

The history of the Dominican Republic is ultimately tied up with that of Haiti. The neighboring population has always acted as a scapegoat for Dominican woes, and popular anti-Haitian sentiment has often been deployed by the Dominican elite to further their nationalist projects, not least under the regime of Trujillo, which is discussed later. A comparison of socio-economic indices between the Dominican Republic, Haiti and the United States, illustrates quite substantial differences between the three countries (Table 2). The severity of Haitian poverty is much greater than that of the Dominican Republic. The United States is a dominant influence in both countries, culturally, economically and politically—not least because the United States military occupied each state during the first two decades of the twentieth century, and invaded the Dominican Republic again in the 1960s and Haiti during the 1990s. Literacy rates, urban infrastructure and health services are generally of a higher standard in the Dominican Republic than in Haiti, which is economically one of the poorest countries in the world.

The Dominican Republic has a stronger economy, which was formerly focused on the export of four agricultural products—sugar, coffee, cacao and tobacco. Sugar production made up 43 percent of export earnings, but its continued decline in importance meant that it represented only 8 percent in the 1990s. The four main export crops now account for only 13 percent of Dominican income, as tourism, export manufacturing and migrant remittances have become the main income generators.

The higher fertility and more rapid population growth rates of Haiti are important for many Dominicans' assessment of the so-called 'Haitian threat'—an exaggerated fear of the 'silent invasion' (through clandestine migration) as a result of which the Dominican Republic will be inundated by Haitians. The key component to this fear is that of race. Despite the malleable and subjective nature of racial difference, Haitians tend to have a darker phenotype or skin color than Dominicans. This difference has been a cause of two centuries of racist antagonism between the countries. It should be remembered that racism flows both ways. Although the focus is upon anti-Haitian sentiment among Dominicans, Haitians share similarly prejudiced views of Dominicans. Dominican women are typically depicted as prostitutes, owing to the relatively large number of Dominican-managed brothels and beauty salons in Port-au-Prince. Haitians naturally resent the frequent, and often discriminatory or violent repatriation of Haitian migrants from the Dominican Republic. Statements of mutual political rapprochement between the two governments have in recent years been announced simultaneously with forced repatriations. Several Dominican authors have suggested that the antagonism between Haiti and the Dominican Republic has been deliberately propagated by foreign powers in an attempt to weaken the island's economy and encourage external intervention. Múnoz (1995, 210), for example, claims that the conspiratorial aims of European and North American powers are the main basis for long-standing enmity and division in Hispaniola.

Table 2. Comparative indices for Haiti, the Dominican Republic and the United States, 1998

	Dominican Republic	Haiti	United States
Population	7.1 million	6.7 million	258.3 million
Population 'doubling time'	31 years	25 years	92 years
Fertility (average number of children per woman)	3.3	6.4	2.0
Child Mortality (per 1000 live born)	43	105	9
Annual GNP per capita	US$950	US$370	US$22,560
Literacy Rate male: female	77:78	35:40	-
Urban Population (% of total population)	60	44	75
Drinking water in urban: rural areas (% of each population)	78:32	59:32	100:100

Sources: UNDP 1997; World Bank 1999

Race and the development of Dominican society

Dominicans frequently talk of the 'race problem.' Dr Joaquín Balaguer (1947, 124), the former President of the Republic, has written that 'the race problem... is the principal problem of the Dominican Republic.' The 'problem' of race is usually deployed in the context of racial mixing, particularly with regard to the immigration of Haitians and the immediate concern to protect *dominicanidad*—an appeal to the elusive identity of the Dominican nation. Guzmán (1974, 42) remarks in her study of the central region of the Dominican Republic on 'the blurry borderline between the races,' which makes the differentiation of people so subtle that distinction at the individual level becomes completely arbitrary and subjective.

Race has been considered, historically, from biological and social perspectives. In the racial theories of the nineteenth century, racist ideology was rooted in biology—race was a physical characteristic determined by genetic heritage. The ideology of scientific racism suggested that the human species could be divided into a number of fixed biological categories, which determined individual behavior and cultural variation. It was argued that the races of the human population could be ranked hierarchically in terms of biological and cultural superiority. Race has since been viewed as a social construction rather than as a natural division of mankind. Van den Berghe (1967) outlines race as a group that is defined socially through physical criteria, and, thus, is devoid of objective reality outside of its social definition. Similarly, Guillaumen (1972) argues that race is found in symbolic form but not as a real object; race exists only in discourse, and racism is transmitted through this discourse to legitimate domination.

The genetic make-up of features evidently influences the perception of race. Hoetink (1982, 188) comments that 'social prejudice against the black was, and is, ... phrased in terms of aesthetic aversion.' A light skin color has continued to be the social and aesthetic ideal, as defined by society. This underlines the simultaneously inclusive and exclusive nature of racial prejudice—by defining oneself or identifying another as 'us', a statement immediately is made about 'them.' Thus, 'where *ego* identifies *alter* as a member of a particular 'race'... *ego* is necessarily also defined as a member of a particular 'race'" (Miles 1987, 27). The social recognition of race often varies greatly from individual appearance, which produces a transient, malleable conception of race in everyday discourse. The concept of race as a 'problem' in the Dominican Republic is fundamental to the perception of racial identity, but first the demographic history of the country must be outlined.

Three broad ethnic groups initially formed the basis for colonial society in Santo Domingo, the name given to the Spanish colony on the island of Hispaniola. These groups were the indigenous population, African slaves and the Spanish colonialists. The first group has left few obvious traces today because of its rapid extinction. When Columbus arrived on the island of Hispaniola in 1492, the indigenous population was around 400,000 (Moya Pons 1995). A census taken in 1508 accounted for an indigenous population of only 60,000. A little over a decade later there were no more than 3,000 Arawaks left, the rest having been killed in combat, through forced labor or by illness brought over by the colonialists and African slaves. Watts (1987, 110) adds that suicide via the consumption of untreated roots of bitter manioc was common. The size and demise of the indigenous population is a contentious issue. Other estimates suggest that this population ranged from 100,000 to four million. If the larger figures are accepted, then the decline of the indigenous groups becomes all the more notable.

The indigenous influence today in Dominican society is limited to certain foods such as cassava bread; the construction of some rural housing; fishing techniques; words such as *bohio* (hut), *huracán* (hurricane) and *hamaca* (hammock), and the names of physical features, places or administrative demarcations. Modern versions of indigenous domestic tools include wooden implements and earthenware designs. Words and artifacts aside, the influence of the indigenous past is most significant in contemporary notions of Dominican racial identity.

The African heritage, long neglected or denied by many Dominicans, is denigrated in both elite and popular cultures. Indigenous heritage has consistently been upheld in contrast to the devaluation of African influences in the Dominican Republic. Hoetink (1982, 185) notes the limited African influence in traditional Dominican folklore. The slavery debate during the sixteenth century sought to determine whether the indigenous people could be potential converts to Christianity, or whether they should be deemed savages, who were unable to be baptized and thus receive the sacrament. Antón de Montesinos first spoke out against the exploitation of the indigenous population in 1511. Bartolomé de Las Casas then argued that the Arawaks were created as humans by God, and should therefore be treated as Christian equals (Sanderlin 1971, 100-

102). His decision, which he later renounced, was to import slaves from Africa to replace the indigenous laborers, since the former were allegedly less able to grasp the Christian faith. Thousands of Africans were employed in the Dominican sugar mills and plantations, which developed from the 1520s onwards. By the middle of the sixteenth century, there were approximately 13,000 African slaves on the island of Hispaniola, and Santo Domingo was the main slave entrepôt for the region (Watts 1987, 123).

The importance of slavery in the Spanish colony of Hispaniola declined with the growing competition for sugar production, especially from Brazil. In addition, most early colonists moved to the mainland of Latin America where silver and gold were said to be abundant. The sugar plantation economy deteriorated during the sixteenth century as the world market for sugar collapsed, and the slave population was severely affected by epidemics during the sixteenth and seventeenth centuries. The economy became concentrated on cattle rearing which was far less labor intensive than sugar production, and limited the supervision required of the slave labor force. In 1794, out of a total Dominican population of 103,000, there were only 30,000 slaves and 38,000 freed former slaves (Hoetink 1982, 82). The number of slaves remained relatively low in relation to the Spanish settlers.

Del Castillo and Murphy argue that the violent imposition of European culture upon African slave labor reduced the possibilities for the transfer of material culture from Africa to the colonies. Thus, 'the contribution of the African ethnic groups to the Dominican society are found predominantly in the areas of religious expression and beliefs, music and dance, certain characteristics of expressive culture and speech, family organization and particular funerary rites' (del Castillo and Murphy 1987, 50). The syncretism of African religions and Catholicism resulted in the fusion of Catholic saints with corresponding African deities. Brotherhoods or *cofradías* existed as organized cults dedicated to specific saints, for example San Juan Bautista in Baní, and Peravia and the Virgen de Dolores in Los Morenos. As part of these cults, specific music and dance forms have developed such as the *sarandunga* in Baní. Dominican Spanish vocabulary shows a similar legacy of African slavery where words have entered common usage, for example *la bachata* (a popular form of music), *el guineo* (banana) and *el baquiní* (a funeral ritual).

Moya Pons (1986, 238) lists the three key factors of *hispanidad* as Spanish heritage, white skin and Catholicism. Spanish laws, religion, architectural styles, political structures and language clearly stamped their mark on the country as an Iberian outpost. The five-hundredth anniversary in 1992 of the arrival of Columbus to the island was a government and Church-inspired celebration of *hispanidad* and evangelization. The myth of the superiority of *hispanidad* was the ideological mechanism used by the light-skinned elites to maintain dominance. This backbone of racist ideology is illustrated by the concern over the immigration of workers from the Lesser Antilles and Haiti to work in the sugar industry at the end of the nineteenth century. Exaggerated fears that the Hispanic culture would be swamped led to subsequent attempts to 'lighten' the population by encouraging white immigration, preferably directly from Europe. As the sugar industry has declined, many Dominicans have expressed concerns over the ability of the state to control potentially restless, unemployed immigrant labor and squatters on the plantations.

Immigration has been important in the development of the Dominican population which grew in influence during the nineteenth century with the introduction of agro-export capitalism, and the development of the modern sugar industry from the 1870s. Large-scale intensive sugar cultivation in the Dominican Republic led to the denationalization of Dominican territory and the growing influence of foreign business interests (Baud 1987). The impact of sugar production was regional: dozens of sugar mills were constructed in the south-west near Barahona and Azua, on the south-east coastal plains and in the north near Puerto Plata, as well as around the outskirts of Santo Domingo. The industry was financed largely by Cuban, Puerto Rican, North American, English, French, German, Italian, Spanish and some Dominican business interests, who soon established themselves as powerful urban elites.

From the beginning of the twentieth century, significant numbers of Chinese arrived in the country, many arriving from other Caribbean islands such as Cuba. Later, after upward socio-economic mobility and the more recent arrival of middle income groups from Taiwan and Hong Kong, many Chinese immigrants established small businesses and manufacturing enterprises. The Lebanese are another influential ethnic minority who began migrating to the Dominican Republic towards the end of the nineteenth century, and who have firmly established themselves in the political, economic and social spheres of national life. Collectively known as *árabes*, migrants from the countries of the Middle East often settled in Santo Domingo, their first port of entry in the Caribbean. It was common for many to change their Arabic names to Spanish equivalents which, combined with success in commerce and politics, aided their rapid assimilation into Dominican society (Inoa 1991). Lighter skin color also helped to limit overt racial discrimination against them.

The *cocolos/as* were black migrant workers who were contracted largely from the British territories of St Kitts, Nevis and Anguilla to work on sugar plantations between the 1880s and 1920s. They faced high levels of discrimination from Dominicans since they worked for lower wages and were a distinctive target for racial prejudice. Complaints were often printed in local and national newspapers that suggested that they were 'ruining the labor market' (Plant 1987, 18). The migration of *cocolos/as* ended during the occupation of the country by the United States between 1916 and 1924 when the North American authorities announced that immigration would be prohibited 'for any race except Caucasian' (Plant 1987, 19). Paradoxically, the Haitian presence increased throughout the 1910s and after, as a result of being contracted to work on Dominican sugar plantations. It has been suggested that racism in the Dominican Republic was given a substantial impetus during this period from the dissemination of racial prejudice by the United States' soldiers and administration (Castor 1983).

Despite anti-*cocolo/a* campaigns and resistance from the white and merchant elites, *cocolos/as* consolidated their presence, founding many Protestant churches and greatly influencing the society of former sugar centers, particularly around the area of San Pedro de Macorís in the south-east of the country. The success of some of the *cocolo/a* population required a social reconstruction of race that employed lighter color terminology. This enabled the immigrants to distance themselves from the increasing numbers of Haitian immigrants:

> Their superior formal education, strict child rearing practices, discipline in the capitalist system, the ability of most to speak to the North American plantation owners and managers in English, and the specialized skills of many, converted the image of these Black immigrants in the Dominican society to that of the *negros blancos*. (Del Castillo and Murphy 1987, 57)

Following the sharp fall in sugar prices during the 1920s, the *cocolo/a* labor force on the sugar plantations came to be replaced by migrant Haitian laborers, who worked for much lower wage rates. Haitian migrant labor has a history of employment in the neighboring Dominican Republic, but the number of workers substantially increased during the United States' occupation of the Dominican Republic and Haiti (1915-1934). Haitian cane cutters have been employed in Dominican sugar mills since the 1880s, although Cuba was the favored destination until Fulgencio Batista ordered the mass expulsion of Haitians from Cuba in 1937. This was the same year during which thousands of Haitians were massacred in the Haitian-Dominican borderlands by the Dominican dictator Rafael Leónidas Trujillo. The policy of the dictatorial regime was to strengthen an Hispanic national identity, whilst contradictorily relying on the exploitation of Haitian labor. Trujillo himself was one of the major employers of Haitian contract labor since virtually all of the Dominican sugar industry came under his personal control by the 1950s. By the time of his assassination in 1961, Trujillo controlled eighty percent of the country's industrial production, and approximately sixty percent of the population relied directly or indirectly upon his patrimony for employment (Hartlyn 1993, 155).

Plant (1987, 69) argues that whilst Dominican migration to the United States acted as a safety valve during the 1960s, a key stage in the development of anti-Haitian rhetoric was the legalized abolition of tenancy arrangements. This, together with the stipulation that tenured lands be granted to the former tenants, played an important part in displacing Haitian labor to other parts of the economy. A recent survey of Haitian labor suggested that whilst under 20 percent worked in the sugar industry, 8.3 percent were employed in the construction industry, 8.3 percent in commerce and 7.2 percent in domestic service (Doré Cabral 1995). Plant (1987) claims that the agrarian reforms in 1972 also encouraged a preference for undocumented Haitian labor. This resulted in heightened antagonism towards Haitian workers as immigrants increased the demand for subsistence plots, and allegedly deprived Dominicans of cash income from casual labor.

Popular media attention highlighted the Haitian influence in the economy, and subsequent pressure led the Dominican government to pursue a policy of forced repatriations which continued throughout the 1990s. Between November 1996 and January 1997, 15,000 Haitians were deported during a renewed wave of government activity. Haitians are scapegoated as the harbingers of moral and medical decay, their presence blamed for the existence of malaria in rural settlements and the spread of AIDS. In an overtly racist polemic, Cornielle (1980) states that the Haitian presence is the root cause of the moral and biological degeneracy that is spreading throughout the Dominican Republic. Haitians are generally excluded from union organization, despite making up an estimated eighty percent of sugar workers in the Dominican Republic (Latortue 1985). The practicalities of providing representation for a temporary or undocumented labor force, and the evident lack of government empathy, maintains the disempowered and unstable position of Haitian workers. The status of dark-skinned Haitian immigrants in the country and the long history of enmity between the two nations are fundamental to the nature of racial identity among Dominicans.

Dominican-Haitian history and *la raza dominicana*

During the latter half of the seventeenth century, Hispaniola was invaded by French settlers who slowly began to occupy the western part of the island. This new French settlement was called Saint Domingue, and tobacco plantations were cultivated which established profitable trade relations with the less developed eastern part. Under the Treaty of Ryswick in 1697, the western part was formerly handed over to France following years of border disputes and tension between the two parts of the island. During the eighteenth century, Saint Domingue continued to develop an affluent plantation economy, extending its export production to sugar, coffee and cotton. The Spanish part also profited from this development, largely through the export of meat to Saint Domingue. In the French territory, the number of African slaves increased dramatically as a result of the massive scale on which they were used on the plantations. Many slaves escaped and fled to the Spanish part of the island. In 1739, there were 117,000 slaves in Saint Domingue, by 1764 there were 206,000 and in 1791 there were 480,000 (Fennema and Loewenthal 1987, 17). By that time they formed nearly ninety percent of the total population.

The 1791 slave uprising in Saint Domingue marked the extreme discontent of the population of African descent. The developing class of prosperous *mulâtres*, which had gained much influence in commerce and agriculture, demanded their own full political rights in a separate battle against the white elite. By 1793, with the country fighting itself, the French governor of Saint Domingue decided to abolish slavery. In 1795, Spain céded the eastern part of the island to France under the Treaty of Basle, and Toussaint Louverture, the general-in-chief of the armies of Saint Domingue and former slave leader, declared the island "une et indivisible." The eastern part of the island was occupied and slavery abolished at the start of the nineteenth century, only for the Haitian rebels to withdraw within two years as a French army landed in the east in 1802. However, the successor of Toussaint Louverture, Jean-Jacques Dessalines, defeated the French forces in the west of the island and declared Haiti independent in 1804—the first independent republic in the western hemisphere with a majority population of African descent. All Haitians, regardless of skin color, were declared *noir/e* under the Constitution of 1805. This included the German and Polish groups who had fought with the liberation movement. Nicholls (1996, 36) suggests that this may have been the first time that 'black' was used in an ideological sense.

The eastern part of the island, reclaimed by the invasion of 1802, remained under French colonial rule until 1809, when a rebellion led by Juan Sánchez Ramírez returned sovereignty to Spain. The Dominican elite continued to fear the abolition of slavery in the eastern half of the island, and the danger that this posed to their position in society. Racial differences fueled their perceptions of the Haitian threat. The inhabitants of Santo Domingo always considered themselves as Spanish, as well as culturally and racially remote from the neighboring population (Moya Pons 1995).

In 1805, Pétion, Geffrard and Dessalines led a series of attacks on Dominican territory and besieged the capital of Santo Domingo, but withdrew when it was falsely rumored that the French had planned a new invasion to reclaim Haiti. Dessalines ordered his troops to ransack Dominican settlements on their return to Haiti. The atrocities committed by the Haitian army formed an important historical basis for popular anti-Haitian sentiment in the Dominican Republic.

A pro-Haitian minority attempted to claim Dominican territory under Haitian sovereignty in 1812. The rebellion was extinguished, and Spanish rule remained until 1821, when an ephemeral declaration of independence was made in the towns of Dajabón and Montecristi by a faction that favored unification with Haiti (Torres-Saillant 1995). The

Dominican leader, José Núñez de Cáceres, responded fifteen days later with another declaration of independence, this time suggesting a federation of Dominican territory with the Gran Colombia of Simón Bólivar. Both declarations were short-lived. The following year, the Haitian president, Jean-Pierre Boyer, invaded and occupied the eastern part of the island for a twenty-two year period.

The Haitian occupation lasted from 1822 until 1844, and has continued to be the key historical referent for anti-Haitian sentiment in the Dominican Republic. Unification of the island under Haitian rule intensified relations between what are now the two countries. Torres-Saillant (1995), contrary to conservative views that the Dominican population never accepted Haitian governance, suggests that during the two decades the populations were brought closer together, notably with the abolition of slavery by Boyer in 1822. During the 1820s the Haitian leader actively encouraged the immigration of former slaves from the United States, and a sizeable community established itself in the Samaná peninsula. Despite emancipation of the slaves, Dominican politics remained restricted to a small, mainly *blanco* elite. In 1844, this elite declared independence from Haiti. Two decades of political strife and violence ensued, resulting in Spanish protection being sought again in 1861. Spanish rule finally came to an end with the War of Restoration in 1865, after four years of conflict between Dominican nationalists and Spanish sympathizers. Moya Pons (1995) suggests that race was an important factor which united the struggle for independence from Spain, transforming a peasant rebellion into a 'war between races' in which dark-skinned Dominicans fought for fear of the reimposition of slavery.

Hoetink (1982, 185) adds that the War of Restoration against Spain created a social cataclysm for the nascent Dominican state. The *blancos/as*, who had remained in the country or had since returned to it, were compromised as collaborators with Spain, while at the same time, the years of war and consequent events enabled numerous *mulatos/as* and *negros/as* to take up positions of responsibility. Despite increased access to power, it was always more necessary for the darker-skinned Dominicans to demonstrate their national and cultural identity in opposition to the Haitian enemy. Phenotypical signs of African descent among the 'well-to-do' or 'respectable' Dominican families were blamed on Haitian atrocities during the occupation. A revulsion for the Haitian enemy legitimized a collective aversion to

African ancestry. Consequently, Dominican *mulatos/as*, condemning the exclusive *négritude* of Haiti, aimed to forge a Dominican nation of Hispanic and indigenous ancestry.

Anti-Haitianism has been, and remains, virulent. The most remarkable and disturbing manifestation of this hatred was the massacre in October, 1937 of around 12,000 Haitian peasants in the western provinces of the Dominican Republic by the army and police of the dictator Trujillo.[6] Racism was a founding component of *trujillismo*, the intellectuals of the era seeking to consolidate the Dominican nation-state on the superiority of *hispanidad*. The creation of enduring myth was a key element to establish the legitimacy of the dictatorship. Firstly, the ideology of Trujillo's regime created the image of a dangerous external enemy to legitimize the nationalist efforts of the dictatorship. The effect of the massacre was to heighten this conception of Haitian laborers in the Dominican Republic as the enemy within. Secondly, it attempted to 'save' the Dominican nation from 'Africanization' and the 'illegal' entry of Haitian immigrants. In this manner, the events of 1937 were justified. Balaguer, then Dominican ambassador to Colombia, defended the massacre as part of Trujillo's nationalization program:

> ... by 1935 there were 400,000 Haitians in our country, resulting in the corrosion of national solidarity; voodoo, a kind of African animism of the lowest origins, became the preferred cult among Dominicans of the border area. The *gourde* replaced the *peso*. Peasants were learning from the Haitians' anti-Christian customs, such as incestuous unions. We were about to be absorbed by Haiti. (quoted in Fiehrer 1990, 11)

Balaguer's political and intellectual life has been strongly affected by Haiti. The border between the two countries is a symbolic ethnic and political divide, and a focus for the prejudice and myth that enters academic discourse. Augelli extrapolates his discussion of the Haitian-Dominican border as a contested space of clashing ethnic stereotypes. He suggests that there are few 'pure blacks' and Europeans in the Dominican Republic: 'The Dominican may be a mulatto or black racially but he [sic] speaks Spanish, is baptized Roman Catholic and 'thinks white'' (Augelli 1980, 21). This form of essentialism forms the backbone of racist ideology in the Dominican Republic.

Haitians are the scapegoats in Dominican society. Cassá (1994) compares their pariah status with that of the Jewish population in Germany during the 1930s. 'Haitian' is a signifier that functions as a switch word, connecting themes of poverty, criminality, *negritud* and backwardness. In this manner it is similar to the term Arab, used as a motif to link terrorism, Islam and a variety of nationalities. Haitians in the Dominican Republic have limited *de facto* rights. The Haitian experience is one of internal colonialism as a core element of Dominican economy, yet peripheral to polity. Haitians exist as an internal colony, marginalized individuals in a society that demands their labor, but refuses to accept their presence beyond that as units of labor. Haitian settlements in the sugar fields are effectively ethnic ghettoes, segregated physically and socially from Dominican society.

Contemporary racist ideology has its basis in nineteenth-century Dominican historiography. Dominican nationalist ideology established the country as part of Hispanic America, and clearly differentiated it from Haiti. After a series of failed Dominican annexations to either Spain or the United States by Pedro Santana and Buenaventura Báez, between the end of the 1850s and the early 1870s, Dominican writers developed a keener sense of patriotism. Rafael Deligne, Emilio Prud'Homme and Salomé Ureña de Henríquez were the leading patriotic authors at this time.

At the end of the nineteenth century, positivism reoriented Dominican nationalist literature. The Puerto Rican writer, Eugenio María de Hostos, was highly influential in the Dominican Republic, particularly through the work of Ramón Lopez and Américo Lugo. The positivist approach argued that Spanish colonialism, particularly the Catholic church, had severely hindered the development of the country. This hypothesis directly attacked the traditional Hispanophilia that had occluded Dominican intellectual production, as well as introducing a dominant element of historical determinism and fatalism within the intelligentsia. Out of positivism grew the depressing voice of the pessimist school. Ramón Lopez, Guido Despradel Batista and Jiménes Grullón were the key writers during the early twentieth century who developed this fatalistic view of *la raza dominicana*. Writing at the start of the twentieth century, Ramón Lopez (1975) contrasted the decadence of consumption in the Dominican Republic with that of the growing degeneracy of its people.

Despradel Batista (1936) published *Las raíces de nuestro espíritu* which lamented the hopeless situation of the Dominican population as a conjuncture of three failing 'races'—the primitive *indio/a*, the libidinous *negro/a* and the lazy Spaniard. Jiménes Grullón (1965) published articles which depicted the statehood of the Dominican Republic as a fiction: it was not, and never could be, a nation-state, but would remain a hollow and meaningless political entity.

The rise of Trujillo and his creation of a dictatorial presidency in 1931 led to a re-evaluation and reconstitution of the Dominican nation. The 1937 massacre of thousands of Haitians and Haitian-Dominicans in the borderlands was the violent expression of an ideology which aimed to fortify and re-build the republic. Two key intellectual progenitors of *trujillismo* were Manuel Arturo Peña Batlle and Joaquín Balaguer. The Trujillist ideology re-stressed the Dominican Republic as an Hispanic, Catholic and white nation. African influences were considered non-Dominican and, thus, subversive of the state. Haiti was the antithesis of the renovated national image. The immigration of Haitians into Dominican territory had been eroding the Dominican homeland, therefore the nation needed to be 'reclaimed' through a Dominicanization program which operated in an overtly racist framework. Haitians were deported or killed, and light-skinned immigrants from Europe were encouraged to migrate to the Dominican Republic. The principal aim of a large-scale agricultural colonization program was to bolster the sparsely populated frontier against Haitian influence. A Jewish enclave was established in Sosúa during the 1930s, following the direct invitation by Trujillo for East Europeans to settle in the country.

Balaguer maintained an anti-Haitian policy and European bias during his time as president (1966-1978 and 1986-1996), following the assassination of Trujillo in 1961. During an interview in the 1992 he expressed his belief in the European basis of Dominican culture (David 1992, 32):

> 'Historically our culture is Hispanic and that's a fact. But it is French too. Our legal texts, for example, are French in origin. Our civil code comes from the Napoleonic Code and so do our labor laws. What is special about the Dominican Republic is its cultural mix.'

Víctor Salmador (1994, 347), a Dominican citizen but Spanish by birth, stresses a sentiment similar to that of Balaguer in his adulation of *hispanidad*:

> Spain continued to be the fundamental, intellectual, spiritual and emotional axis of our culture. It is the epicenter in which the Dominican Republic wishes to keep itself in order to preserve the sacred values of our spirit and the permanency and steadfastness of our beliefs, of our idiosyncrasies, of our way of being. It is the unique geopolitical orbit to which we all belong with our hearts and souls.

These views have been criticized, but the critiques often substitute eulogy for pessimism, rearranging words rather than replacing sentiment. Pérez Cabral (1967, 157) criticizes the cruelty and the corruption of the Dominican political culture, which he blamed on the servility and *blancofilia* of the Dominican *mulato/a*. More recently, Núñez (1990) has defended *dominicanidad* against anti-Hispanic and anti-nationalist attacks from the Dominican political left. He laments that the defense of the nation is frustrated by contemporary Dominicans who have lost their identity and show little understanding of the historical values which underpin Dominican nationality. *Dominicanidad*, he suggests, should be protected against the increasingly incursive nature of Haitian culture, in order to perpetuate *la raza dominicana* as a viable cultural and ethnic reality.

Anti-Haitianism

Shared insularity is an important part of explaining perceptions of race in the Dominican Republic. The sharing of an island territory between two separate states is unique in the Caribbean—unless one includes the tiny island of Saint-Martin/Sint Maarten, which is divided between French and Dutch authorities, respectively. Other islands which are partitioned between two states, for example Ireland, New Guinea and Cyprus, often have histories of tension and conflict as rival authorities compete for dominance or maintain fragile truces. Overt and widespread violence between Haiti and the Dominican Republic, however, has not occurred in recent history.

The main language of the Dominican Republic is Spanish, and that of Haiti is Haitian Creole. Language variance, however, is only one of several factors which have marked two centuries of hostility between the two countries. Differences between the two populations have their origins in the different colonial regimes which governed each country and their subsequent economic development. During the eighteenth century, Haiti was the most important French colony, providing half of the metropole's transatlantic trade. A booming plantation economy produced sugar for the extensive market in Europe. The intensity of production meant that thousands of Africans were brought to the French colony as slave labor for the plantation system.

The situation was somewhat different in the eastern part of Hispaniola. After initial interest during the sixteenth century, the Spanish colony of Hispaniola was largely ignored by the new colonists, who were more inclined to enter the rush for the alleged gold and riches to be found in Mexico and Central America. The eastern part of the island, in contrast to the sugar-slave economy of what is now Haiti, had fewer requirements for slave labor. This colonial legacy is the cornerstone of racial differences between the two countries. Haitian control meant the formal end of the Spanish colonial regime of slavery, but it also meant that the Dominican Republic would gain its independence not from a metropolitan colonial power, but from Haiti—a former society of African slaves. The twenty-two years of Haitian occupation and subsequent liberation from Haitian control are fundamental for an understanding of Dominican-Haitian relations and the Dominican racial complex.

High fertility rates and the more rapid population growth rates of Haiti have fueled fears of the so-called Haitian 'threat.' The migration of Haitian workers into the country is posited as the 'silent invasion' or the 'Haitian problem.' The perception of an increasingly visible Haitian labor force in the fields or on the streets raises a growing 'voice of alarm' and demands for action, which range from a census of Haitian workers to mandatory expulsion:

> We are neighbors, but... we could never tolerate the neglect of our national origins, the integrity of our citizenship and social influences... without realizing the dangers which threaten our future. We must defend the Dominican Republic![7]

The preceding extract is from a national newspaper article concerning the Haitian population in the Dominican Republic. A Dominican geography student described the Republic as 'an island surrounded everywhere by water and Haitians' (Yunén 1985, 183).

The very foundations of nationhood would appear to be at grave risk—a view shared by Dominicans from all backgrounds. Almost a fifth of people interviewed during research in the city of Santiago suggested that Haitians should not be allowed to work in the Dominican Republic (Howard, 1993). Thirty percent agreed to temporary migrant labor only with strict legal documentation—the majority was very much concerned with the increase in Haitian labor. Nearly a half of the interviewees in Santo Domingo and Zambrana were opposed to Haitians gaining any form of residency in the Dominican Republic. The higher level of opposition may be due to the inclusion of a rural survey site, but also reflects a heightened awareness of Haitian residency following the Dominican presidential elections in 1994.

The number of Haitians living in the Dominican Republic is a highly contentious issue. Estimates vary widely, some suggest up to 1.5 million, but there are probably around 500,000 Haitians and Dominicans of Haitian descent on Dominican territory. The size of the population of Haitian descent in Dominican Republic is said to have doubled in the past ten to fifteen years (Corten and Duarte 1995). Despite a history of annual labor contracts between the Dominican and Haitian governments, the Dominican military regularly deport Haitian workers. A quota system in which the Dominican government paid the Haitian authorities for each Haitian laborer existed up until 1986. It continues to operate today, albeit informally or via agreement and payment between the countries' military forces. The Haitian sugar workers live mostly in rural communes, called *bateyes*, under conditions that have been equated with slavery by international human rights organizations. An increasing number of Haitians have been incorporated into coffee production, heightening the dependency of the Dominican economy on Haitian migrant labor (Grasmuck 1982). A widely published account of the oppression and discrimination suffered by Haitian laborers in the Dominican Republic has been written by Lemoine (1985).

Many Haitians remain as seasonal laborers after being brought to the Dominican Republic. Their continuing residence in the country, the indeterminate nationality of their offspring (without Dominican or

Haitian citizenship) and the scale of undocumented Haitian immigration are emotive issues. My sample of interviewees were evenly divided when questioned on their opinion of Haitian workers being allowed to gain residency in the Dominican Republic. They were asked if, in principle, they would allow existing Haitian laborers to legalize their residency in the Dominican Republic. The concept of residency is an important issue in Dominican society. *La residencia* is a term frequently used in the context of Dominicans attaining residential rights and citizenship in the United States. As such, it is a much sought-after status and a significant sign of prestige. Dominicans often compare their attempts to gain residency in the United States with those of Haitians trying to acquire legal status in the Dominican Republic—although interviewees tended to assume that most, if not all, Haitians lived without legal documentation in the Dominican Republic.

Overall, the opposition to Haitian residency is apparent across all study sites. The respondents in the Los Guandules sample were more favorable to the Haitian presence in the country. This may be due to their greater contact with Haitians as low-income urban dwellers. Respondents from the rural sample, however, opposed Haitian residency to a greater extent, outlining their hostility in often vehement and overtly racist terms. Two-thirds of the interviewees in Zambrana disputed Haitians gaining residency in the Dominican Republic. They were more likely to castigate Haitians as *vodú* worshippers and malefactors who meant harm to Dominican society. High levels of anti-Haitian sentiment among this rural group may be explained by the vulnerability of their economic position and the perceived threat from Haitians who are assumed to work for lower wages.

The threat from Haitian labor is more imagined than visible in this region. The agricultural labor force of the Zambrana region has an extremely low presence of Haitian workers and none were encountered during field interviews. The lack of visual or social contact with Haitian laborers allows racial stereotyping to become escalated and exaggerated since very few Haitians are present in Zambrana to dispel myths or to dispute the typecast images.

Haitians are perceived by many interviewees to be totally incompatible with Dominicans. Haitian culture represented the antithesis of Dominican society. Haitians were commonly linked to *vodú* or with 'black' magic. A middle-class *trigueña* describes Haitians thus: 'They work like dogs, but they have feelings, a religion and a language which we just can't share, and their governments are run by dictators. There's a lot of witchcraft. It's a backward country—they live by witchcraft.' Haitian witchcraft was associated with evil or mischief, unlike Dominican *brujería* which was typically referred to as a form of good or 'white' magic.

In the rural sample, much was made of Haitian vampire-like qualities. Haitians, it was said, suck Dominican blood and eat human flesh. The verb 'to suck', *chupar*, can also be used as a vulgar expression for having sex, which in this context, implies that Haitians are sexually attacking Dominican 'bloodlines.' The myth of Haitians who eat children was particularly evident during discussion with interviewees from the rural lower classes. Gladys Sánchez, a long-term resident of Zambrana, wryly yet doggedly expressed her concern: 'Haitians? No, things aren't good. They're brutes—they harm children and eat people. They won't eat me though, because I'm too old. They want young, fresh meat.'

Dominicans who described themselves as lighter-skinned, for example, *blanco/a*, *indio/a* and *trigueño/a*, more frequently opposed the granting of resident status to Haitian workers in the Dominican Republic. Those who used darker racial terminology, such as *mulato/a*, *moreno/a* or *negro/a*, tended to tolerate Haitian residency more readily. Just under a half of the Dominicans with whom I talked agreed in principle to allow established Haitian laborers some form of legal residency in the Dominican Republic. The more significant total is the similar proportion who refused outright to acknowledge any form of residency, however limited, for Haitian workers, many of whom were contracted to work in the sugar industry by the Dominican government.

Comments recorded during interviews with those who opposed Haitian residency perhaps illustrate more than figures alone. The vehemence of anti-Haitian feeling and the extreme comments expressed are not revealed in the numerical data. A phrase often heard whenever the subject of Haitian labor enters discussion is, 'Ellos por allá, nosotros por aquí'—'them there, us here'—emphasized with abrupt hand gesticulation. *Haitiano/a* is often used as a term of abuse against Dominicans with a dark skin color. Similarly, many dark-skinned Dominicans tend to pre-empt suspicion by emphasizing their Dominican citizenship. Dalys, describing herself as *india*, was sure to avoid any doubt when describing her friend's ethnicity: 'My friend, he's *prieto haitiano*, but he's Dominican.' Her friend had very dark skin color, by implication like that of an Haitian, but, she adds pointedly, he was definitely not Haitian.

Racial prejudice against Haitians is self-evident. The rural Haitian population is physically segregated as a racial labor enclave in the rural *bateyes*, and socially by racism and popular opposition to assimilation. Dominicans recognize a necessity for Haitians as units of labor, but condemn their presence to one of marginalization and inferiority. Ramón Gutierrez, an agricultural worker who confidently described himself as *indio oscuro*, was sure to separate the economic and cultural acceptability of the Haitian presence: 'Their labor is necessary— Dominicans don't cut cane—but, I'd never want to see any child of mine marry one of them. Each to their own. It's not the color of their skin, but they themselves—they're Haitians and we're Dominicans.' Dominicans have traditionally scorned work in the canefields, which is seen almost exclusively as Haitian labor. Ramón was one among many who argued that the Haitian physiology was more suitable to working outdoors than the lighter-skinned Dominican population.

Is anti-Haitianism functional to the Dominican state? Haitian migrants provide low-cost labor, especially in the sugar industry, and increasingly in domestic service, commerce and construction. It could be argued that wages are depressed and conditions worsened for Dominican labor, who then vilify the darker-skinned Haitian laborers. The presence of low-paid Haitian workers in the country has been suggested in the media as a restricting influence on the modernization and development of the economy. Bernardo Vega, a former Dominican ambassador to the US and Governor of the Central Bank, proposes that, 'large numbers of Haitian workers (who make up between five and ten percent of the foreign population) keep wages down and sustain a non-mechanized system of farming' (David 1992, 23). It may be suggested that anti-Haitianism is a divisive force manipulated by the Dominican government to weaken labor alliances, thus forcing a false racialized hierarchy upon the Dominican working classes. Even restrictions on immigration and residency, imposed by the Dominican government, deliberately place Haitian labor in a vulnerable, servile position of illegality, in the context of widespread racial prejudice.

Hoetink (1992) has outlined the key aspects of Dominican attitudes towards Haiti. He sees animosity being fostered by Dominican national historiography *vis-à-vis* the Haitian state, which emphasizes an alleged preoccupation of the Haitian government to unify the island. Nevertheless, a history of mutual political and financial support has existed between the ruling elites. There is also an awareness of the open border between the two countries, which has for many years been crossed by both Haitians and Dominicans. Vega (1993, 30) has suggested that Haitian and Dominican forces co-operated with each other during the nineteenth-century Haitian occupation, and that Haitian troops helped Dominican rebels to defeat Spain during the War of Restoration. He adds that at the end of the nineteenth century there was little anti-Haitian sentiment among the Dominican population. However, it would be naive to underestimate the strength of antagonism between the two populations. Anti-Haitianism provided a strong element for national cohesion during the nineteenth century, and was the focus of much nationalist rhetoric.

The influx of Haitian labor to Dominican sugar plantations at the end of the nineteenth century led to the fear of a passive invasion. Dominican employers have frequently deplored the immigration of Haitian workers in terms of their demographic and social influences, while simultaneously employing their labor at extremely low wages. Many Dominican merchants also prosper from the Haitian domestic market. This trade gained world attention during the early 1990s with the breaking of international trade embargoes against the Haitian military regime imposed by the United Nations.

Race is the dominant factor which underpins the fear of Haitian immigration. Despite the malleable and subjective nature of racial difference, Haitians tend to have a darker phenotype, or skin color, than Dominicans. This difference has been the cause for two centuries of racist antagonism between the countries. Anti-Haitianism not only influences political discourse, sentiment and action, but also has been institutionalized in many Dominican schools. An extract from a school textbook used during the era of Trujillo is cited by Bueno (1992, 45), who concludes that anti-Haitian prejudice remains evident in the Dominican education system:

Haiti is inhabited by a mob of savage Africans. We Dominicans should be in debt to our blood. The Haitian is an enemy. Haitians should be transferred to French Guyana or to Africa. The Dominican race and civilization are superior to that of Haiti. Haiti has no importance in the world. The poorest sectors of the Haitian population are an ethnic group incapable of evolution and progress.

Bueno studied anti-Haitian prejudice in three Dominican schools located in different regions of the Cibao. One school was situated in a predominantly rural area where frequent social and economic interaction occurred between Haitian workers and Dominicans. Another school was located in the city of Santiago, where the students could expect some contact with Haitians, principally through their employment in the construction industry or street vending. The third school was located in the highlands southeast of Santiago, where very few Haitian immigrants reside. Bueno aimed to investigate how levels of anti-Haitian prejudice varied with Haitian-Dominican interaction. He concluded that the degree of social interaction had little significance in determining the relatively high level of prejudice. Much of the anti-Haitian sentiment, he argued, developed as children grew up in a social environment that had always seen the Haitian population as a 'natural' enemy. He suggested that the most significant event that continues to shape such prejudice is the Haitian invasion of 1822. A reminder of the salience of the past for the construction of the present.

Prejudice against Haitians similarly expresses itself in contemporary Dominican politics. Anti-Haitianism was the major stimulus for the deportation, decreed by President Balaguer in June 1991, of all undocumented Haitian immigrants aged under 16 or over 60 years old. Within three months, around 50,000 Haitians had been deported by the Dominican army, or else had left the country voluntarily to avoid maltreatment. There were alleged abuses of human rights by the Dominican forces who used violence and split up families. Second generation immigrants of Haitian descent, though born in the Dominican Republic, were forcibly deported to a country where they had never lived. The government received popular support for the deportation program. The history of antagonism between the two countries was revived and retold extensively by the national media. Dr Leonel Fernández, Dominican president between 1996 and 2000, expressed his intention to improve relations with Haiti, distancing himself from the policies of previous president Dr Joaquín Balaguer. The deportation of Haitians in the Dominican Republic, however, was re-intensified within months of his inauguration in August 1996.

Many Dominicans supported the removal of Haitians as a legitimate and necessary government action. Higher income groups could look upon the poor Haitian immigrants from a disdainful distance, whereas the lower income sectors were more attuned to the problems that widespread poverty presented for all inhabitants of the Dominican Republic. However, the theme of anti-Haitianism was manifest in many interviews across all socio-economic groups, and the similar experiences of poverty often did little to appease Dominican contempt for their neighbors.

Anti-Haitianism lies at the core of Dominican racial identity, but provokes the question, anti-Haiti or anti-*negritud*? The influences that feed perceptions of Haiti have largely been negative in terms of the historical and contemporary manipulation of the subject. The enemy of the Dominican nation is Haiti, and Haitians are identified directly with African ancestry. Nation becomes closely associated with race, incorporating characteristics of nationalism with overt racism.

Few Dominicans have grown up without hearing private or public defamation of the neighboring country. The Haitian population, subconsciously and consciously, becomes a threat. A phobia is openly promoted through the racist discourse of politicians, or, more subtly, through everyday language and stereotypes. Typical of this attitude was a cartoon in a national daily newspaper, illustrating a harassed Haitian worker forced to cross the border into Haiti.[8] The image professed sympathy for the plight of the neighboring population, but at the same time bolstered the general view of Haitians in the Dominican Republic as undocumented immigrants, treading unwelcome steps on Dominican soil The Haitian migrant is characterized as illegal, destitute, and desperate. The same migrant may have arrived in the Dominican Republic as a contract worker or 'guest-worker' following inter-governmental negotiation.

The hatred of many Dominicans for Haiti is not based solely on nationalist sentiment. Overt racism has etched itself on popular opinion to such a degree that it has gained a level of respectability. Individual and institutional biases have led the way to continuous sources of racial prejudice. The danger of racialized politics is clear since 'racist ideologies have severe practical consequences particularly where they become institutionalized through the power of the state' (Jackson 1989, 151). Those Dominicans who speak out in favor of Haitian workers and who acknowledge African descent incite treason in the opinion of others.

Ambiguity and the *indio*-myth

Anti-Haitian sentiment is aligned with the use of the term *indio/a*, which extends across all classes in Dominican society. *Indio/a* is an ambiguous term, not least because the vast majority of the indigenous population of Hispaniola died or was killed within fifty years of Columbus' arrival. Historically, *indio/a* has been used as a term to describe a brown skin color, and it was not until the dictatorship of Trujillo that *indio/a* was established as an official and popular description of Dominican race. The Haitian massacre of 1937 has been mentioned as part of Trujillo's 'lightening' project to distance somatically the Dominican nation from its Haitian neighbor and African ancestry. Parallel to physical violence, *indio/a* was the ideological assault. Today, most official identity cards describe the color of their holder as *indio/a*. Popular usage added the embellishments of *oscuro/a*, *quemado/a*, *canelo/a*, *lavado/a* and *claro/a*—dark, burnt, cinnamon, washed and clear.

Over half of those interviewed in Santiago described themselves as *indio/a*, but of these, over 70 percent refused to consider themselves as *mestizo/a* (Howard, 1993). A similar study in Santo Domingo showed that 43 percent of the sample perceived themselves as *indio/a* (Silvestre 1986). In other parts of Latin America, the latter term generally refers to a person born of indigenous descent. In the Dominican Republic, this term corresponds with what might be referred to as elsewhere as mulatto. *Indio/a* and *mestizo/a* (the latter is seldom used) have therefore developed meanings and identities specific to the context of Dominican historical and spatial relations.

In Gazcue, the twilight zone of the traditional elite, interviewees more frequently described themselves using lighter terminology, although *indio/a* was by far the most popular. When more affluent respondents describe themselves as *indio/a*, it is usually qualified by lightening adjectives such as *claro/a* or *fino/a*. The former refers to clear, pale skin; the latter to 'finer' facial features. Adjectives such as *oscuro/a*, *quemado/a*, and *canelo/a* acknowledge the darker skin color of the individual, but their incorporation with *indio/a* maintains a somatic and cultural distance from African ancestry.

In the lower-income sites of Los Guandules and Zambrana, the term *indio/a* is more prevalent, either on its own or with darker adjectives. The affectionate diminutive ending of *-ito/a* is often added to lessen the impact of darker racial terminology; for example, *indiocito*, *morenita*, or *negrito*. Describing himself as *trigueño*, shopkeeper Rafael de los Santos used the diminutive to acknowledge the darker skin color of his friend: 'My friend has darker skin. He's *indiocito*. I know *indio* doesn't exist... Well, my friend's color is equal to mine, but he's *indiocito*, you see?' A professed lack of color bias is negated by his need to soften the potentially derogatory ascription of a lower aesthetically derived status.

Most interviewees described the race of the majority of Dominicans in their own image or as *indio/a*, although interesting anomalies appear. Almost two-fifths of the total survey sample considered the majority of the Dominican population to be *indio/a*, and a half of these were from the Zambrana sample. A further twenty percent believed the majority to be a racial plurality which they described as *ligado/a*, translated as mixed or alloyed, or *mestizo/a*. Over a fifth of the total sample described the majority population as *mulato/a* or *negro/a*. These respondents, in general, lived in the urban survey sites, and almost a half described themselves as *indio/a*, perhaps reflecting a greater willingness to accept an African past for the population at large, rather than for themselves.

Two-thirds of those interviewees who believed the majority of the population to be *blanco/a* were from the low-income neighborhood of Los Guandules. The concentration of opinion may be explained by the frequently-heard phrase, 'Los dueños son blancos'—'the bosses are white.' This refers to the white power bias in business and political spheres. Most members of the elite have light-colored skin. Ownership, or the control of power, is equated among the lower classes with whiteness. Those respondents who described themselves as *blanco/a*, 16 percent of the total sample, perceived themselves as a minority group, describing the majority of Dominicans as *indio/a* or as having a darker skin color. In addition, those who saw themselves as *blanco/a* frequently took on the role of an embattled ethnic minority, remnants of a white Hispanic tradition under threat from the process of *mulatización*.

The following interview quotes illustrate the confusion surrounding the use of *indio/a* and its reference to a mythical racial heritage. A female interviewee from Gazcue was clearer on what *indio/a* did not mean, than what it represented in positive terms: 'I'm an *india*, but that doesn't exist.

We Dominicans aren't *blanco* or *negro*. We're *indio*, but that's a Dominicanism.' Another resident from Gazcue, describing himself as *indio*, suggested: '*Indios*... we're very *blancos*, but not *blancos claros*.' There is confusion between the use of *indio/a* as a reference to an indigenous descent and as an expression of color. Acknowledging the term as a color designation, but also linking it to the presence of African ancestry, Alberto Velez tried to elucidate further: '*Indio* isn't *negro negro*, but *chocolate*. We're a mixture—everyone's got *negrita detrás de la oreja* ('a little bit of black behind the ear').' He was countered by a neighbor: 'The term *indio* is used poorly... It refers to *la raza*, not to the color of indigenous people.'

The use of *indio/a* evidences a denial of African ancestry and a rejection of Haiti—a racial cover-up. The situation is similar to Degler's (1971) concept of the Brazilian 'mulatto escape hatch' in which a racial category is created that cannot claim to be white, but somatically distances itself from being black. Rejection and the aesthetics of color are closely tied together. A resident of Gazcue, Maria Torres was keen to distance her race from her color when discussing issues of ethnicity: 'They say that the majority is *negra*, but there are no *negros* here, only *indios* and *blancos*. My parents are Spanish, so even though I look like a *mulata*, I'm definitely *blanca*.' Aesthetically she may be *mulata*, but her self-defined race was *blanca*, with a definite Hispanic bias.

It has been argued that the term *indio/a* functions as a neutral term in relation to color (Fennema and Loewenthal 1987). Hence, a variety of adjectives has been used in conjunction with the word *indio/a* to acknowledge darker and lighter skin tones in the population. This explanation of *indio/a* as a 'colorless' term is untenable in a society so conscious of light and dark aesthetics. The use of coloring adjectives merely illustrates the underlying bias in Dominican society. The majority of interviewees describing themselves as *indio/a* would be unable to validate a secure claim to a perception of whiteness.

Three main hypotheses have been suggested for the origin of the term *indio/a* as a Dominican expression of ethnicity. Firstly, the term may refer purely to skin color, providing an alternative to *mulato/a* without the connotation of African origins. The color was perceived, historically, to be similar to that of the population of India or to that of the indigenous Americans. Secondly, it has been suggested that *indio/a* is derived from the belief of Columbus that he had actually arrived in India. Thirdly, the use of *indio/a* has been linked to the rise of *indigenismo*. Knight (1990) gives an account of *indigenismo* in Mexico, where the generic concept was part of Spanish rather than indigenous vocabulary. *Indigenismo* in Mexico was an important element of post-revolutionary ideology, emphasizing the indigenous element in Mexican national culture, as in Gamio's *Forjando patria* (1960).

The influence of *indigenismo* was limited in the Dominican Republic. Unlike other Latin American countries, the indigenous population was quickly eradicated with the development of European colonization. Attempts were made to resurrect an indigenous heritage towards the end of the nineteenth century. Haiti experienced a similar resurgence of interest in an indigenous past at that time. Knight (1990, 76-77) comments on the more successful endeavor in Mexico where the indigenous population is still an important constituent of society. Nevertheless his comments are apt for the Dominican experience:

> When later *indigenistas* set out to recover a pristine Indian culture, they either attempted the impossible, or, more realistically, they took the syncretic culture of the colonial Indian as their yardstick... *indigenismo* thus represented yet another non-Indian formulation of the 'Indian problem', it was another white/mestizo construct.

The evolution of the term *indio/a* in the Dominican Republic attempted a historical-racial fix that continues up to the present. This involves the blocking out of a reality, and the denial of an African ancestry which has led to an uneasiness over issues of race. The tension between a racially complex reality and the logic of a preferred indigenous and Hispanic heritage frames any discussion of race in the Dominican Republic.

The most obvious example of history and literature combining to emphasize the indigenous past is the narrative surrounding Enriquillo. Manuel de Jesús Galván (1989) wrote *Enriquillo* to recount the story of the indigenous leader in the former colony of Santo Domingo. Franco (1979) suggests that this novel, first published in 1882, marks the zenith of *indigenismo* in the Dominican Republic. In 1519, Enriquillo led an insurrection against the Spanish colonizers which resulted in peace negotiations with the Spanish authorities. In return for a form of self-government, Enriquillo agreed to pursue and return runaway slaves. Galván describes Enriquillo as a Christian hero, a faithful adherent of

Spanish culture and Christianity. *Enriquillo* represents the archetypal 'noble savage', the effective syncretism of Spanish civilization and indigenous heritage.

Hoetink considers *Enriquillo* to be an attempt to fulfil a national psychological need. It aimed, 'to establish a continuity between the earliest inhabitants and the present population and, by so doing, to legitimate the latter's historical claim on the land they inhabit. The custom, still very much in use today among many classes, to name one's children after a native *cacique* flows from this same need' (Hoetink 1992, 137-138). *Enriquillo* aims to establish a racial authenticity for Dominican society through the pursuit of an ancestry perceived as distinguished and legitimate.

The descendants of Dominican slave society wished to distance themselves from the legacy of enforced servitude. This necessitated the denial of African slave ancestry and the forging of a contemporary identity which marginalized *negritud*. African slaves who fled enslavement in the French part of the island during the eighteenth century established themselves in Santo Domingo as *indios/as*. This was a psychological attempt to break with the stigma of slavery, but it undermines those who wish to employ the term *indio/a* as an emblem of non-African descent. The concept of *indio/a* invokes a past in order to mould the roots of the present:

> In the formation of the Dominican nation [the merging of the identity of colonizer and colonized] served as a point of reference for all those Dominicans who, for the color of their skin, could never hope to be called white and Spanish, but desperately wanted to get rid of the negative stamp of being black and African... Thus, the word '*indio*' became current, instead of *mulato*, invoking an indigenous and romantic past rather than that of African tribalism and slavery. (Fennema and Loewenthal 1987, 28)

Cohen (1969, 349) argues that 'one of the most important functions of myth is that it anchors the present in the past.' *Enriquillo*, and a similar period work entitled *Fantasías indígenas* (1877/1989) by Pérez, became platforms for the construction of a national and personal myth. This literary basis provided one influence, although the *indio/a* identity was most keenly worked into popular and official psyches during the era of

Trujillo. School textbooks, the press and political discourse propagated the indigenous illusion to dispel an African heritage and separate the Dominican Republic from Haiti. Hoetink (1992) warns against stressing the exclusivity of the term *indio/a* for the Dominican racial complex. However, its use can be singled out as having special importance in the Dominican Republic, primarily due to its effectiveness as an institutionalized myth during the *trujillato*. The legacy remains potent. An editorial in a former Dominican American newspaper heralded the importance of *indio/a* as an affirmation of 'our identity as a people.'[9]

The *indio*-myth has, historically, played a significant role in Dominican anti-Haitian racist ideology. The potency of *indio/a* illustrates the power of racial ideology in a Dominican society that superficially treats race as benign. It is an attempt to legitimize and vindicate the construction of a false history inspired by racial prejudice. The use of myth is often 'a device for blocking curiosity and the search for further explanations' (Cohen 1969, 348). Myth blocks off the false presence (*indio/a*) from the true absence (*negro/a*), justifying the mistaken identity of the former through an elaborate historical and ethnic rationale.

In 1992, Dr Joaquín Balaguer, the former Dominican President, made a speech to the second Ibero-American summit in Madrid, which eulogized the synthesis of indigenous and Hispanic cultures, and made no reference to African influence in Dominican society:

> '*El mestizaje*, the violent alloy of two heroic metals which are mixed in the blood of our indigenes and the descendents of those who arrived with Columbus from the other side of the Atlantic, is perhaps not the cosmic race described in the fascinating rhetoric of the master, José Vasconcelos. However, with certainty and without reservation, it is the fusion of two cultures, or one could say, two civilizations.'[10]

The display of Hispanophilia by Balaguer was extravagant. He extolled Spanish as one of the most dignified languages for human thought, arguing that it was the basis for one of the best literary works, *Don Quijote*, which came a close second to the Bible. The idea of the *indio/a*, and with greater resonance, Hispanic cultural heritage, form the bedrock of Balaguer's conception of *dominicanidad*.

The indigenous heritage of the Dominican Republic is a popular topic for study. In 1992 it was the subject of a series of educational cartoons in the national daily newspaper, *Listín Diario*.[11] The premise of the series was to illustrate the significance of the indigenous past. The Castilian language, it was argued, has been 'polished and enriched' by 'thousands' of indigenous words. The fervor to produce a verifiable indigenous heritage has led to a number of scientific studies of dubious merit. Many authors have attempted to show the salience of an indigenous past, although Veloz Maggiolo (1986) cautiously suggests that it is more often found in attitude than contemporary Dominican reality.

Alvarez Perelló (1973) attempted to discover the extent to which there is indigenous ancestry in the present population by analyzing blood groups. He concluded that there is a strong suggestion of such a component in the population today, but that it is more evident in the highlands where Spanish influence was limited during colonial times. The study pinpointed the indigenous genetic component of the current Dominican population at 17 percent, regional differences having been taken into account and was originally published in the United States in 1951. The methodological and theoretical merits of the research are doubtful, although its eventual publication in the Dominican Republic, twenty-two years later, says much about the enduring legacy of the *indio/a* term.

Another study which purported to verify biologically the *indio*-myth was undertaken by Omos Cordones as recently as 1980. From an analysis of language, color vision and tooth shape in a village 'renowned' for its indigenous ancestry, the research failed to find conclusive proof of direct indigenous descent. However, the author does provide five photographs which allegedly illustrate indigenous phenotypical characteristics among the local children. The author relies heavily on the subjective construction of race to enable the reader to envisage such characteristics. The five children appear little different from children in any other part of the Dominican Republic.

Finally, the contemporary manifestation of the *indio*-myth finds its institutional support through the personal identity card issued by the government. All residents in the Dominican Republic over the age of eighteen are expected to have a *cédula*, which is renewed every five years. In order to vote, the possession of a *cédula* is necessary, which has provoked protests against governments accused of withholding cards from opposition voters. Many Haitian-Dominicans are disenfranchised by this system, since they cannot afford to purchase the necessary personal documents to prove their birth status, or else fear deportation as undocumented immigrants if they approach government officials.

The *cédula* carries personal details of the holder, including skin color which is assessed either by the clerk issuing the identity card, or alternatively, the individual herself or himself may be asked to describe their own color. The descriptive terms authorized by the government illustrate much about the reproduction of the *indio*-myth. Over two-thirds of interviewees were holders of *cédulas* which described their color as *indio/a*.

In Gazcue, almost half of the interviewees had *blanco/a* on their cards, illustrating the subjective nature of color allocation by the Dominican authorities, who tend to 'lighten up' residents of higher-status neighborhoods. Only four percent of the interview sample from that neighborhood described their race as *blanco/a*. Anecdotal evidence suggests that affluent Dominicans were more likely to be described as *indio/a*, or in lighter terms, on their *cédula*. This may be a result of self-description, but is most probably due to the interplay of status and power relations with color-coding by government officials. Clerks working in the offices which issue identity cards are unlikely to risk offending members of the affluent classes by describing them as *indio/a*. This show of deference is possible since few affluent Dominicans would renew their *cédulas* themselves. They will often send an employee with the relevant papers to deal with the bureaucratic requirements. The employee is unlikely to insult an employer by ascribing her or his color as *india/o*. Several respondents who wanted to state their color as *mulato/a* recounted stories of having to insist that this term be placed on their personal identity cards. Each card has a color photograph of the holder, but the government clerks were reluctant for these affluent residents to describe themselves by dark aesthetic terminology, especially since they could easily have 'passed' as *blanco/a*.

The use of the term *indio/a* focuses attention away from African ancestry as a response to racial prejudice:

We live with our backs turned to the Caribbean because we do not want to see ourselves as blacks... we believe that we are whiter than the Spanish. (Andújar 1992, 9)

African heritage is swapped for an indigenous, non-African past. The function of myth is important, because it shapes perceptions and connects the individual to a shared sense of ethnicity. The lived falsehood of *indio/a* is founded on racist discourse, and thus, constitutes a major obstacle to encountering racial identification without prejudice at the individual and national level in the Dominican Republic.

3.

Race, Color and Class in Dominican Society

'Race and color are shorthand designations of class, but they often
overwhelm all other connotations.'
—Lowenthal (1972, 134)

Race and class are two analytically distinct concepts fundamental to the stratification of Dominican society and to Caribbean social formations in general. Lighter-skinned elites and darker-colored lower income groups in general typify Caribbean societies. A glance at the 'society' pages in any newspaper confirms this generalization. An edition of *Ritmo Social*, a weekly supplement, contained photographs of 274 members of Santo Domingo's elite.[12] The vast majority of the week's social revelers could be described as *blanco/a*, only two could have been *negro/a*, or more probably *indio/a oscuro/a*. *Negros/as* and *mulatos/as* are disproportionately represented among the lower social classes in the Dominican Republic. In general, they have considerably lower incomes than *blancos/as*, experience less social mobility and are more likely to be in the urban informal market.

Darker-skinned Dominicans tend to have lower occupational and socio-economic status, but the relationship between race and class cannot be represented by a simple empirical correlation. Class represents a status negotiated between economic attainment and social standing. Economic attainment corresponds to the level of an individual's access to income, and social standing is based on an individual's standard of living, level of formal education and prestige associated with birth or occupation (Weber 1947, 394). Definitions will always contain authorial bias. An observation of Dominican social classes in the 1950s provides a clear example, where the author equates class and race, combining snobbery with racism. Mejía-Ricart asserts that class represents a group of individuals who share forms of conduct, language, dress, education and social norms. He defined a concept of class that reifies Eurocentric culture and 'breeding', and lamented:

... the non-existence in Santo Domingo of a class with clearly superior cultural roots and wealth, equivalent to those in the great countries of Europe and America. (Mejía-Ricart 1953, 23)

In the Dominican Republic, he argued, there was no upper class of sufficient social and economic standing compared to European standards. He outlined the psychological inferiority of the lower classes, suggesting that the origins of Dominican social stratification were threefold—racial, economic and cultural. His analysis of Dominican social classes provides an inaccurate and racist overview of society, painting images of a false racial democracy:

In our country, there are no extremist attitudes: there is no violent racial discrimination, and no social color barriers exist outwardly. (Mejía-Ricart 1953, 27)

The study is itself a product of a discriminatory society. Higher social classes aspired to be *blanco/a* or to protect the 'gift' of whiteness where it existed. Only exceptional merit, it was proposed, had allowed *negros/as* into the highest classes. The middle classes were *mulatos/as*. Most of lower classes were *negros/as* or dark *mulatos/as*. Ultimately, social advance was perceived in terms of white cultural superiority: '... *los blancos* will predominate, since they have the indispensable cultural traits for relations with people of a superior level' (Mejía-Ricart 1953, 29).

Mejía-Ricart's analysis gives much significance to the factors of class and race. His framework of reference for social classes was social status. According to Wolch and Dear (1989, 8), social status has profound importance: 'a central dynamic in life is the innate human tendency to strive for security and status, and to protect those gains that have already been achieved.' Race and class are the key variables that locate an individual's status in Dominican society—both require close analysis.

Analytical distinctiveness is more apparent in theory than in practice, which impedes the disentanglement of race and class factors in complex social matrices. Race, color and class are often conflated, and distinct analytical terms lost in composite descriptions of Caribbean societies. Hall (1980, 167) has described Caribbean societies in terms of 'the profound stability of a system of stratification where race, color, status, occupation and wealth overlap and are ideologically mutually reinforcing.' The response is twofold, although Hall himself would surely question the starkness of his comment. Firstly, the complex social experiences of over thirty-five million people living on more than fifty islands within the Caribbean cannot be reduced to a single explanatory system. Secondly, the dynamics of race, color and class are such that societies are constantly changing and challenging societal frameworks. Dr José Francisco Peña Gómez was an established politician in the Dominican Republic, yet his Haitian origins and dark skin color do not correlate with the normal status markers in Dominican society.

Analyses of Caribbean societies which aim to determine the dominance of either race or class-based theories of stratification cannot arrive at a succinct answer, but they are able to summarize complex realities, provided that the summaries do not bolster oversimplification at the expense of explanation. Clarke (1991) has developed a four-fold typology of Caribbean societies, expanding the work of Lowenthal (1972) and M. G. Smith (1984). The typology outlines the dominant cleavages in Caribbean societies by adopting four frameworks of stratified or segmented pluralism, class stratification and folk communities. Hispanic territories are categorized as class-stratified societies since class structuration is considered to be dominant over racial and cultural stratification. The development of sugar plantation economies during the nineteenth century and the relatively higher incidences of white immigration or conditions of free labor meant that these countries evolved as societies with slaves rather than slave societies.

Hoetink (1970, 96) argues that historical relations of slavery are insufficient to explain the concept of race in the Dominican Republic, which experienced a relatively late development of its sugar plantation economy after the abolition of slavery in 1822. The Spanish-speaking countries, Cuba, Puerto Rico and the Dominican Republic, generally have lighter-colored populations due to their demographic histories of slavery and migration. In the eastern part of Hispaniola, the predominance of cattle rearing rather than labor intensive production between the sixteenth and eighteenth centuries, limited the number of African slaves in that region. Hoetink (1967) earlier suggested that the Moorish influence in Iberia was an important aspect of the Spanish and Portuguese colonial regimes, allowing narrower chromatic bridges to ease social relations and to influence perceptions of race following emancipation and during the post-colonial era.

Several Caribbean scholars have used the concept of caste as a structuring term. Leyburn (1941) and Lobb (1940), for example, recount Haitian history using the framework of a rigid caste society, in which class variation is reinforced by color differentiation. Hall (1980, 162) remarks that following emancipation, slave societies became colonial societies, which later changed to decolorizing societies. As colonialism developed, the racially based caste systems of slave societies evolved into class systems. Post (1978), also adopting the concept of caste, viewed early Caribbean slave societies in terms of a class-caste system. The growing class cleavages of miscegenated populations created groups of intermediate social status—the result not of the economic mode of production, but the outcome of reproduction.

The concept of caste, however, confuses the situation by conflating notions of race, class and culture, providing a conceptual bucket without proposing a framework for rigorous analysis. Balibar's conception of class racism, constructing a medley of race, caste and Weberian and Marxist class variants tends to confuse the issue further. Previous studies have tried to tease out distinct and separate concepts of race, color and class in the context of Caribbean social stratification. The studies by UNESCO (1977), Williams (1944) and Girvan (1975), for example, emphasize class relations. Lowenthal (1972, 92-93), however, focuses on race and color in his description of social stratification:

> Race and color have always supplied critical distinctions among creoles. Segregated by law or by custom since the seventeenth century, white and non-white have played distinct social roles. Codified differences forced each class to institutionalize separate modes of organization and ways of living... Race and color are not the sole determinants of status in the West Indies. But class distinctions are mainly seen, and grievances expressed in racial terms. Color in the sense of physical appearance carries extraordinary weight.

Phenotypical difference is a significant social marker. Skin color, Banton (1991, 125) argues, 'is a feature which varies along a continuous scale when measured by a light meter, but in social life it is used either as a discontinuous or a continuous variable in ordering social relations.' Discontinuous categories are the semi-fixed 'racial' groupings of, for example, black, brown or white. Continuous categories assign color a place on a scale of social status. Color, as the dominant index of phenotypical difference, is thus perceived as a sign of wealth, education, accent or demeanor. It becomes a matter of culture, which is formulated with respect to appearance, social associates and ancestry.

Color adds a chromatic scale to levels of social interaction in Caribbean societies. Emancipation freed the Caribbean from the strict color lines that demarcated society under slavery. The legal strata of citizens, freeman and slaves readily translated into the social hierarchy of whites, browns and blacks in most parts of the region (Clarke 1984). Color exists as a social, rather than simply biological, construction that tends to correlate with social mobility and economic status, and is an important element in the aesthetic formation of race. Elites tend to be lighter colored than the rest of the population, and the saying that 'money lightens' holds true throughout the Caribbean region. Ambitions of 'marrying lighter' express the widely recognized view that marriage to a lighter partner may enhance social status, or increase the opportunities for offspring by 'improving the color' of a darker-skinned parent.

Studies have recognized the color continuum as a fragmented and blurred marker of status in Caribbean societies. An interviewee in Los Guandules, who described himself as *indio*, remarked: 'Some people here are racist, but many colored people have positions of importance—there is no color discrimination here like in the United States.' Wade (1997) argues that the recognition of a black-white continuum has created an ambiguity and ambivalence towards black identity in Latin America. The lack of anti-racist pressure groups can be attributed to the ability of many *mulatos/as* to dissociate themselves from *negritud* and be accepted as socially distinct. There are only two small non-governmental organizations, Identidad and Onérespés, which directly confront racial prejudice in the Dominican Republic, despite the high level of inequality that comes from pervasive racism, and despite a semi-official ideology of racial democracy that denies racism.

The myth of racial democracy tends to strengthen a perception that race has little or no effect on life chances, at least for individuals of similar socio-economic position. Persistent racist practices may thus seem less conspicuous, or become channeled via a scapegoat, frequently under the banner of nationalism. Haitians are scapegoats in Dominican popular prejudice, the majority stereotyped as poor and *negro/a* or *prieto/a*. The absence of clearly defined racial categories in official statistics or legislation diffuses the intensity of discriminatory labeling, but also limits coherent terms of reference for anti-racist policy. Color aesthetics are a major element of racial prejudice, but racism cannot be understood adequately without accounting for the wider economic, political and ideological context. State legitimization of racism, which reproduces racially structured situations in the public sphere, is a key consideration.

The historical role of the state in the structuration of race and class in Caribbean societies was most apparent under the colonial system of slavery. The system of labor incorporation under slavery involved the exploitation of African slaves by a minority ruling class of European descent. Slave society was constructed on:

> a regime of labor exploitation which itself depended on sufficiently gross disparities of race and power between the exploiters and the exploited to establish, 'legitimate' and sustain the slave 'mode of production'... That being so, the rigid 'class' lines that distinguish planters from labor, whether free or slave, are clearly entailed by the political, demographic and racial structures of these societies. (Smith 1984, 122)

Smith refuses to adopt Marxist terminology with respect to class relations since, he argues, slavery was not dependent on relations of wage labor. Only with the abolition of slavery could capitalist relations of production between the proletariat and the bourgeoisie be established. The slave system, nevertheless, sought to accumulate capital through the appropriation of surplus value from an exploited labor force. Miles considers racism to be a historically specific ideology that structured economic relations in order to bring about and reproduce the colonial system of production. He bases his observations on colonial Kenya where:

> ...racism became a relation of production because it was an ideology which shaped decisively the formation and reproduction

of the relation between the exploiter and the exploited: it was one of those representational elements which became historically conducive to the constitution and reproduction of a system of commodity production. (Miles 1989, 111)

Class and race were the dominant markers of status in Caribbean societies. Miscegenation resulted in the creation of ambiguous racial categories which gave further strategic emphasis to race, since lighter coloring could procure a higher-class status for *mulatos/as*. Recognition of the importance of race and class, however, does not disentangle the complexity of their influences on the social matrix. Nor does it resolve the debate over the concepts of race and class themselves.

Wade (1997) argues that sociological studies in Latin America have not helped to dispel the ambiguity and ambivalence about the relations of race and class. He generalizes that racial discrimination is recognized, but that class is more important: poor blacks suffer more because of their low income rather than their color. Wade suggests that class is a more accurate way of accounting for group composition in general; race, although a deeply rooted identity, can never dominate as a principle of stratification. In the United States, Wilson (1978) propounds a neoliberal view that suggests that the significance of race declined in North American society during the second half of the twentieth century, as labor relations became dominated by market forces. Despite racial division within and between communities, it is argued that class relations stratify society at large.

One of the first contemporary writers to address the composition of race in terms of class analysis was Cox (1970). Racism, he suggests, grew out of capitalism as a means to further the use of labor as a commodity. Racial inequality, thus, is not a 'natural' phenomenon, but an outcome of the interests of the capitalist class in exploiting sections of the working class. Having aligned racial prejudice with class interest, Cox could argue that racial antagonism was essentially political class conflict since racial exploitation equaled a specific form of labor proletarianization and exploitation. Miles (1980) agrees that the essential relations are those of class, overlaid by distortions of racism, but sees that racial categorization, as a product of consciousness, does not in any way alter class determination since it leaves the dominant mode of production unaffected. He, thus, overlays the influences of race and color on society, but maintains that social relations are ultimately governed by class.

It is, however, not possible to refer to class as a unitary category. Anthias and Yuval-Davis (1992) assert that classes are heterogeneous in terms of race, ethnicity and gender, and that these social divisions cannot be seen as 'epiphenomena of class.' Social classes must be considered as the product of struggles within concrete historical processes which will include relations of gender, ethnicity and race, as well as economic, political and ideological relations. Class conflict occurs not only in the workplace but via all spaces of social interaction and over a variety of issues. Some would argue, though, that a broader focus away from the economic relations of production diverts attention from the key Marxist analysis of class structure.

Class formation itself is predicated upon race structuration, whereby race and class are separate but connected sets of relations in which antagonism is a primary driving force. Gilroy (1987) sees racial meaning as embedded in culture, 'the life-world of subjects' who have different, but connected, histories. Race and class, as factors of this life-world, are analytically distinct concepts, but cannot be treated as two distinct sets of relations. Class position is structured by racism in society, although racism on its own cannot be used as an explanation for economic position. Racism is not always functional to capitalism, since the latter simultaneously undermines and reproduces the former. The commodification of labor tends to reduce racial discrimination, yet the dynamics of the class struggle aim to intensify racial discrimination as a basis for a 'divide and rule' agenda. Race exists within and between classes, but class relations do not structure the effects of race.

The crux of the discussion rests between the extremes of separation and conflation of race and class terminology. Race and class may be separated theoretically, as the framework within which social formation ferments. However, practical analysis cannot separate the influence of the two terms, nor should it attempt to demand answers to 'critical' questions such as:

... under what conditions in biracial and in multiracial Caribbean societies of differing size and composition does political conflict develop on bases of race or culture rather than class; on bases of class and race rather than culture; on bases of class and culture rather than race; or on the basis of class, independent of race and culture? (Smith 1984, 129)

Race and class are legitimate terms of analysis, but their effects and results are not independent. Each is irreducible to the other, making it impossible to define any simple relation between racism and class struggle. To determine the dominance of either, particularly for a society as a whole, is an unrealizable task. Race and class impinge on one another according to the individual, the situation and the time— as aspects of identity, their influences are temporal and situational. The core of research is the articulation between the two in historically specific contexts.

The irreducibility of class and race relations ought not to lead to theoretical conflation or essentialism. Analytical terms should be concise, distinct, but not deterministic. They are the glasses through which the field is surveyed. Location, scale and history condition the framework of study. Race and class are place-bound and temporal factors that situate individuals and groups in specific contexts. The focus of the following sections describes the development of social classes in the Dominican Republic, before addressing issues of race and class.

The development of social classes in the Dominican Republic

Dominican society has been characterized by a light-skinned elite and *mulato/a* majority since the seventeenth century. The lack of directed economic growth under the Spanish colonial system, an extensive cattle rearing economy which limited slave labor, and the late expansion of the sugar plantation economy provided the basis for the country's racial demography. Slaves made up fewer than 30 percent of the population in 1794, with another 35 percent classified as non-white freemen (Hoetink 1982, 182). Following the demise of slavery after the Haitian invasion in 1822, color maintained its importance in Dominican society. The *mulato/a* population formed the bulk of the emergent middle class, lighter skin color allowing a greater chance of social mobility than for darker-colored Dominicans.

After the War of Restoration between 1861 and 1865, which finally confirmed Dominican sovereignty from the Spanish, the military became an important mechanism for upward social mobility, especially among the poorer and darker-skinned families. Luperón came from a low-income background, and both Guillermo and Heureaux were *negros* from poor families. All three were military officers who went on to become presidents. In 1865, there were at least forty-five generals vying for power. A decade later, there were over one thousand officers of similar rank (Hoetink 1980, 107). The Dominican Republic has had more *negro* or *mulato* presidents than any other Hispanic country in the western hemisphere (Wiarda and Kryzanek 1992, 58).

Economic growth, based on sugar production during the last two decades of the nineteenth century, created new avenues for social mobility. Limited profitability had brought the Dominican sugar industry to a virtual standstill during the seventeenth century, but Cuban and North American growers revitalized export production in the 1870s and 1880s. While the colonial system and slavery established the racial bases of Dominican society, the expansion of the merchant groups was the main influence on contemporary social class formation in the Dominican Republic. The growth of the sugar industry similarly parallels stages in the development of the class structure.

Small-scale sugar production had existed in the Dominican Republic since the sixteenth century. Large-scale production began with the sugar boom of the late nineteenth century, although agriculture in the country was unevenly developed. Economic power rested with the large capitalist sugar plantations in the south and export-oriented, agricultural, petty commodity production in the northern Cibao valley. Smaller-scale coffee, tobacco and cacao production, however, was soon overshadowed by the dominance of southern agricultural production at the end of the nineteenth century.

Sugar production had been encouraged by a series of external events: the Ten Years' War which disrupted the Cuban economy between 1868 and 1878, and led to the migration of Cuban producers to the Dominican Republic; the demise of sugar beet production due to the Franco-Prussian War of 1870, and the Civil War which affected sugar plantations in Louisiana between 1861 and 1865. Betances (1995) suggests that two important phases followed these initiating events. Firstly, the emergence of large-scale plantations with the investment of Cuban, Italian, German, Puerto Rican and North American capital which encouraged the growth of a Dominican business class. Secondly, after 1907, the dominance of large sugar conglomerates, incorporating the Dominican Republic into the world economy. In 1907, the

Dominican-American Convention established a relationship whereby the debt-ridden Dominican Republic would have its finances controlled by the United States. The Dominican Republic became a semi-protectorate of the United States. The affluent upper classes had profited as internal creditors to the Dominican government, but reduced access to government stunted the growth of an incipient national bourgeoisie.

At the end of the nineteenth century, global overproduction of sugar reduced prices and slowed down Dominican production. A new elite of sugar planters had been established, who, along with the merchants, formed an emerging bourgeoisie. However, the continuing dominance of foreign capital interests, and their close relationship with the state, limited the development of a national bourgeoisie. Instead, the influence of the United States became dominant. United States sugar corporations and banks replaced other foreign resident sugar planters and merchants. Despite early competition from the smaller scale production of coffee, tobacco and in particular, cacao, sugar was now the dominant crop. Agricultural production in the interior was limited by poor and expensive communications to the export market.

Two schools of thought have suggested explanations for the class structure in Dominican society. Firstly, Bosch (1992) has suggested that no bourgeoisie existed in the Dominican Republic in the nineteenth and early-twentieth centuries. It was the occupation of the country by the United States between 1916 and 1924 which laid the basis for the creation of a bourgeoisie, but it was not until the era of Trujillo that a bourgeois class was able to develop under the umbrella of the dictator. Bosch (1992) suggests that there was only one class, the petty bourgeoisie, which was subdivided into five hierarchies: high, medium, low, lower poor and lower very poor. Political conflict was therefore of an intra-class nature. However, the fivefold hierarchy fails to account satisfactorily for the position of the landed oligarchy and the very wealthy merchant class.

A second school of thought, followed here, considers the Dominican merchants of the eighteenth and nineteenth centuries as an incipient bourgeoisie, operating within the full sphere of capitalist relations. Betances (1995) views the development of Dominican social classes at the turn of the twentieth century in terms of an embryonic bourgeois class, arguing that the structural weaknesses of the state could not cater for local and international capitalist development. A weak state, unable to respond to the needs of advancing capitalism, was vulnerable to the influences of imperialist powers, seeking to restructure the weaker states as theaters for capital accumulation. The Dominican Republic thus became a site for United States intervention in 1916, and the consequent political restructuring of the state.

The development of modern capitalist agriculture on the sugar plantations created a salaried rural proletariat and an incipient national bourgeoisie. Whereas Betances considers a structurally homogenous bourgeoisie and fails to mention the intertwining factors of race and class, Hoetink (1982) argues that the last quarter of the nineteenth century heralded notable social and political changes in the Dominican Republic. Racial criteria gained greater emphasis as a means of maintaining social control and access to power. In particular, he contends that society became more organized, incorporating a vertically structured patronage system where color was an increasingly significant factor. The occupation of the Dominican Republic by the United States at the beginning of the twentieth century propagated further changes in Dominican society.

The occupation between 1916 and 1924 aimed to establish a national government favorable to United States interests. A national guard and road network was developed, and local elites were weakened through the creation of national tariffs. Local industry could not develop, given the negative influence of high export tariffs, but an import-export merchant class emerged.

Regionalism and the importance of local *caudillos* had restricted the earlier development of a national bourgeoisie following independence in 1844. The declining importance of the timber industry and the *hateros* in the eastern part of the country had helped to establish an incipient commercial and agrarian bourgeoisie in the Cibao in the mid-nineteenth century. Hoetink (1980) described the Cibao as the heart of the nation, with a traditional peasantry and relatively prosperous medium-sized tobacco, cacao and coffee farmers, plus a strong economy and traditional customs, making it a characteristic 'national domain.' However, the strength of the Cibao upper classes, already weakened by the sugar boom in the south, was further challenged by the United States' intervention in domestic affairs. The absence of effective communications during the eighteenth and nineteenth centuries restricted the development of a national elite and bourgeois class, but the modernizing process of the occupation firmly established national and international capitalist relations.

Following the withdrawal of occupation forces, whose position was made untenable partly by opposition groups from the urban middle classes and the peasantry, conflicts between the political and military elites developed. The discord enabled Trujillo, leader of the national guard, to gain power in 1930 as a national military *caudillo*. He had sufficient influence to prevent the re-emergence of regional elites, and succeeded, through political and economic power, in subordinating all social classes. Betances (1995) suggests that Trujillo was not simply a product of United States largesse, but the result of continuing weakness from nineteenth-century social and political history.

According to Betances (1995), Trujillo personified the dominance of the national bourgeoisie and upper classes. In contrast, Bosch claims that Trujillo was a surrogate for a bourgeois class, arguing that the *caudillo* restricted its development. Either way, Trujillo clearly had his own agenda for Dominican ethnicity and the nation. *Trujillismo* dominated Dominican life for over thirty years until his assassination in 1961. Vast socio-economic differences characterized Dominican society for most of the twentieth century, but only during the 1960s did civil conflict surface to the point of war.

The election victory of Bosch and the Partido Revolucionario Dominicano (PRD) in 1962 represented a success for the urban and rural masses over the traditional ruling upper and upper middle class. The PRD was elected on a platform of economic reform and social justice—a democratic social revolution for the country. Conservative opposition from the military, the church, the economic elite and the United States government were united through anti-Communist fears. In 1963, a military coup overthrew Bosch after seven months in office, and replaced him with a three-man civilian *junta*, headed by Donald Reid Cabral. On 24 April, 1965, a PRD-led coalition force of politicians and renegade military officers attempted to seize power, aiming to reinstate the constitutional government of Bosch. The following four months was a period of bitter fighting between the Constitutionalists and the ousted conservative military. The latter were assisted by 23,000 United States marines who had intervened, ostensibly to protect United States citizens resident in Santo Domingo, but in reality were there to prevent a leftist group from gaining power.

Cassá (1982) argues that the short-lived civil war essentially reflected the opposition of the lower and middle classes to domination by the upper classes of the national bourgeoisie. The main combatants in the revolution, however, were the inter-class pro-Bosch factions and the former supporters of Trujillo. Both Constitutionalist and conservative forces had members of all classes, although the former received the majority of support amongst the lower classes.

Economic development and socio-economic gains since the mid-1960s have been unevenly spread through Dominican society. An attitudinal and material chasm separates upper and lower classes, the haves and the have-nots, as economic growth has left behind the urban and rural poor. The 1970s Dominican 'miracle' of economic growth created an expanding middle class. New middle-class neighborhoods, shopping malls, cinemas and businesses were developed in Santo Domingo as the affluent suburbs moved to the north and west. In the countryside, where 300,000 families own tracts of two hectares or less, economic gains were less evident (Wiarda and Kryzanek 1992). Land reform in rural areas has traditionally been blocked by the landed upper classes, due to the association of land ownership with social standing. Rural unemployment affects over half the economically active population, according to government statistics, and illiteracy stands at 80 percent. Incomes are noticeably lower in rural areas, where life expectancy is 10 years less than for urban zones.

Bray (1984) argues that the high prices of the 1950s reactivated the process of class differentiation in Dominican rural areas. The rural middle class expanded land-holdings and diversified production, whilst also investing capital in urban areas. This led to a more rapid process of proletarianization. These rural capitalists were able to survive times of lower prices during the 1960s by cutting production costs and resorting to debt. Export agriculture provided the base for the rural and urban merchant classes to expand, but high rates of international migration began to influence the Dominican economy and demography.

During the 1960s, President Balaguer relaxed restrictions on migration to the United States and on foreign investment in mining, sugar, tourism, cattle ranching, communications and finance. By the mid-1970s, huge profits were being repatriated by multinational companies, with 125 United States subsidiaries operating in the country. High sugar prices enabled the Balaguer government to invest in construction and middle-class housing projects. Building permits for relatively expensive modern homes nearly doubled between 1966 and 1972, and the value of savings increased from US$8 million to US$111 million (Bray 1984).

The urban middle class boomed. Between 1966 and 1973, the number of registered cars more than doubled and the number of telephone lines increased fourfold, with over three-quarters of new installations in Santo Domingo (Reyes 1991). The number of university graduates per annum rose from around 600 in the late 1960s to 4866 in 1977. In Santo Domingo during the 1980s, 44.1 percent of the economically active population worked in the informal sector and 48.5 percent of informal workers were self-employed. Modern industries have been unable to absorb labor, leading to a greater expansion in the informal than the formal sector.

Despite these growing differences, there appears to have been little class conflict within the Dominican Republic since the 1965 rebellion. Wiarda and Kryzanek (1992) summarize three reasons for this lack of conflict. First, Dominican society has tended to respect traditional social norms. The civil conflict of 1965 was, thus, an anomaly. Secondly, popular opposition groups have never achieved a strong united front, and government repression, particularly under Balaguer during the 1970s, subdued radical forms of discontent. Thirdly, personal agendas rather than party policies have dominated Dominican politics. The 1965 rebellion, for example, could be seen as an explicit reaction to replace the weak leadership of Donald Reid Cabral.

Economic depression caused some contraction of the middle classes, but in general, the upper and middle classes have survived the economic downturn during the 1980s and 1990s. These same groups were nurtured during the Balaguer government of the 1970s, having been associated with the patronage of Trujillo. Dominican society is composed of several elite factions. The established landed gentry, the business-commercial classes who emerged at the start of the twentieth century, and the new upper class which developed under Trujillo, whose wealth has been concentrated in finance, agribusiness, the professions, light industry and tourism.

The Gross Domestic Product increased by over five percent per year during the 1970s, but the last two decades have experienced low or negative rates of growth, and per capita income has stagnated at around

US$1,000. The Dominican Republic is an economically vulnerable state. The 1980s were described as the 'lost decade', when the country, in line with many other Latin American and Caribbean states, achieved minimal economic development. Wealth creation has focused on the existing elite, exacerbating income differentials. Unemployment is consistently over 30 percent of the economically active population, underemployment affects another 20 percent. Life expectancy and literacy rates showed only slight improvement during the last decade, while infant mortality has almost doubled since 1978 (Wiarda and Kryzanek 1992). Life is a constant struggle against poverty for the majority of Dominicans, a struggle that worsened during the 1980s and 1990s as earnings became increasingly concentrated among the upper and middle classes, leading to greater levels of economic segregation (Contreras 1991).

There is no overt racial segregation of the type studied in the United States and Europe, largely due to the existence of a large mixed population. Neither does the Dominican experience agree with inferences from Brazilian cities. Telles (1995) argues that social transformations in Brazil during the 1980s support the hypothesis of increasing segregation by race and by class, in which greater class segregation also meant greater race segregation. However, in Santo Domingo middle- and upper-class neighborhoods tend to have lighter-skinned residents. Nevertheless, residential location corresponds to economic differentials and historical factors rather than contemporary forces of racial-residential segregation.

Within Gazcue, there is no racial segregation at street or household level, though this is not to say that racial prejudice does not exist. One *mulato* interviewee reported that he was initially not offered a rented apartment in a housing block because the owner did not like blacks in the neighborhood. The owner himself was *mulato*. Only subsequently, with the intervention of a mutual white friend, was the respondent able to rent the apartment. The landlord was reassured on discovering that the potential tenant could pay the relatively high rent 'up-front.' As the interviewee remarked, 'You can improve your race [mejorarse su raza] with cash.' With money, a *negro* may become a *negro blanco*. Thus, although residential segregation is not overt, racially prejudiced gatekeepers may have some influence upon a neighborhood's ethnic mix. People living in the same neighborhood, often hold strong, antagonistic feelings towards certain racial groups.

Social and economic exclusion rather than residential segregation characterize Dominican society. One Dominican author has framed this separation in terms of the alienating coldness of the modern supermarket, affordable for the affluent, against the openness of the popular *colmado*, or local store. Two markets which have their separate clientele divide Dominican society: 'one, more participatory with features typical of the national character, and the other, foreign and tempting, cold and alienating' (Sáez 1991, 68).

Race and class in three study sites

Four characteristics obtained during interviews were rated to assess an individual's class or social status: the occupation of the household head; the monthly household income per capita; house quality and standard of living, and the level of formal education. Each was assessed on a seven-point scale and the ranks totaled to indicate an overall class rating. The influence of remittances from former household or family members who have migrated overseas make income the most significant indicator of social class. Many Dominican households with an income from a migrant overseas are able to adopt a class position that is not immediately indicated by their occupation alone. The rankings were not weighted to express the importance of a particular status characteristic, although the level of household income is emphasized indirectly as an enabling factor; higher incomes allow the achievement of higher-status household type, and higher educational-level and occupational-group indices.

The Gazcue sample was predominantly middle-class, though over a half of the total sample of three hundred was from the lower classes, and located mainly in Los Guandules and Zambrana. Gazcue was the only survey site to have interviewees in the upper and upper middle classes, though Los Guandules and (to a lesser extent) Zambrana, had a few middle-class and lower-middle-class residents. Men and women were evenly represented throughout the class groups.

The occupational status of the household head was used as an index of class. Respondents adopted the same class position as the head of their household, if they themselves were not the head. This is important for the analysis of class where a married woman in the Dominican Republic usually adopts the status of her male partner. In cases of similar household type, income level and educational attainment, the occupational group of the household head is the key factor that explains higher-class status.

As expected, the upper classes are associated more with professional and non-manual employment, while manual work characterizes lower-class occupations. The only manager, and nearly all the professional workers in the sample, resided in Gazcue and were predominantly upper middle-class. Skilled and semi-skilled manual workers in the upper and upper middle classes achieved their class positions as a result of an elevated income status from migrant remittances, particularly in the Gazcue sample

The majority of respondents in Los Guandules and Zambrana were unskilled manual laborers employed in the informal economy. Both samples, however, accounted for over a half of the non-manual labor, other than the managerial and professional categories. These non-manual workers were normally university students or employed in small-scale retail and commerce. In Zambrana, it was evident that shopkeepers tended to earn more and have a higher social status in the community than many farmers, even though the latter owned land. However, such status is highly place-specific. Felipe Perego, a small-scale farmer, but leader of the regional agricultural co-operative in Zambrana, had a high social status by virtue of his institutional position. His role as local activist and statesman was a source of pride and authority that gave him influence far beyond the boundaries delimited by numerically based class analysis.

Researchers often face difficulties in obtaining accurate income details, therefore occupation is frequently used as a key factor in analyzing class. Misinformation, due to modesty, or more normally, a reluctance to divulge personal income, affects the assessment. In general, income was underestimated, although the ranking of mean monthly household income per capita provided a useful indicator of class. An analysis of household income was important, since the influence of migrant remittances may allow a more affluent level of living than would be expected from an interviewee's occupation alone.

Very low incomes are characteristic of the lowest classes in Los Guandules and Zambrana. In the rural area, subsistence farming was an important aspect of household survival. The general appearance and condition of the house incorporated into the class analysis, as well as the acquisition of certain consumer durables, such as radio, television, car or van, moped or motorbike, tricycle (often used by low-income traders or *chiriperos/as*), electric fan, cooker, refrigerator, telephone or video. House quality and standard of living was evidently of a better condition or status in Gazcue than in Los Guandules or Zambrana. The rural location had no electricity supply other than car batteries, though the standard of living could be judged at times higher than the low-income urban neighborhood.

Patriarchal values have traditionally discouraged some women from completing formal education before entering a union or marriage. Thus, upper- or middle-class women in some cases have received limited schooling. However, continuing education beyond secondary school is increasingly common among younger middle- and upper-class women. Higher levels of education, as expected, are concentrated in the upper and middle classes. Nearly 80 percent of the upper and upper middle classes had attended university or another form of further education, the vast majority of these living in Gazcue. Similarly, the majority of respondents who had completed secondary education was in the middle or upper classes and resided in Gazcue. In contrast, over 70 percent of the lowest classes had been unable to complete basic primary education.

How does class influence perceptions of race, and does race affect an individual's socio-economic status? Many respondents considered both to be closely linked, in particular, light skin color and upper class status. 'To be white is to have a profession' is a commonly heard phrase in the Dominican Republic, indicating greater social and economic opportunities for people with lighter-colored skin. It also recognizes that a *blanco/a* phenotype probably means that the individual already occupies a privileged position in society. Frank Acuña, an apprentice mechanic remarked, 'The rich people are *blancos blancos*', stressing that they stand out as the 'most white' in a predominantly *mulato/a* population. In the well-to-do suburb of Gazcue, Juan Manuel Domínguez affirmed his identity as *mulato* and expressed his resentment, 'With white skin and straight hair, you have more job opportunities. The *negro* has always been downtrodden.' His white neighbor, joining the conversation and recognizing the advantages of his own skin color with a limited attempt at sympathy, continued, 'The boss is always the little white guy. I'm *blanco*. I'm lucky not to face these problems, but that's the way it is.' Owners of large businesses were presumed to be white and separated from the darker-colored workforce: 'The boss is often *blanco*. He'll never hang around with the *negros*', added Juan Manuel's neighbor, now on a roll. The upper and middle classes were perceived to be more racist, even among their own ranks.

More affluent Dominicans invariably use lighter color terminology to describe themselves, such as *blanco/a* and *trigueño/a*, as well as *indio/a* if qualified by lightening adjectives such as *claro/a*. The frequent use of *indio/a* among the lower middle, lower and lower lower classes is evident. These three classes account for four-fifths of those interviewees who described themselves as *indio/a*. It would appear paradoxical that the term *mulato/a* was used almost exclusively in the largely middle- and upper-class neighborhood of Gazcue. *Moreno/a* is expressed to a greater extent among the lower classes of Los Guandules and Zambrana. The term is used less frequently in liberal anti-racist discourse than *mulato/a*.

Dominicans of established middle- or upper-class status, and sure of their position in society, can afford, socially, to be more aware of, or explicit about, their African ancestry. Self-description as *negro/a* may be the result of a more liberal education and socialization process among these more affluent groups. Race becomes an affordable declaration among the upper and middle-classes—with a comfortable economic base, racial discrimination is less likely to prejudice employment and life chances.

An individual's color on her or his *cédula* is usually ascribed by the clerk at the government issuing office. *Blanco/a* and *indio/a* accounted for 86 percent of the *cédulas* issued to upper-, upper-middle and middle-class interviewees, each accounting for approximately 43 percent of the total. *Indio/a* was the most popular term for the *cédulas* of lower class interviewees, making up 81 percent of the two lowest class categories. Among the middle classes, *indio/a* accounted for over half, and *blanco/a* for a third, of all *cédulas* issued.

The applicant may request the color term used, but this is not the norm. There is a tendency for upper-class individuals to be ascribed lighter colors. The issuing clerk automatically assumes that an affluent Dominican would be considered as *blanco/a* rather than *indio/a claro/a*. Dulce Torres Menéndez lives comfortably in the leafy neighbor of Gazcue. She, unlike many whom I interviewed in similar situations, lamented the everyday racism against darker-skinned Dominicans and positively challenged her wealthy friends to acknowledge African influence in Dominican society, even within the walled patios of their affluent neighborhood. She described her skin color as brown. None of her social circle, she said, would feel comfortable stressing their African ancestry when distant European roots could be traced instead. Her experience when obtaining a new identity card exemplified similar frustrations for her. Only after a prolonged verbal tussle was she able to persuade the clerk not to type *blanca* on her *cédula*. She was not *blanca*, she argued, but the clerk had contested flirtatiously that with such beautiful fair skin, she must be *blanca*. Dulce's *cédula*, to the disbelief of her bemused friends, describes her as *mulata*.

Nearly 40 percent of the total sample perceive Dominican society as a predominantly *indio/a* population. The use of the term was more prevalent among the lower classes, in particular in the Zambrana sample. Although only eight respondents consider the majority of the Dominican population to be *blanco/a*, five of these were from the lowest two class groups. These respondents alluded to the continuing dominance of the lighter-skinned traditional ruling classes. Approximately a quarter of those interviewed believed the population to be of mixed origin—*una mezcla*. Dominicans who used terms such as *negro/a*, *mulato/a* and *moreno/a* to describe the Dominican population (23.6 percent of the sample) tended to be from the lower classes, though *mulato/a* was a popular term among the more liberal middle and upper classes of Gazcue.

When questioned about the relative advantages or disadvantages of having white or black skin, nearly half of the sample believed that to be *negro/a* was a disadvantage in the Dominican Republic, a recognition that increased with social status. Similarly, 46 percent believed a white skin to be advantageous, the highest proportion again being in the upper classes. This suggests that the perception of racial advantage or disadvantage is greater among the upper classes, either as a mark of their own prejudice or as a result of a greater awareness to the problems of racism in the Dominican Republic. However, lower class *indios/as* or *mestizos/as* tended to be more aware of the disadvantages of dark skin in the Dominican Republic: 'The *blanco* here discriminates against the *negro*... The *blancos* treat the *negros* like slaves.'

Lower-class interviewees often made a distinction between elite racism and their own antagonistic feelings towards Haiti. Carefully considering her skin color and pronouncing herself as *mestiza*, Gladys

Ramos Ortiz differentiated her dislike of Haitians from the prejudices of the more affluent: 'Real racism belongs to the upper classes. There's racism here in Los Guandules, but it's against Haitians.' There was even greater objection to the Haitian presence among the predominantly lower class rural respondents compared to urban interviewees. The general distrust and fear of Haiti and Haitians is repeated across all classes, although the majority of urban dwellers in Gazcue and Los Guandules consider that Haitians who work in the Dominican Republic should be granted residency for the term of their employment. Respondents, however, emphasized that only those Haitian laborers necessary to the Dominican economy should be allowed to reside in the Dominican Republic. Many believed that attempts to formalize the Haitian presence through residency permits would be the most effective way to minimize and monitor a controlled Haitian population in the country. The majority of interviewees did not welcome Haitians without employment; while some respondents professed their acceptance of Haitian labor in the Dominican Republic, comments expressed later during the interview signified their hostility.

Race, class and the Dominican nation

Race and class differentiate as well as unite Dominicans within the social system. *Dominicanidad* constitutes a national collectivity which is internally divided by race and class. First- and second-generation Haitians in the Dominican Republic, as a racial and ethnic minority, hold a much lower social status than Dominicans, although they share similar lower-class characteristics. They are a class apart, located outside *dominicanidad*. Dominican *negros/as*, whilst not excluded, are perceived as marginal to the Dominican nation, contesting and negotiating the discriminatory light bias of *dominicanidad*.

Racism and nationalism form a focus of interest which displaces class inequalities from mainstream political and social agendas. The politicization of racial identity has been suggested as a means of negating the discriminatory ideals of the nation (Anthias and Yuval-Davis 1992). The priority inclusion of multicultural and multiracial policies on the political agenda is designed to promote social equality. Race has been politicized in the Dominican Republic, but its politicization has been in a manner which heightens its discriminatory value.

Racism is prevalent throughout all classes in Dominican society. Racial discrimination cannot be reduced to the outcome of class relations, because racism is not a necessary prerequisite of class exploitation. Race, like gender, however, often facilitates class-oriented oppression. Racism may crosscut class relations, as exemplified by prejudice among the middle and lower classes towards middle-class *negros/as*. Racism, conversely, may be incorporated into class relations to further the interests of specific groups within the ruling elite, where racial supremacy comprises the privileged exploitation of, or access to, economic or political resources. Labor from Haiti reduces the costs of sugar production and restricts the effectiveness of trade unions, leading a large proportion of Dominicans across all classes to resent the Haitian presence. The Dominican Republic is a class-structured society, where race often subverts class interests.

4.

Race and Ethnicity: Gendered, Domesticated and Sanctified

'"Tell me the hen doesn't peck when the rooster crows," said Chucha with heavy sarcasm.'
—Alvarez (1991, 259)

The domestic sphere is a key site for the expression of patriarchal culture, but it is also a location for the reproduction of racial stereotypes and the expression of Afro-syncretic beliefs, out of the view of more public Catholic worship. Consequently, aspects of race in everyday life are inherently gendered, domesticated and sanctified. This chapter begins with a theoretical consideration of patriarchy and culture, then, with reference to the survey material, discusses the contemporary issues of household structure, women's work, the aesthetics of sexuality and images of the body, and finally, the influence of religion in Dominican society.

Gender, crosscut by race and class, refers to the socially unequal division of society into forms of masculinity and femininity, based on the biological differences between male and female. Gender relations are social constructions, giving social significance to biological attributes. The impact of race cannot be added to gender analysis, and *vice versa*. The categorization and influence of race and gender relations are mutually constitutive, each operating within or around the other. Thus, any concept of race will be gendered, and any notion of gender racialized.

Patriarchy, class bias and racism overlap as forms of oppression. Patriarchy is defined as 'a fluid and shifting set of social relations in which men oppress women, in which different men exercise varying degrees of power and control, and in which women resist in diverse ways' (Hondagneu-Sotelo 1992, 25). Analysis cannot aggregate the variables of gender, class and race, though commonalties exist and reinforce the impact of each. Patriarchal structures uphold race and class prejudices and discrimination. Slavery has left its legacy in the formation of both race and gender relations. Racial terminology is frequently used in combination with the presuppositions inherent in a patriarchal culture.

The household, a unit of domestic reproduction and shelter, is a source of two contradictory currents. First, the domestic sphere is the location for the formation and reproduction of race and gender relations through the process of socialization. Secondly, and conversely, the household is also a site of resistance to patriarchy and racism. Households incorporate complex social relations, which may adopt consensual or confrontational aspects at various times in differing situations.

The household acts as 'a conduit for wider familial and gender ideologies', providing the context for the reproduction of patriarchal and racist culture (Chant 1996). Theories of socialization propose that gendered social and cultural attributes are formed principally during childhood, hence the importance of the household environment. Children acquire socially ascribed norms in the domestic arena, learning the appropriate behavior for their sex. Acculturation to perceived adult roles occurs as boys help their fathers in the garage, or girls assist their mothers in domestic chores. Socialization occurs not only in the household as a young child, but later through schooling and in the workplace. The domestic sphere, however, is a fundamental context. In a similar manner, racial ideas and values are expressed within the household and form part of the socialization process. Perceptions of race and forms of xenophobia and racism are copied or understood from the social surroundings.

Members of many Dominican families vary significantly in terms of skin color or phenotype. Thus, while racism is evident in Dominican society, race may not play a discriminatory role within the domestic sphere. However, race still is an important part of identity construction. The darkest child in a family is often known as *negrito/a* as a term of endearment; the underlying tones, however, are racist. The darkest child is singled out, isolated from the lighter siblings. Hooks (1984) argues that the family becomes a site of resistance for black women, providing solidarity against racism. Household structure, thus, mitigates the impact of racial discrimination and is not the prime cause of subordination that it is for white women. Structure and headship are central to the nature of household relations.

The household head is the person who gives most economic support to the family and who has the greatest responsibility in decision making. The traditional domestic code assumes headship to be male. Household structure, thus, is important for the formation of patriarchal and racial perceptions. The predominance of male household heads reproduces the patriarchal domestic structures. Women-headed households, however, erode the traditional norms of patriarchy in the domestic sphere. The established domestic code and the patriarchal culture of Dominican society are discussed in the following section.

Cultures of patriarchy

How does race influence gender analysis, and *vice versa*? Men and women face changing forms of inequality, which vary according to their racialized or gendered positionality. First, racial variation differentiates the experiences of women *vis-à-vis* those of men in the labor market; secondly, men and women of similar race will be exposed to differing forms of gender discrimination. Consequently, racism and patriarchy are not constant influences but vary according to time, place and context. Class relations also impinge on racial and gendered experiences. The women's liberation movement during the 1960s, for example, was initially a white middle-class assault on patriarchal relations (Westwood and Radcliffe 1993).

Patriarchy has developed a variety of meanings. Initially referring to a system of government in which men from their position as patriarchs ruled societies, the concept now focuses on the domination of women by men. The dualist framework of analysis theorizes patriarchy as an independent social system which exists alongside capitalism. Alternatively, the patriarchal structure is viewed as a by-product of the domination of capitalism over labor. The former framework considers that both systems are equally important in determining gender relations; patriarchy provides a system of social control and order, while capitalism structures an economic system. The latter approach argues that class relations and the economic exploitation of one class by another are the central features of the social system. Capitalist relations determine gender relations; women as mothers and homeworkers provide cheaper labor by supporting and reproducing the household without receiving a wage. Capital therefore benefits from the unequal sexual division of labor within the household.

A psychoanalytical approach to patriarchy describes gender acquisition as a product of the unconscious, existing beyond the bounds of conscious manipulation. Chodorow (1978) focuses on the role of mothering as the central and constituting element in social organization and reproduction of gender, which limits women's role in adult life to one that has a reduced status in patriarchal society. Gender differentiation arises as a girl follows the nurturing role of her mother, while the boy, identifying with his father, adopts a less caring personality. The analysis provides an active attempt to resolve gender inequalities, but in addition to veering towards an essentialist view of the woman as mother, fails to address the social structures of patriarchy which devalue women.

Patriarchal structures are culturally specific and change through time. Walby (1990) argues that patriarchy in westernized societies has shifted from the private sphere towards wider public realms. In contemporary Britain, for example, domesticity is less central to women's identities; notions of motherhood and fatherhood have become more flexible, weakening the sexual division of household labor. While progress in Dominican society is also evident over the last century, analyses of European or North American countries can only be transposed to other societies after careful revision. The influence of patriarchy is dependent on the historical and contemporary surroundings, forming part of the specific cultural context.

Subsumed within this context is the idea that popular culture represents mass, or, more specifically, class culture. Kipnis (1986) considers mass culture to be a coded form of class discourse. Popular culture serves as an instrument of capitalist culture, appropriating and transforming meaningful elements in society to support the dominant capitalist hegemony. Popular culture is therefore reactionary but not revolutionary, since it operates within the existing hegemonic framework. The main element embodied in these definitions of culture is shared experience. Culture represents a shared set of meanings or meaningful activities, the sharing of which establishes a collectivity or group identity. Identities are necessarily influenced by prevailing concepts of race and gender in languages, activities and cultural institutions.

The variable experiences of masculinities and femininities are hidden by popular culture and the blunt definition of gender as a duality. Spender (1980) claims that languages are patriarchally structured. The colloquial register frequently voices a male bias; for example, the predominant use of 'he' or 'mankind' hides female existence. Languages employ expressive forms in which femininity is often conveyed by diminutive patterns of speech. Spender's analysis concentrates on the English language in which nouns lack gender, but a study specific to Spanish, for example, must take into account the significant use of masculine and feminine nouns and pronouns. The name of the most influential museum in the Dominican Republic remains unchallenged as *El Museo del Hombre Dominicano*—the Museum of Dominican Man. If language is perceived as expressing a patriarchal structure, then it would seem that a solution to the oppression of women would be to create a non-patriarchal language. Discourse analysis brings to light the importance of representation and questions the subliminal imagery of patriarchy, but tends to neglect the importance of the everyday political and economic realities through which patriarchal structures operate and are experienced.

The influences of race and gender in Dominican society are analyzed in the following section from the everyday experiences of men and women in the three survey sites—at work, in the home, through sexuality and via religious beliefs. These relations are the changing outcome of the structures outlined above by Walby: the patriarchal mode of production, and patriarchal relations in paid work, in the state, male violence, in sexuality, and in cultural institutions.

Household structure and the role of women

A popular Dominican children's song presents an image of women which reproduces in verse the social structures of patriarchy. The man sets out his requirements for a woman with whom he would consider marriage. The lyrics suggest that the ideal wife should be a wealthy widow, skilled at sewing and cooking. She must have all the necessary domestic skills to fulfil the role of a 'good housewife'. The repetition of such lyrics by young children indoctrinates and reproduces patriarchal structures during the formative years of social development. It encapsulates the conventional and widespread conception that domestic matters are women's issues. A group of supermarkets have been considering the creation of rest areas, 'as an alternative for husbands who become bored in the supermarket, while their wives buy the family shopping.'[13] Women, it is argued, take much longer to buy the groceries; men spend more, but purchase rum, whisky and 'nibbles' to entertain guests at home.

Socialization theory, while negating biological determinism, fails to explain gender relations adequately in several respects. First, the process does not account for the initial formation of gender identity, leaving the attributes of masculinities and femininities to be appropriated as gendered baggage during childhood. Secondly, the emphasis on socialization during very early childhood underestimates later influences; the varying social implications of gender identity are experienced, and elicit reactions, in a variety of locations at various stages of life. Thirdly, the theory operates through standardized views of gender, limiting an explanation of the differing masculinities and femininities within similar social and historical circumstances. Finally, socialization fails to emphasize notions of masculinity and power. Patriarchy is a side-product of socialized gender development; indeed, gender attributes attained through the lens of socialization theory appear to be an inevitable outcome of passive acceptance.

Socialization of gender and race must be considered beyond the domestic sphere and at work. The traditional domestic code locates women's work in the household, and subordinate to the male household head. The historical precedent of a male-dominated economy has meant that the majority of women have had to rely on their male partner's support, thus maintaining the relations of patriarchy. Despite relative numerical equality with men, the structures of patriarchy serve to marginalize women in many aspects of Dominican society. Women have increasingly been entering paid employment, but the degree of inequality between men and women with respect to remuneration, work conditions and opportunities for promotion have improved only slightly. Quantitative change has not been matched by qualitative improvement in employment. Women continue to experience greater levels of social, cultural, economic and political discrimination, evidence of which is outlined below.

The role of the woman as mother is critical to the social structures of patriarchy. Human capital theorists would argue that women's position in the family restricts involvement in the labor force due to a limited acquisition of necessary work skills, thus reducing the development of their human capital potential. The imposition of the mothering role, however, has become less dominant with the greater acceptability of female employment and smaller families.

The current annual national birth rate is 30.1 births per thousand inhabitants, and the average number of children born per woman is 3.3, ranging from 4.4 in the rural areas to 2.8 in the cities (Population Reference Bureau, 1998). Despite persistent differences between rural and urban areas, the birth rate is decreasing steadily. This reduction has been achieved through extensive family planning programs. The majority of Dominican women now have access to methods of contraception, although the patriarchal relations of sexuality remain dominant in issues of male responsibility. Safe sex practices were frequently treated with scorn by male interviewees; the use of condoms often being seen as an infringement on male sexual enjoyment. Among sexually active adolescents a survey reported that 87 percent did not take precautions against contracting HIV-related illnesses (Aizpun 1994). Family planning remains very much a 'women's issue' (*una cosa de mujer*) throughout Dominican society.

The type of union in which a woman is involved, in addition to her role as mother, conditions their position in a patriarchal society. A recent summary of survey material by Báez and Taulé (1993) provides useful information on the position of women in Dominican society during the 1980s and 1990s. Consensual union accounted for 28.2 percent of women's relationships in 1981; 24.5 percent were married, 32.0 percent were single and 5.9 percent were widowed. At the national scale, there has been a decline in consensual union and marriage, with decreases of around 4 percent since 1960, accompanied by a rise in the level of divorce or separation from 1.9 percent in 1960 to 9.4 percent in 1981

There is a marked variance in union type according to socio-economic background. Consensual union accounted for two-thirds of partnerships in the lowest classes, particularly in Los Guandules. The predominance of consensual union among these classes is explained by the greater social acceptability of concubinage, and the potentially prohibitive cost of a formal marriage ceremony. Couples often stated that they were reluctant to formalize their partnership; they saw no immediate need if the relationship had been established for a significant period of time.

The middle classes have a high proportion of married interviewees, and correspondingly fewer consensual unions. In the Gazcue sample, virtually all couples were married, either by civil or religious wedding. The older age of respondents in this neighborhood is reflected in the high proportion (one tenth) of widows and widowers. Lower classes tend to marry or start living together at an earlier age, while the middle and upper classes increasingly delay marriage to complete further education or pursue a career.

A study in the 1960s of residents in low-income settlements in Santo Domingo indicates that there has been a substantial decrease in the number of marriages, and an increase in the frequency of consensual union. The survey showed that 49.4 percent of interviewees were in a consensual union, 45.1 percent were married, and 5.0 percent were either single, separated or divorced (Corten and Corten 1968). In my study, unmarried couples living together accounted for 48 percent and 38 percent of interviewees in Los Guandules and Zambrana respectively. The greater occurrence of formal marriages in Zambrana reflects the more conservative nature of rural society and the stronger influence of Catholic and Protestant churches in the locality. Marriage is of greater importance in rural areas as a mechanism for land acquisition and for the transfer of legal tenure.

The low proportion of single interviewees in Zambrana is accounted for by the greater reliance of rural households on family labor to survive in a subsistence economy. The higher rates of divorced or separated women in Gazcue and Zambrana are difficult to explain conclusively, but are most likely due to the limits of sample size. In both locations, the women receive support through family ties. In Gazcue, the women are more likely to have spent most of their adult lives in the same area, or even the same house, and now live alone. The tendency to have larger families in rural areas means that the widowed women in Zambrana live predominantly with close family members and relatives in extended households.

A comparison of the type of union and the race of an interviewee shows that Dominicans who describe themselves with lighter terminology are more likely to be married, reflecting the concentration of marriages in the middle and upper classes. The predominance of *indio/a* as a category of racial self-description meant that, as expected, no correlation was evident between union type and race in Los Guandules and Zambrana. Racial preference, however, proves significant when interviewees' descriptions of their partners' race are examined.

Respondents were asked to describe the race of their partner, irrespective of whether they were married, in a consensual union, cohabiting or not; those without a current or previous partner described the race of a girlfriend or boyfriend. Interviewees tended to agree with the general strategy of 'marrying lighter,' or at least seeking a partner of similar color. When questioned about marriage, over a third of the respondents across all classes in my survey sample, expressed the desire to marry lighter (*mejorar la raza* or *blanquearse*). Two-fifths of interviewees who described themselves as *moreno/a* and *negro/a* referred to their partners with the aesthetically lighter terms of *blanco/a*, *indio/a* or *mestizo/a*. Given the *indio/a* majority, however, the opportunity to have a lighter partner is limited; when one marries lighter, the partner, by definition, marries darker—one third of respondents, both male and female, who declared themselves to be *blanco/a* described their partner using the darker term of *indio/a*.

Household structure is an important factor that influences patriarchal relations. Between 1971 and 1991 woman-headed households in the Dominican Republic increased from 19.6 to 25 percent of all households (Báez and Taulé 1993). Woman-headed households are more numerous in urban than rural areas, accounting for 29.4 and 18.0 percent of urban and rural households respectively in 1991—a result of a strong patriarchal culture and the traditional male dominance of land tenure (Báez and Taulé 1993). Eighty percent of interviewees in the total sample lived in households where the head was male; seventeen percent of households were headed by a woman, whether divorced, separated, widowed or single.

The relatively high proportion of women-headed households in the lower and middle classes is the outcome of high rates of divorce or separation, combined with the effects of male migration. There were relatively fewer woman-headed households in the rural sample, compared with the urban locations, which concurs with the national trend. Upper and upper-middle class households are headed predominantly by married men, though male headship is the most common in each sample site and across all class groups. In Gazcue, three-fifths of the households are headed by the husband where the union is based on a civil or religious marriage. Conversely, the male partner in a consensual union heads two-thirds of the households in Los Guandules.

There is no clear correlation between household headship and the race of interviewees. Self-description of race corresponds more directly to class. Upper and middle classes have a higher proportion of male household heads, describing themselves with lighter racial terminology. Interviewees in a household headed by the male partner in a consensual union will be more likely to describe themselves as *indio/a*, due to the predominance of this household type in the lower classes.

The mean household size for the country is 4.6 persons, with little difference between rural and urban areas—4.8 and 4.6 persons per household in 1991 (Báez and Taulé 1993). The corresponding figures for Gazcue, Los Guandules and Zambrana are 4.4, 5.1 and 5.5 persons per household respectively. The advantages of larger household size in the lower-income areas include stronger extended family networks and the economies gained from pooling domestic resources. The mean size of women-headed households in each sample were no different from those of the location as a whole, with the exception of Gazcue, where there was a relatively higher proportion of widows living on their own.

The changing structure of households is a consequence of unstable economic conditions, marriage or union breakdown, and the increasing participation of women in the labor force, predominantly in the urban sphere. The following section analyses women's employment outside the household and considers its impact on the structures of patriarchy.

Work and the relations of patriarchy

The increasing economic activity of women outside the household is an additional factor which may weaken structures of patriarchy. Pessar (1985) has outlined the ways in which women's wage labor is changing traditional domestic codes. First, the female domestic and male public sphere have merged. Secondly, ideas of the male-only breadwinner have been challenged. Thirdly, women's wages are a negotiating point for more equality in household labor. Finally, the growing number of women-headed households has meant has reduced the privileged position of nuclear families in the traditional domestic code.

Wage labor, however, is not always a liberating experience, nor does it necessarily weaken patriarchal structures. Women still confront gender inequalities and discrimination at work. Female headship may be not the result of choice, but an unplanned outcome. Too much emphasis on wage labor leads to the further devaluation of domestic work. The latter is not remunerated with wages, but it may be a source of status within the household and lessen the dominance of patriarchal relations.

Between 1981 and 1990, the female labor force of the Dominican Republic doubled from approximately a half to over one million workers. The number of women described as economically active by the government census (which excludes many informal workers, students and women working in their own household) increased from 41 to 55 per hundred male workers. Despite this growth of women's economic activity, unemployment among women increased from 19.9 percent in 1981 to 35.1 percent in 1990; the result of a greater number of women seeking entry into the labor force. More household members are seeking employment to support the household economy as a result of economic recession and government austerity measures. The rate of economic activity for the total population over ten years old increased from 34.0 percent in 1981 to 43.2 percent in 1990 (Báez and Taulé 1993).

Gender inequalities remain evident in the analysis of male and female occupational groups. Men are still three times as likely to be employers than women, who have a substantially lower probability of being self-employed. Men have a higher likelihood of working as non-remunerated family workers when agricultural labor is taken into account. In terms of occupation type, women are more concentrated in manufacturing, commerce, restaurant and hotel work, community and personal services than men.

The increase in female economic activity rates is partly due to the growth of foreign-owned light manufacturing industries in the expanding free trade zones. Women represent three-quarters of free trade zone employees; almost a third of all workers employed in this type of manufacturing industry (Báez and Taulé 1993). A study of the impact of export manufacturing in the Dominican Republic indicates that women wage earners tend to have more negative attitudes to marriage, thus creating less stable partnerships. These workers, however, can expect greater help with domestic tasks from other members of the household, albeit women, and more control over resources (Finlay 1989).

The greatest numerical incorporation of women into the workforce over the last two decades has taken place in the tertiary sector. Duarte (1989) argues that the gain in tertiary sector employment has occurred principally through the increase in women employed as 'household workers', though employment in tourism has made a significant contribution. Unskilled manual work is the most common source of employment for women in the three survey sites. Respondents were asked to describe their main occupation, though several interviewees, especially among the lower classes, earned income from two or more jobs.

Tertiary non-manual work accounted for 88.0 percent of men's employment in the Gazcue sample, reflecting the middle-class majority. A male bias occurs within the skilled manual, unskilled manual and agricultural occupational groups. Women, however, predominate in the occupational categories of semi-skilled manual and personal service and unskilled workers. Within the former occupational group women often worked as domestic servants, or, in Gazcue, were employed in one of several beauty or hairdressing salons. The predominance of unskilled manual labor as the most common occupational group for women is a result of the prevalence of women working as non-remunerated workers in their own household.

Interviews in the three survey areas revealed a concentration of women's activities in their own households. From the total sample of women interviewed, 45.9 percent said that their principal occupation was as a 'housewife' or unwaged domestic worker in their own home. Only 2.5 percent described themselves as domestic servants. Rather than refute the importance of domestic service as a source of women's employment, the low figure obtained in the survey is more a result of the locations studied. In Zambrana, a remote rural location, the opportunities for employment as domestic servants were severely limited. No domestic servants were interviewed in Gazcue, though some lived in their employers' households. In Los Guandules, four percent of women were employed in domestic service as their main occupation, however, eleven percent occasionally worked in other households outside the neighborhood.

The national census in 1981 indicated that domestic service, at 27 percent of the total, is proportionally the most important economic activity for women in the Dominican Republic; 96 percent of all household workers are female. Domestic servants earn among the lowest incomes in the country. Employers are currently entitled to combine cash with payment 'in kind', such as board and lodging, to bring the overall income of a household worker up to the national minimum wage. The minority of male domestic workers, however, still earn nearly three times as much as women (Báez and Taulé, 1993, 14).

Duarte (1989, 201) compares the characteristics of domestic service to a form of serfdom, the life of the worker dictated by the owner of the household. The employee may be responsible to the 'mistress of the house', but more often than not, the power structure of the household will ultimately rest within a patriarchal framework. While domestic service is an important form of employment for women, it arguably serves only to reinforce the dominance of patriarchal social structures. The 'mistress of the house' is removed from domestic responsibilities, but she merely places another women in a subordinate position without lessening the effects of patriarchy.

Census material rarely gives information concerning employment in the informal labor market due to its irregular status and the flexibility of definition; informal employment acts outside state regulation. Báez and Taulé (1993) suggest that an increasing concentration of women, 52.9 percent in 1983, is employed in the informal sector and domestic service. These sectors have the lowest salaries and minimal legal protection. Male employment in the informal sector and domestic service remains at 39.1 percent of economically active men. Without a coherent definition of what the authors consider to be informal employment, these figures only serve to illustrate a broad trend— women's work continues to be concentrated in sectors characterized by low remuneration and employment vulnerability.

The traditional domestic code is challenged by the increasing numbers of women who have undertaken paid employment outside the home. The position of women workers still remains subordinate to that of men overall, but gender relations within the household have been modified. Changing daily routines, varying forms of household structure and the differing management or allocation of resources alter the domestic sphere in which gender roles are constructed and socialized. Are the shifting relations of patriarchy within the household and at work transforming gendered perceptions of race?

Race, gender and images of the body
Darker-skinned women in the context of a highly racialized and patriarchal society would predictably suffer twice from racist and sexist

subordination. The relationship between the two forms of discrimination was rarely established during interviews in the three sample sites. There is also little evidence from my survey that racial self-description varies on the basis of gender. Men and women in the lower classes describe themselves as *indio/a* to a similar extent. Men from the upper classes defined themselves as *blanco*, though a relatively high proportion of middle-class women described themselves as *blanca* (10.8 percent of all women in the sample). The relationship between race and gender, however, is more apparent when considered in the context of popular culture; specifically through the racialization of sexuality.

Sexuality incorporates the aesthetics of the body through the lens of patriarchal relations and racial perceptions. Just as the personal is political, the body is sexualized and politicized. Brittan and Maynard (1984, 219-220) emphasize the body as a site of oppression:

> It is the sphere in which the consequences of oppression are most readily felt. How an individual experiences his or her body will depend, to a large degree, on the 'others' in the immediate environment, who continuously monitor and interpret his or her bodily processes. To an extent, the body is society's creature. It will live through the image of those who watch, nurture, punish, and reward it. The body becomes an 'it' when it is experienced as a thing among things.

Thus, sexual objectification turns a body into an 'it', but is this objectification a compulsory component of male and female sexual relationships? Brittan and Maynard (1984, 220) argue that sexual objectification is a historical result of the power relationship inherent in hierarchy, 'a social concept and practice, with its basis lying in the meaning given to the division of activities between men and women in society.' A hierarchy was established as men began to value their work above that of women. The devaluation and appropriation of women's work extended to the body. Furthermore, heterosexuality set the parameters for male and female sexuality, the acceptable or popular sexuality. The body is politicized, sexually objectified with respect to the established political and social force of heterosexuality.

Given the dominant relations of patriarchy, sexual objectification tends to be focused on the female body in society. Walby (1990, 108) suggests:

Abstinence from paid work is no longer such a central element of femininity. Overall there has been a shift in the discourse of femininity away from private domesticity towards more public aspects of sexual attractiveness to men, outside as well as inside the family.

It could be argued that although a dominant form of femininity has always existed in the public domain, the aesthetics of feminine beauty vary across cultures. However, all societies socially construct beauty and create space for the exhibition or expectation of beauty in society.

A book of popular Dominican stories illustrates a common masculine conception of female beauty—blond hair, blue eyes, and white skin. One of the protagonists laments that he will stay celibate unless he finds what he considers to be the essence of beauty:

'... I have an idea fixed here in my head, that I'll never get myself a woman. I'll not marry unless she's blond, blue-eyed and beautiful; neither will I have lovers.' (Bautista Lopéz 1995, 67)

The collection of narratives illustrates the prevalent sexual objectification of women by heterosexual men. Another story derides the non-aggressive sexuality of a young man when he fails to develop a sexual relationship with a woman who is attracted to him. His male companion, ridiculing the man for being too effeminate by calling him *el palomo*, 'the dove', advises him that a woman, like bread, must be 'taken while hot,' since later on, nobody will want her.

Men in the Dominican Republic, as in all patriarchal societies, have greater sexual liberty with respect to the social acceptability of multiple relationships. It is not unusual for a man to have at least two current partners; *la mujer* and *la querida*. Women who maintain similar sexual relations face far greater social condemnation. The commonly used term, *el tiguere*, illustrates the reification of sexually active *machismo* or masculinity in the Dominican Republic. A Dominican male author celebrates the forms of *el tiguere*, a colloquial term for 'tiger' referring to a male scoundrel. He characterizes *tigueres* as amorous, valiant, shrewd, tricky, suave or deceptive (Collado 1992). All *tigueres* are most definitely heterosexual and born patriarchs. The opposite of *el tiguere* is *el pariqüayo*, a word invented by the author to describe a 'man without character.' The author aims to address a popular readership but is not entirely light-hearted in his study; he wishes to make a social observation and unwittingly provides an example of the cultural acceptance and incorporation of patriarchal relations. First published in 1992, the book sold enough copies for a second edition to be published, and remains popular in Dominican bookshops.

Gilmore (1990) argues that the cultural dominance of masculinity over femininity in the vast majority of societies finds its expression through the concept of the male as Impregnator-Protector-Provider. Masculinity, he argues, is created via the competition between men to achieve these ideals in a patriarchal, heterosexual-dominated society. Gilmore's understanding of masculinity, and ultimately aspects of femininity, focuses specifically on sexuality. Sexuality is a key social structure in the production and maintenance of patriarchal relations. Conceptions of race are entwined with sexuality and beauty. Aesthetic values tend to discriminate against *negro/a* features, which are deemed ordinary or ugly. Aesthetics are defined variously in terms of perception by the senses, the appreciation of beauty or in accordance with the principles of good taste. The lighter the skin color, the straighter the hair or the narrower the facial features, the greater the tendency to define beauty within these terms. A national television channel had two dark-skinned presenters for an evening program. The station soon became known in popular conversation as the 'Channel of the Uglies'. 'Good taste' is conditioned by preference for lighter skin color.

Employment advertisements seek potential employees of *buena presencia* or *apariencia* who are *bien parecida*. These solicitations for 'a good appearance' conform to the light color bias, and are normally aimed at young women interested in secretarial or restaurant work. Advertisements for employment oriented towards men tend to use the term *dinámico*, suggesting that men are more likely to adapt to changing commercial needs or thrive in the rugged world of business.

Advertising may be envisaged as a moment of suspension between production and consumption in the circulation of commodities (Winship 1980). Consumption itself is a process or moment of production since it reproduces the consumer. Consequently, advertising focuses on this instance of consumption—adverts suggest what or who we should be through the acquisition and consumption of the commodities represented. Successful advertising produces consumers, the adverts sell images of how to construct our relationships with the surrounding physical, cultural or emotional environments.

Sexually and racially biased advertising, often overt, is commonly used in the Dominican media. A brand of Dominican rum has an established marketing campaign featuring light-skinned models with the slogan, *una cosa de hombres*; the bottle of rum and the woman are 'men's things'. The broadcast times for a new television commercial for the brand of rum were advertised in newspapers days before the commercials were due to be aired during the summer of 1994; the adverts were eagerly awaited by the Dominican male audience.[14] The *india clara* model was clothed in a transparent white shirt, playing a saxophone on a beach. The newspaper advertisements attempted to tease the reader with a photo of the model: 'You have to see it! It's sensual, it's daring... it's a man's thing.'

A widely sold tonic for improving male sexual potency, *Fórmula Árabe*, reinforced the sexual, and racial, message of its market strategy during the summer of 1995. The packaging of the tonic has a photo of a muscular, bearded and tanned man squeezed into a pair of jeans, sporting a turban and standing in a sexually assertive pose. Between his straddled legs, clinging onto his thigh, and gazing upwards, sits a white model with long blond hair in a small white silk dress. A magazine advertisement for the product, striking by its overt display of sexuality, showed the naked front torso of a *blanca*, with two male hands reaching for her breasts from behind.[15] Race and sexuality sell products, but more specifically it is the image of a women's body, *blanca* or *india clara*, which sells in the Dominican Republic. The male body has not received as much advertising space as, for example, in Europe or North America.

Racial aesthetics are prevalent in the choice of partner. Partners are frequently described with lighter terminology to emphasize their aesthetic standing. Every week, a national newspaper recently produced a color supplement with photographs of light-skinned women, often tourists, in swimwear on the beach. Many shots were taken using a zoom lens in a highly voyeuristic manner.[16] Very few women were aware that their photograph was being displayed in the national media to increase sales.

The white bias in beauty challenges the desirability of black sexuality. The contradiction is clear—popular male and female opinion reveres the beauty of the *blanco/a*, yet popular sexual myth imbues the *negro/a* or *mulata/o* with vigor and skilful prowess. Bastide (1961, 18) outlines the sexual stereotypes that surround racial classification:

> ... the Dusky Venus hides the debasement of the black woman as a prostitute; and the Black Apollo is seeking revenge on the white man. It is not so much that love breaks down barriers and unites human beings as that racial ideologies extend their conflicts even into love.

Bastide (1961, 13) describes miscegenation in terms of the 'bitterest sexual competition.' Similarly, Fanon (1986) views the desire of dark-skinned women for lighter men as an attempt to obtain whiteness, to gain legitimacy and bear children in the 'white world.' The craving for revenge, Fanon relates, drives darker-skinned men's desire for white women. The *negro/a* sexuality-*blanco/a* beauty dialectic is the basis for the success of the Dominican sex tourism industry. A Dominican tabloid newspaper ran a front-page article on the alleged exodus to Europe of dark-skinned Dominicans with lighter-skinned European tourists, a product of casual and calculated holiday romance:

> Wow! Black Dominicans strolling through European capitals arm-in-arm with stunning blondes who are now their wives, thanks to Cupid's legendary arrow. These women came here, fell in love and took home their men.[17]

Popular images portray *la negra* as lower-class street sellers, prostitutes and single mothers. Darker skin color is associated with the erotic, but also with the more secretive and potent aspects of popular Afro-syncretic belief. *Brujería* and the magical powers of *vodú* are commonly associated with *negritud*, and Haiti.

Religion: racialized and gendered

Religion is a key institution which reinforces relations of patriarchy in Dominican society. The prevalence and powerful influence of Catholicism continues to reinforce gender inequality, strengthening social norms with religious and moral precepts. The household is an important location for the expression of Afro-syncretic beliefs, which are practiced away from the public, and Catholic, gaze. A paradox of emotions exist among Dominican believers who are outwardly hostile to Haiti, yet inwardly subscribe to beliefs and superstitions which mirror Haitian *vodoun*. Gender relations in patriarchal Dominican society reinforce historical and contemporary images of *la raza dominicana* and support racist prejudice.

Ninety-two percent of the people interviewed professed Catholicism as their main form of religious belief, a figure concurrent with the national average. This is more a public acknowledgement of the official state religion rather than a faithful reflection of active religious practice. People were more likely to criticize the Church, or to express no religious conviction if they lived in the middle-income neighborhood of Gazcue, although there was no significant correlation between class and religious belief.

The Catholic Church is one of the most powerful institutions in the Dominican Republic. The close alliance between Church and state is evident through the high profile of religious leaders as mediators during election periods, and during the government celebrations in 1992 of the five hundredth anniversary of the 'discovery and evangelization of the New World.'

The importance of the Church is reflected in its influence on patriarchal relations in society. The Church considers the nuclear family with a married male household head as the socially desirable norm. Men are expected to lead religious as well as familial matters; patriarchy receives a divine mandate which may be defended with Biblical authority. Daly (1975) argues that the Church has been fundamental in justifying the subordination of women as the second sex. Virginity is considered as a prime virtue amongst unmarried women. It becomes the right of the man to initiate sexually his female partner when married, but the Church appears to be more tolerant of men's sexual infidelities or parallel sexual relationships. During 1992, an intense campaign by the Church forced the defeat of a motion in Congress which aimed to allow greater flexibility for abortion on medical grounds. Unable to support a successful campaign on medical issues alone, the Church used notions of moral condemnation—a vote for greater flexibility was a vote against religion. Women seeking abortion face not only legal punishment, but the guilt of divine censure.

Nevertheless, women make up the majority of the Catholic congregation and, amongst interviewees in Gazcue, Los Guandules and

Zambrana, are almost twice as likely as men to attend church on a regular basis. Although excluded from the upper hierarchy of the Church, women are the main organizers of most popular religious activities. Men participate in religious ceremonies or celebrations, but do not maintain them.

González (1973) has studied the preparations for the *Carnaval* in Santiago, when the *lechones*, or devils, are let loose to run through the streets of the city on Ash Wednesday. Whilst not an official part of the Easter celebrations, the Church engages in *Carnaval* as a popular cultural institution. The *lechones* are men dressed in colorful masks and bright clothing. The creation of such costumes takes much time, effort and expense, the latter increasingly limiting the participation of low-income earners. Women usually assist in the production of costumes, but may not participate as *lechones* in the *Carnaval*. The most visibly important female role is that of the Queen of *Carnaval*, elected from amongst the daughters of the organizers. The family of the chosen Queen must pay for her dress and entourage, thus, restricting possible candidates to the higher-income, and usually lighter-skinned, groups.

Evangelism is an increasingly important influence in Caribbean societies. Mormon, Adventist and Pentecostal churches have established expanding missions throughout the Dominican Republic. However, they were not a significant influence amongst interviewees in the survey. Catholicism is undoubtedly the most influential and widespread religion, although syncretic religious practices may be found throughout Dominican society. The syncretic belief system is a synthesis of formal Catholicism and *vodú*. Davis (1987) outlines similar religious manifestations in the Dominican Republic and Haiti. The secrecy of *vodú* is strongly associated with Haitians and Dominicans with darker skin color. The latter, however, it is commonly believed, cannot be possessed by spirits to the same extent. Religious difference symbolizes racial difference, but the separation is as ambiguous as racial identity itself. The 'darker side' of religion correlates with skin color in popular perception. In border regions it has been commonly believed that Haitian women could fly like the spirits (Derby 1994).

In rural areas interviewees more readily discussed the influence of Dominican *vodú* and expressed their belief in *brujería* and *los santos* (the saints), referring frequently to elements of African-Christian syncretic religion. In the Zambrana region, *brujería* is more widely acknowledged as common practice, reflecting a strong influence of local *brujos/as* and local belief system. One *brujo* is well known in the area and regularly receives visitors from the provincial capital of Cotuí seeking spiritual advice on a variety of matters. These clients come from all social backgrounds; most noticeable were the richer clients who would arrive in expensive four-wheel-drive vehicles.

In general, however, a reticent attitude existed amongst interviewees to discuss *brujería*. Such beliefs were highly personal, open to ridicule by non-believers and discouraged by the Church, particularly in the urban areas. Unlike Haitian *vodoun*, the African-Christian syncretic belief in the Dominican Republic is hidden from general view, though the majority of the population share some form of belief in *los santos*. The latter are saints of the Catholic Church whose religious characteristics and powers have become fused with African deities, a legacy from the period of slavery. Each saint represents certain emotions or is connected to an occasion, with specific prayers and offerings presented to him or her, usually at a small shrine in the home. Every believer will worship a patron saint, amongst a few others, for protection and spiritual guidance.

Given the antagonism at state and individual levels between Haiti and the Dominican Republic, *vodú* is generally perceived to be a Haitian vice—the black magic of an uncivilized, violent, dangerous African society. Many argue that *vodú* is purely a Haitian phenomenon, but studies have shown the close evolution and linkage between variants of *vodú* across the island (Ducoudray 1975). *Vodú* is an island-wide phenomenon, with certain sites regarded as being of particular religious importance, such as Arcahaie in southern Haiti (Krohn-Hansen 1995). *Brujería* incorporates notions of fear and respect. Faith in *brujería* may take the form of advice with lottery numbers or in issues of love, to the more sinister, though no less common, *mal de ojo*, the casting of an 'evil eye', often cited as the root cause of a strange or sudden illness. Such ailments are often deemed to be the result of a malicious spell cast upon an opponent via the medium of the *brujo/a*.

Women play an important role in popular syncretic religion at all levels and functions. Spiritual leaders may be men or women, and the lack of gender bias is expressed in the importance ceded to the various spiritual categories. The Dominican pantheon consists of twenty-one divisions; five contain female figures—these are Legbá, Ogún, Guedé,

Radá and India (Albert Batista 1993). Anaísa, for example, is the popular goddess of love, fond of drinking, dancing and perfumes. Formerly a prostitute, she is a specialist in matters of love. The Barón del Cementerio is the most widely known *luá*, or god, in the Dominican Republic. He governs cemeteries, protecting bodies and helping the dead purge their sins. Both gods, Anaísa and the Barón, have their corresponding Catholic saints, Santa Ana and San Elías respectively, a portrait of whom would be placed in the home of devotees. The deities are from African and European religious traditions, having characteristics recognizable and sympathetic to their followers' needs. The gods are highly gendered entities, maintaining characteristics and stereotypes pertinent to the influences of contemporary society. Several saints, such as the Virgen de Regla and San Juan Bautista in Baní are represented as *negro/a*, though the majority are lighter-skinned.

Gender division is evident in instruments played during celebrations. Men play the various sizes of drum, which themselves are considered as sacred objects, since they summon the gods, while women play the tambourines. Religious associations may exhibit patriarchal relations in the allocation of posts—for example, the treasurer is often a man due to the traditional masculinization of financial matters. Women normally prepare the food and make the arrangements for religious celebrations, whilst the men focus upon enjoying the social occasion. Religion and gender codes differentially incorporate men and women into Dominican society and thus emphasize the socialization of racial perceptions and patriarchal structures.

5.
The Dominican Republic: A Transnational Society

'Sometime during 1996, at the very least, Latinos surpassed Blacks as the second largest ethno-racial group in New York City.'
—Mike Davis (1999, 3)

'If I win the presidency, I am going to turn the Dominican Republic into a little New York.'
—Leonel Fernández (*El Siglo*, 9 August 1997)

Latinos/as have been making a big noise in the States. Mambo and salsa first rumbled the New York club scene several decades ago, and now contemporary artists continue to project *latinidad* to a widening mainstream audience. As more Hispanic authors become resident on the lists of English-language bestsellers, Latino/a singers and actors leap not only between film screen and recording studio, but also from the Latin Top Ten to Dr Fox's Pepsi Chart. Dominicans form an integral part of this cultural and demographic growth of Latino/a society.

Accounting for one tenth of the US population today, Latino/as or Hispanics will make up over a fifth of the total population of 383 million by 2050 (Castro 1993). Dominicans, principally located in the northeast, but with significant communities stretching from Florida to Alaska and Rhode Island to California, are now among the fastest growing ethnic groups, and the largest Latino/a immigrant community in New York City. The Dominican Republic supplied more migrants to New York City than any other country during the 1980s. In 1990, 511, 297 Dominicans were permanent residents in the United States, of whom two-thirds lived in New York state (U.S. Bureau of Census 1993). Most families in the Dominican Republic share some experience of migration, either directly or via relatives. The former Dominican president (1996-2000), Leonel Fernández, grew up in New York and attended college in the US. He has openly declared his wish to return to live there at the end of his term of office. Given the notable increase of Dominicans living in the United States and their impact on Dominican society, how has this experience influenced perceptions of ethnicity and race?

The constant interchange and two-way flow of people, capital and culture across international boundaries is the subject of the burgeoning literature on transnationalism. The migration of Dominicans to the United States, in particular, has dramatically shaped the country's development over the last three decades. The Dominican Republic is a transnational society that increasingly relies on migrant remittances and commerce. Proximity and the expanding web of familial, social, political and economic ties facilitate an array of linkages that play an important part in everyday lives (Itzigsohn et al 1999). While not suggesting that the majority of Dominicans are in a constant state of airborne flux, jetting between JFK and the Airport of the Americas in Santo Domingo at the drop of a ticket, the links between Dominicans on the island and those Stateside form a crucial backbone to Dominican society.

The community provides the social base or context for the highly variable outcomes of the migratory experience. Social embeddedness reaffirms the importance of the migrant community or ethnic enclave, in which 'individual profit-making is enmeshed in a dense grid of social expectations and reciprocal obligations' (Portes and Guarnizo 1991, 104). The significance of the Dominican experience is the international nature of this grid of social and cultural interaction, which has dramatically increased in density since the 1960s. Sites of emigration and immigration are dynamically interconnected, with transnational households often perceived as somehow bridging two or more locations (Grasmuck and Pessar 1991). Rural sending areas adopt aspects of urban and transnational cultures, while New York neighborhoods become transformed into Dominican economic and cultural enclaves. Sutton and Chaney (1992) describe the development of 'transnational socio-cultural systems', whereby an increasingly globalized economy has respatialized communities. National boundaries have been blurred in certain realms, but it is as well to recognize that the mounting literature on transnationalism has been accompanied in many cases by tighter citizenship requirements and colossal expenditure on surveillance at many international borders.

Whereas much emphasis has been placed upon the changing notions of race among Dominicans in the United States, I argue that stasis or the direct transferal of existing conceptions of race may be as equally important an aspect of the migratory experience. Sørensen (1997) and Duany (1996) contend that transnationalism leads to a developing awareness among Dominicans of 'their black roots and reaching out to other Caribbean and Latino peoples' (Duany 1996, 269). Nevertheless, Duany (1998) acknowledges the reinforcement of Dominican ethnicity, categorizing it as a form of resistance to the prevailing racial order in the US. Undoubtedly, the experience of living in the United States impacts upon conceptions of ethnicity and self-representation, but within the Dominican community, racialized terminology and perceptions of race socialized within Dominican society persist.

The history of Dominican migration

The incorporation of the Dominican Republic into the periphery of the world economy in the late nineteenth century established the basis for the migration of Dominican labor overseas. The United States was the major destination for Dominican migrants during the twentieth century, in particular after the 1960s. International migration was limited during the era of Trujillo (1930-1961) with fewer than 10,000 Dominicans going to the United States during the 1950s. Trujillo restricted the migration of the national work force, in order to maintain maximum control over domestic labor.

Following the assassination of Trujillo, restrictions were lifted and the number of Dominicans migrating to the United States grew rapidly. Between 1960 and 1963, Dominican documented migration to the United States increased from just over 5,000 to 66,919 (Georges 1990, 37). Migration was perceived by the Dominican government as a necessary and obvious safety valve to relieve social and economic pressures. Corresponding to the premises of equilibrium theory, the positive influence of migration for the development of the country was emphasized.

The domestic political situation promoted migration to the United States in 1966 and 1978; both years reflect political turning points, when a change of government provoked the emigration of political opponents. The number of legal visas issued in 1966 increased by 74.0 percent to 16,503, compared with 9,503 during 1965, the year of the

April Revolution and subsequent invasion by the United States (Georges 1990, 39). Those who feared repression as a result of their opposition to the new United States-backed government paradoxically found themselves seeking exile in the Dominican community of New York. The PRD election victory in 1978 was another cause for politically motivated migration. During that year, 19,458 Dominicans were admitted as residents to the United States. A deteriorating economy, the prospect of a more radical government and changing networks of patronage following three terms of PRSC government, induced a sixty percent increase in legal residency applications and approvals.

Migration to the United States has continued to grow in scale and importance. Dominican nationals are now second only to Mexicans among Latin American nationals arriving in the United States—since the 1970s the number of immigrant and non-immigrant Dominicans arriving every year averages 150,000 (Cosgrove 1992). When assessing the scale of Dominican migration to the United States, the illegality or non-documentation of many arrivals must be taken into account. Between 1961 and 1981, 255,578 Dominican immigrants legally entered the United States. The importance of undocumented migration is clear if estimates of up to 1.5 million living in the United States today are to be believed. The figure probably lies at around 800,000. Whilst an exact total remains elusive, Dominican neighborhoods are evidence of the scale of the migratory flow, especially in New York City, the destination for approximately ninety percent of Dominicans (Pessar 1995). Over a half of the Dominicans living in the city reside in the north Manhattan neighborhood of Washington Heights—a highly visible enclave. There are an estimated 20,000 Dominican-owned businesses in New York City, with Dominicans owning approximately seventy percent of the city's grocery stores or *bodegas* (Portes and Guarnizo 1991, 111).

The relatively recent process of return migration to the Dominican Republic has attracted a growing amount of research on transnationalism. The 'myth of return' does not apply to the transnational community (Anwar 1978). The reality of re-migration or return has become part of the migrant ethos; a national study of Dominican migrants indicates that a relatively high proportion return to the country—39 percent at the time of the survey (Ugalde, Bean and Cardenas 1979). Duany (1994) confirms the strength of a return ideology in his research on the Dominican community in Washington Heights. Two-thirds of interviewees expressed a desire to go back to live in the Dominican Republic, and three-quarters had visited at least twice during the previous five years. More and more Dominicans have decided to make roots in the United States. Nevertheless, despite the growing recognition and self-realization of Dominican Americans, the tension between ideas of assimilation and a continuing attachment to the island remains apparent.

Migrant characteristics

Dominican communities have become established across the world. A survey of 8,000 households in the Dominican Republic showed that 16.7 percent had members living overseas (Profamilia 1993). Puerto Rico, Haiti, Venezuela, Spain and the Netherlands were all countries in which interviewees had lived at some stage, but the United States was by far the most common destination. Two-thirds of the thirty-seven returned migrants who were interviewed in the Dominican Republic had migrated to the United States. They were relatively young, generally from urban backgrounds and the majority was middle-class. There were more returned male migrants, though the small sample size restricts a detailed analysis of gender variation among migrants. Three-quarters of the sample resided in the neighborhood of Gazcue, where the returnees were on average older. All had migrated in order to improve their employment opportunities, while several had also studied overseas.

International migrants are defined as those Dominicans who have lived outside the Dominican Republic for a substantial period, rather than temporary migrants on social, medical or business trips. However, even short-term visits abroad add to the collective experience and external contacts of a transnational community; the most popular destinations for short-term travel among interviewees being the United States and Puerto Rico. Almost a third of all respondents had traveled outside the Dominican Republic. This includes the thirty-seven respondents (12.3% of the total sample) who were returned migrants at the time of interview. A quarter expressed the intention or desire to return to the United States at some stage for family or employment reasons.

Due to the obvious issue of sensitivity, the question of the legality was not raised. Nevertheless, two returned migrants, both aged 18, were content to tell something of their clandestine journeys to Puerto Rico. Eduardo recounted in adventurous terms his trip across the Mona Passage in an open launch; a voyage, which he admitted, had terrified him, but which he would do again if life worsened in Santo Domingo. Joel was a stowaway on a merchant ship. Although more reticent to elucidate in greater detail, he had hid on a vessel heading for San Juan with several friends, seemingly with the captain's knowledge and thus perhaps for an undisclosed fee. Whereas Eduardo returned of his own volition after several months of work, Joel was arrested and deported a few weeks after arrival. The latter's misfortune and bashful account of the experience was in stark contrast to Eduardo's more successful, and hence upbeat, chronicle of events. Other respondents were far more reluctant to mention their work experience overseas, presumably due to a lack of legal documentation at the time of migration and during employment. Pérez (cited in Grasmuck 1984) found that 17 percent of a sample of Dominican migrants in New York had no legal documentation for their residence, though over a third had been living illegally in the United States at some point of their migrant history.

A number of studies on the social composition and characteristics of the migrant flow have reached different conclusions concerning its origin and form. The analyses are derived mainly from regional samples, rather than from a national survey. Earlier studies assumed that most migrants were former peasant farmers, with small to medium-sized land-holdings, or rural proletarians (Sassen-Koob 1979). González (1970) studied the migratory experience of peasants from the Cibao, while Hendricks (1974) focused on the growing economic dependency on international migration in a rural highland settlement. The former suggests that the Cibao has reached saturation point with respect to peasant production. Key problems were the division of land under inheritance laws into plots too small for efficient cultivation, the lack of modernized farming techniques due to limited capital and knowledge, and oscillating prices for agricultural products. Soils have been overworked, while deforestation has decreased fertility and increased rates of erosion.

Migration from rural areas in the Dominican Republic during the 1950s created an average annual urban population growth rate of 9 percent, almost double that of today. Net migration from rural areas accounted for at least half of the urban population increase during that time. Relatively cheaper international flights and fewer travel restrictions have subsequently made emigration a real possibility for an increasing number of Dominicans.

Ugalde, Bean and Cardenas (1979) were the first to oppose the dominant view that Dominican migrants originated from rural areas. Their analysis of the only national-level survey of 12,500 households in the Dominican Republic suggests that just 24 percent of all international migrants had rural origins. There is now general agreement that most migrants are from urban areas, though many may have migrated initially from the countryside. They tend also to come from the middle and lower middle classes, rather than from the lowest classes or least-skilled section of the labor market. While the reasons for migrating are most often cited as wage and profit earning, migrants are less likely to have been unemployed than non-migrants. Georges (1990) suggests that the majority of migrants had jobs in the Dominican Republic and that the desire for higher earnings was a key motive for international migration.

Báez Evertsz and d'Oleo Ramírez (1986) characterize Dominican international migrants as members of the urban lower middle and working classes, while Bray (1984) emphasizes a middle-class origin. The latter has suggested that a 'middle-class bottleneck' developed during the 1960s as a result of political discrimination and economic constraints experienced by the relatively well-educated Dominican middle class. The economy did not meet the employment demands of this class, and political patronage frustrated those not aligned with government interests.

Bray challenges the dependency and orthodox economic theories which focus on migration originating from low-income rural areas. Dependency theory posits that the penetration of capital into rural areas results in the proletarianization of subsistence farmers, creating a surplus labor pool which drives internal and international migration. Orthodox economic theory emphasizes the forces of supply and demand, particularly with respect to wage differentials, thus suggesting that the rural labor force is likely to migrate in search of higher incomes.

In contrast to Bray, Piore (1979) contends that middle-class migration is transitional, thus, any 'bottlenecks' will be temporary. The Dominican Republic, she argues, is a 'shift case.' Dominican migrants were originally from the urban middle class, but the contemporary flow now consists of rural and lower-class migrants. My present research, however, shows that Dominican migration does not fit the 'class shift' model. Middle-class migration is an enduring feature of Dominican development.

Several studies have shown that international migrants from rural areas of the Dominican Republic originate primarily from the sector of 'medium and large farmers' or among the 'rural capitalists', many residing in urban areas before leaving for the United States (Bray 1984). Given the varied range of research results concerning the composition of the migrant flow, it is feasible to propose that all levels of Dominican society are directly incorporated into the transnational community, except perhaps for the very low-income groups. Grasmuck (1984) has suggested that migrant characteristics range between the categories of unskilled labor and professional workers. Only migrants from the lowest stratum are under-represented. Over a half of the returned migrants interviewed during my research were professional or non-manual workers, though a quarter were unskilled. Respondents who had experience of overseas travel were over-represented in the higher status occupational groups. Unskilled manual workers were under-represented among returned migrants, despite accounting for over a quarter of the sample.

The predominance of upper- and upper-middle-class migrants reflects the high academic attainment of the sample. Nearly a half of the returned migrants had attended university, and over three-quarters had completed secondary education—levels well above those of the total sample. Interviewees who had traveled outside the Dominican Republic similarly had reached levels of education well beyond those of the total sample. An unexpectedly high proportion of migrants (8.1 percent of the sample) had received no formal education. This anomaly is accounted for by the small sample size—the three interviewees who had no schooling were unskilled manual workers from Los Guandules and Zambrana.

Influences of migration in the sending society

By the start of the 1990s, the impact of contemporary international migration was evident throughout Dominican society. International migrants made strong impressions not only as consumers and investors, but also by influencing popular culture, the arts, music and media. The reaction of non-migrants to returnees in rural and urban areas also became more diverse, reflecting their perception, often grossly stereotyped, of North American lifestyles and influences.

During the 1960s and early 1970s, the image of those who migrated to the United States was generally positive in the Dominican Republic. Migrants were perceived as pioneers, saving diligently for the return to the Dominican Republic and living frugal lives. Migration provided the possibility, or at least embodied an aspiration, to increase income earning and social standing, and to improve opportunities for dependants. International migration provided an outlet for the movement of 'excess' population. The perception of emigration as a demographic and economic pressure valve was promoted by government indifference to stemming the flow.

Migration is a prominent theme in everyday life. An American visa or the journey to the United States is increasingly seen as necessary for personal advancement. A similar migrant syndrome has been observed by Reichert (1981) in Mexico, where relatively high dollar earnings in the United States encouraged more people to migrate, exacerbating imbalances by disintegrating rural economies and increasing dependence on migrant remittances.

As the 1970s progressed, an increasingly hostile reception was given to returned Dominican migrants. The positive image of the majority as honest and hardworking became tarnished. The ostentatious display of wealth by some returnees, combined with the growth of the drug trade among Dominicans in New York, sullied previous perceptions. Dominican migrants are now commonly associated with drug dealing. The head of the North Manhattan drug squad commented, 'It is unfair to assume that all Dominicans peddle drugs... although 18 months in the drug trade will earn you enough to go back to the Republic.'[18] Social problems in Dominican society were increasingly blamed on influences brought to the island from the United States.

During the 1990s, the non-migrant Dominican elite, who felt challenged by the younger migrant generation of *nuevos ricos*, promoted images of these migrants as villains, involved in illicit trading, generating inflation, crime, violence and drug problems in the Dominican Republic. Everyday language incorporates disparaging epithets such as *dominicanyork* and *cadenú*. The latter term refers to the gold jewelry often worn by Dominicans who have lived or still reside in New York, the *dominicanyorks*. One returned migrant, interviewed during a separate study, had harsh words for *dominicanyorks*, whom she perceived to be wholly unlike the earlier generation of Dominican migrants. *Dominicanyorks* were:

... ill-educated Dominicans who emigrated to the United States and got drunk on that culture. They scraped around to make easy money and so spent it without any care. They live, dress and act to catch the attention of others. The *dominicanyorks* are discriminated against because of their scandalous behavior and because they change quiet neighborhoods for the worse. (Bueno 1995, 24)

Returned migrants face heightened alienation from the dominant class and earlier migrants. Wealthy returnees have experienced social exclusion from businesses, associations, social clubs and schools. Paradoxically, returned migrants may have helped to reduce class polarization in Dominican society by transferring capital through remittances and savings during the 1980s, when the urban middle class contracted as a result of a deteriorating national economy. Guarnizo suggests that the lower classes still admire returnees as successful adventurers who challenge the non-migrant traditional elite. This may be true at an individual level, but the negative image of the *dominicanyork* is evident across all class groups. Respondents in the present survey were united in their negative perception of what the term *dominicanyork* meant to them: 'bad news', 'drug peddlers' and 'crooks.' Many lamented the wealth inequality which they exemplified, combined with their apparent rejection or loss of *dominicanidad*—they were neither Dominican nor American.

The illegal or undocumented nature of many migrants' movements between the United States, Puerto Rico and the Dominican Republic has contributed to the negative image of *dominicanyorks*. To enter legally into the United States, a valid immigrant or temporary visitor's visa is required. The dominance of demand over supply has made the visa a potent icon and status symbol in Dominican society. There is a general saying: 'To have an American visa is to have a profession.' A returned migrant commented on the importance to her of having US residency status, and her misfortune at not 'getting' citizenship:

We kept our residents' visa, and I would have liked to get citizenship, but I didn't qualify for it because during my time living there, I visited here more than I remained there. My children won't forgive their dad for not getting residency for them. Both of them are mad to get away. For me citizenship is important—when you reach retirement age you can claim a pension. (Bueno 1995, 10)

Visas and United States citizenship are highly valued commodities. A citizen has access to the benefits of welfare and pension programs, and this provides a concrete basis for the establishment of a transnational household.

Popular folklore has evolved around methods of visa application. There have often been rumors which circulate in rural and urban areas concerning the latest scam or short cut in the application process. González (1970) describes the events of the alleged 'Day of Grace' in November 1966 when Thanksgiving and the anniversary of President Kennedy's assassination coincided. The size of the queue for visa applications outside the American Consulate in Santo Domingo increased fivefold to over one thousand people, after a radio announcement reported rumors of the unrestricted issuing of visas. The importance of an American 'friend' putting in a good word for a visa applicant is also part of the visa folklore which illustrates the prominence of paternalism in Dominican culture. This notion is very much part of reality. González (1970) suggests that Dominicans with 'friends' at the United States Consulate managed to get visas.

Visas have become increasingly difficult to obtain, hence the dramatic rise of illegal migration. The difficulty of obtaining an immigrant visa in Santo Domingo has meant that many Dominicans apply for temporary visas and overstay the legal visiting period. Formal and informal businesses have responded to the demand for visas or illegal entry into the United States. Agents, brokers and lawyers have all gained financially through the aspirations of potential migrants. In Santo Domingo, several legal consultancies now advise clients specifically on how to obtain residency in the United States. Brokers, or *buscones*, arrange undocumented entries into the United States for aspirant migrants via Puerto Rico, making use of Puerto Ricans' US citizenship to pass through mainland migration control, with the aid of false Puerto Rican identity. The passage to Puerto Rico is usually by boat, or sometimes light aircraft, and Dominican newspapers regularly have reports of failed attempts, involving the deportation or death of aspirant migrants.[19] Puerto Rico is the second most popular destination for legal and undocumented Dominican migrants, with about 60,000 Dominicans living there. Other undocumented entry routes to the United States are via Mexico or the US Virgin Islands.

The importance of migration in Dominican society is illustrated by the relative success of the country's two most recent films to gain international recognition. *El Pasaje de Ida* (1991) is based on the true story of a dozen Dominican stowaways who hid in the ballast tanks of a Puerto Rican ship, later drowning when the tanks were flooded. *Nueba Yol* (1995), the colloquial Dominican name for New York, recounts the life of Balbueno, a Dominican migrant, who struggles to find work, but eventually makes a successful return to the Dominican homeland. Heavy with stereotypes, the film attempts to portray the contradictions within a migrant's life—the support and demands of kin, the stresses placed upon Dominican family values, the limited opportunities for employment, the insecurity of undocumented status and the struggle to return.

These experiences have created a 'reactive cultural identity' among migrants (Guarnizo 1993, 43). When abroad, the cultural values of the society of origin become the dominant aspect of the migrant's identity. Conversely, on temporary or permanent return, values adopted from abroad become exalted by the migrant, yet the migrant is perceived as a foreigner in both societies. Bueno (1995) suggests this layering of identities preserves cultural values among Dominican migrants while in the United States. Migrants aim to maintain something of their origins—among Dominicans one aspect that remains unchanged, and reacts against mainstream norms, is racial identification.

Implicit in the reactive identity of migrants is the underlying tension or conflict between different cultural or racial experiences and traditions. This discord provides an unstable basis for transnational identity. One Dominican writer expresses the stress of this experience and its importance for the perception of her own *dominicanidad*:

The New York experience, which was so crucial to my discovery of my Caribbean and racial identity, has made me a very, very critical person with respect to my own society. Things I never noticed before, I now see. Like racism, for example. Class differences. Santo Domingo is a very societally structured city. The situation of women is atrocious. I get almost rude about this because I can't stand the kind of sexist behavior that exists in my country. And for that, you pay the price of ostracism. It's really hard. By dint of having lived in the United States, I am considered a 'liberated woman,' which means that the men feel they have a green light to harass me sexually while the women distrust me. That's the most painful part... And then you realize that you symbolize all the things that she has never been able to do, and perhaps never will; leave the country, study what she wants to. (Vicioso 1994, 274)

The suffocating nature of patriarchy in the Dominican Republic is similarly evident in the writing of another Dominican woman, who has lived in the United States for over thirty years. The extract illustrates how the relationship between a young Dominican man and his female cousins is entirely dependent on the location and context:

When he's in the States, where he went to prep school and is now in college, he's one of us, our buddy. But back on the Island, he struts and turns macho, needling us with the unfair advantage being male here gives him (Alvarez 1991, 127).

Dominican patriarchal norms are subdued in the United States, but are revived on return to the homeland. Racial identity, however, is not only re-established when back in Dominican society, but arguably remains intact and active whilst outside the Dominican Republic.

An element of conservatism is present in the tense fusion of transnational identities. Georges (1990) agrees with Rhoades (1978) by suggesting that the social effect of migration is often conservative, or even preservative, promoting the traditional structures of the country of origin. Rhoades suggests that the cultural hearth of the homeland remains the social frame of reference against which the changing status and fortunes of migrants are measured. The sending community provides the social and economic template, though the effects of migration are the stimuli for change. The concept of a racial hearth is apt for the subsequent discussion of migration and race.

González (1970) suggests that among Dominicans working in the United States, the importance of their class status on return to the Dominican Republic is of greater significance than their social standing in the United States. This reaffirms the importance of the cultural hearth, points to the suggested transformation of class structure through return migration. New forms of social segregation between migrants and the non-migrant population have been created as a result of different levels of education, income and cultural influences. In New York, Dominican migrants have established ethnic enclaves, reproducing the cultural and social 'baggage' brought over from the homeland. The development of transnational communities involves not only the transfer of people and culture, but the flow of capital.

Remittances

Remittances sent by migrants back to the Dominican Republic are crucial to the Dominican economy as a major source of foreign exchange and an aid to the balance of payments. Estimates placed the value of these remittances at between $230 and $280 million per year during the 1980s, equivalent to 10 percent of the Gross National Product, and a greater source of export earnings than the sugar industry (Georges 1990). By 1989, remittances equaled the sum of the three traditional exports from the Dominican Republic, sugar, coffee and tobacco. Only income generated by tourism challenges the importance of migrants' money. Jaime Fernández succinctly argued that the majority of families in the Dominican Republic depended on work in the United States, outlining the growing dependence of the country on external contacts: 'The Dominican Republic has always been dependent on other countries—the second city is not Santiago at all, but New York. Everything comes from there.'

The impact of remittances increased during the 1990s as the Dominican economy deteriorated. Georges studied a Dominican village in which one-third of the community's income was generated by remittances sent from the United States. Most of the money goes towards household consumption rather than investment, and remittances are sometimes sent on a regular basis as a dependable source of household income. González (1970) stresses that even after a migrant's death the dependants may receive survivors' benefits from the social security system if the migrant had obtained United States citizenship.

Remittance checks may be cashed informally, never going via the Central Bank to add to the country's dollar reserve. As a result, the exact influence and size of remittance capital is difficult to ascertain on a national basis. The International Labor Organization advises that although remittances selectively aid some families in the sending society, the net positive effects are debatable. Grasmuck's (1984) study of three sending communities in the Dominican Republic suggests that remittances may provide temporary relief for individual families, but in general, migration has promoted a dependency on these payments, which has undermined the productive base of communities. Inequality among household incomes has increased, and highly unequal land tenure patterns have worsened in rural areas. Middle to large landholders are most likely to receive remittances, enabling them to cutback on low-return investments in farming. The demand for occasional or seasonal labor, important for many low-income households, is then reduced.

Georges (1990) argues, however, that migration has had little effect on the class structure in her rural study area, and not led to the disorganization of communities. Remittances have maintained, rather than created, the middle class, since most migrants in her sample originated from privileged households. Migration, thus, represents a 'holding strategy' for the middle strata. The movement of people and capital has undoubtedly allowed many middle-class families to maintain their social and economic position, but such a holding strategy neglects the dynamics of change inherent in a transnational community. Class structures and social status are changing under the influence of international migration. Perceptions of, and expectations among, returned migrants have modified Dominican society since the 1960s. A holding strategy has limited relevance for the variety of neighborhoods in which the increased incomes of migrant households has improved the relative socio-economic standing of those households. An inherent outcome of a remittance-based local economy is the growing wealth disparity in sending communities, most noticeably at the level of individual households.

Household transformation in the transnational community

Transnational migration has led to the formation of a special type of household, involving the spatial dispersion of the domestic unit across two or more countries and the creation of multinuclear families. The changing structure of migrant households causes tension when patriarchal norms are challenged. Pessar (1985) argues that the social mobility of a migrant is usually achieved at the level of the household rather than the individual. Household structure is therefore an important factor for assessing the effect of transnationalism on gender relations.

Women are more likely to work beyond the domestic sphere if living outside the Dominican Republic, providing the basis for a relatively more independent lifestyle. In migrant or transnational households, relations of patriarchy may, thus, be less severe, since more women work outside the household and earn separate wages. Women, however, frequently lag behind men in occupational and economic attainment during the migration process (Guarnizo 1993). They are also more likely to return due to family reasons, especially those concerning the education of children. The dynamism of a household functioning across national boundaries means that it is uncommon to find complete nuclear or extended family networks based permanently at either end of the migration stream, hence the prevalence of transnational families or multinuclear households.

Multinuclear family structure has helped to challenge traditional domestic codes, though it has been viewed as a major cause of reduced family solidarity—one of the most reliable sources of social capital. Stress may fracture familial bonds when expectations are placed on migrants to provide remittances for extended families, or when relatives are forced to care for non-migratory or returned family members. Gilbertson and Gurak (1992) argue that cyclical migration and the greater number of migrants, who were single before migration, have produced higher rates of female headship. The majority of households with returned migrants were male-headed, though nearly a quarter were headed by single women—higher than the sample as a whole. The over-representation of households headed by women with returned migrants is accounted for by the relative high proportion of widows in the migrant sample. Very few woman-headed households had respondent members who had traveled overseas, an indication of their lower household incomes. Almost two-thirds of the households in which returned migrants resided were nuclear, though this reflects the bias towards older, more affluent migrants who returned to retire in the neighborhood of Gazcue.

The return to the Dominican Republic for many female migrants has meant regression to a more repressive patriarchal system. Pessar's (1985) study showed that many Dominican women in the United States were reluctant to come back to the island. In the United States, they have more freedom to work and to travel independently. Additionally, if the household income is sufficient, then women may be restricted by a male partner from wage working on return to Dominican society.

The relations of patriarchy often remain intact during the migration process. Women still tend to assume responsibility for childcare and domestic tasks, acting out support roles essential for migration. Bueno (1995) emphasizes the sacrifices that women make for the family, working in productive and reproductive spheres to make re-migration possible. Women frequently leave the United States when their own position would be enhanced by staying. Alvarez (1991, 143-144) describes the reluctance of a wife to return with her husband to Dominican society, but she remains unable to dissent openly:

> But Laura had gotten used to the life here. She did not want to go back to the old country where, de la Torre or not, she was only a wife and mother (and a failed one at that, since she had never provided the required son). Better an independent nobody than a high-class houseslave. She did not come straight out and disagree with her husband's plans.

International migration has clearly had an impact on gender relations. Its influence is less evident, however, when perceptions of race are analyzed.

Transnationalism and racial identity

International migration has changed a range of migrant and non-migrant realities and expectations. Migrant household structures are shaped by transnationalism, incomes depend on remittances, and relations of patriarchy are often challenged. It would seem logical to extend the influence of change to a reappraisal of race. Dominicans confront a sharper racial and ethnic segregation in the United States. Given the strong negation of African Caribbean or black identity in Dominican society, migrants who would not consider themselves as *negro/a* or *mulato/a* in Dominican society find themselves being considered as black Hispanics, Latinos/as or African Americans. While

Dominicans living in the United States 'invariably overcome the legacy of denial regarding the African part of their heritage' (Torres-Saillant and Hernández 1998, 145), the much-vaunted dynamics of transnationalism so far have failed to create a full re-evaluation of racial awareness, both on the island and within the United States.

The racial hearth remains the dominant reference for racial perception among migrants. Observations from the present survey of returned migrants support this stasis of racial perception and challenge several contemporary writers who perceive a shift in Dominican racial identity. At an individual level, Vicioso (1994, 272) expresses the impact that living in New York has made on her own racial identity:

> In the United States, there is no space for fine distinctions of race, and one goes from being '*trigueño*' or '*indio*' to being 'mulatto' or 'black' or 'Hispanic.' This was an excellent experience for me. From that point on, I discovered myself as a Caribbean *mulata* and adopted the black identity as a gesture of solidarity.

Moya Pons optimistically points to the 'discovery of Dominican negritude', arguing that the social discrimination experienced by thousands of Dominicans in the urban ghettoes of New York made them aware of their real 'racial constitution.' Dominican migrants were able to share their experiences with Caribbean counterparts:

> Their parochial outlook was expanded and they went back to Santo Domingo, their hometowns outwardly and inwardly transformed in their thoughts, their clothes, their feelings, their language and their music. Now black is beginning to be beautiful in the Dominican Republic... The real discovery of black origins has been the result of the behavior of the returning migrants who go back to their communities transformed into new social agents of modernity, capitalism, and racial emancipation. (Moya Pons 1981, 32-33)

After the end of the *trujillato*, and with more Dominicans migrating and gaining experience of life overseas, Moya Pons contends that long-standing racial ideologies were questioned, and in part, overturned.

Thousands of Dominicans migrated to the United States at a time when issues of race and racism were being re-evaluated. Dominicans realized that, 'they were descended from Spanish fathers and African mothers, and that half of a Dominican's origins was not so different from those of a Haitian' (Moya Pons 1981, 244). But why did it take migration to New York for them to discover this? The forced socialization and the abrupt realities of a dichotomized racial classification allegedly necessitated a change in racial ideology.

Moya Pons (1981) argues that the 'discovery of Dominican negritude' occurred in two different spheres. Firstly, during the second half of the 1960s, Dominicans were meeting other ethnic and racial groups within the civil rights movement. Secondly, professional and intellectual groups began to bring attention to the social alienation of Dominicans in the United States. While not sharing the optimistic opinion that returned migrants will themselves change racial perceptions, Jiménez predicts that attitudes will evolve through the liberalizing influence of Dominican intellectuals, resident in the United States, who frequently publish, visit and lecture in the Dominican Republic.[20] The evolution of racial awareness would, thus, come from external sources, and from the 'top down.'

Gradually, the myth that Dominicans are a white people with indigenous ancestry would give way to the understanding that the population was largely *mulato/a*. The long-standing *indio*-myth has no relevance in mainstream North American society; however, it has found a role in the reconstituted social and cultural environments of the transnational communities of Dominicans in New York. The very success of the Dominican social and cultural regenerative experience has reproduced racial norms, rather than dispelled them. In the 1990 census, 25 percent of New York's Dominicans classified themselves as black (Pessar 1995, 143). Most Dominicans considered themselves as white or 'other'. North American mainstream society was not made privy to the 'other' category of *indio/a*.

An analysis of returned migrants and those who had traveled abroad in the survey sample showed similarly entrenched views in their racial perceptions—41.3 percent of returned migrants described themselves as *blanco/a* or *indio/a*. Given the predominance of middle and upper classes in both samples, the over-representation of *blanco/a* as a self-description is not surprising. A fifth of returned migrants described themselves as *indio/a*, less than the sample as a whole, but significant in the context of the bias towards the middle and upper classes.

A reappraisal of racial identification, however, misleadingly appears evident among the returned migrants and interviewees who have had experience of travel outside the Dominican Republic. Twenty-seven percent of returned migrants described themselves as *mulato/a* or *negro/a*, and all were from the upper three classes.

While the difficulties and inaccuracies inherent in ascribing race are evident, this categorization is used to illustrate cases where the author's description of race and the self-described race of the interviewee varied. Those respondents who defined themselves as *negro/a* or *mulato/a* were described as *mulato/a* by the author, and, as members of the middle and upper classes, were more likely to conform to the suggested 'discovery of negritude.' Racial awareness and expression is often the result of higher levels of education, or originates from a sympathetic liberal background where the possibility of racist rejection or abuse is limited. Evidence of the restricted renewal of racial identification among Dominican migrants is illustrated by five interviewees who had very dark skin color, categorized by the author as *negro/a*, yet who described themselves as *blanco/a* or *indio/a*.

The hypothesis that racial identity is expressed more intensely with ascending class contradicts the 'straight-line assimilation model'. The latter explanation posits that the assimilation of migrants to the receiving society will increase with rising levels of income. Gans suggests that low-income groups may assimilate to a greater extent than more affluent migrants or second-generation migrants who have the opportunity to create their own ethnic niche (cited in Waters 1994, 800). As the second generation of Dominicans in New York establishes itself, the Dominican transnational community strengthens. Waters' (1994) study of ethnic and racial identities among adolescent second-generation Caribbean Americans in New York City suggests that the key factor for self-identification is a personal experience of racial discrimination. Respondents frequently expressed the need to separate themselves from black or African Americans by defining themselves as immigrants or ethnic Americans, for example Dominican-Americans. Peer culture reproduces the stereotyping of the former as lazy, good-for-nothing and of a lower social status. 'The darker the skin, the louder the Spanish' was a common refrain which related to the desire of black Hispanics in New York to separate themselves from African Americans. Paradoxically, the dress, vocabulary and the 'cool pose' of the stereotypical young black American has been reproduced as a desirable image by many Latinos/as, who aspire to black culture, but without the racial affirmation.

A respondent in a recent survey of female migrants summed up the problems of living in the United States. The evil of drugs and blackness were casually intertwined: 'There's black folk. There's drugs. You know' (Bueno 1995, 27). Dominican migrants who were interviewed tended to adopt racist stereotypes of other groups, despite their own negative experiences of racism as immigrants. A respondent had problems in attending night school due to the make-up of the class: 'It was full of colored people, and since everyone knows that blacks aren't very friendly I didn't want to go to the school.' Another classified the students in the school as 'Chinese, Americans and blacks', reinforcing the racial ideology that North Americans are white and that African Americans belong to a different society.

Gurak (1987) speculates that migrants from the Caribbean may be re-addressing the black-white racial dichotomy in the United States by importing a racial continuum. A sorting of immigrants into 'slow' and 'fast' integration categories operates with the selection mechanism being primarily racial in nature. In some instances this may occur, but a reproduction of the racial hearth serves only to perpetuate existing racisms. Color-coding along a continuum may merely create a more expansive grading of racial prejudice.

Most migrants and those who had traveled overseas in the research sample, however, appeared to be more aware of the advantages that light skin color afforded in Dominican society. Several migrants expressed highly racist sentiments, despite, or perhaps because of, several years of living in New York. Old antagonisms with Haiti were quick to surface. A sixty-two year-old woman, waiting to re-migrate to New York, was quick to reject Haitian immigration to the Dominican Republic: 'Each to their own place. I'm not giving away my nationality to anyone.' Despite the widespread desire to acquire United States residency or citizenship, Dominican sovereignty is aggressively defended by migrants, most vigorously in the context of Haitian migration to the Dominican Republic. Over a third of the returned migrants who were interviewed believed that Haitians should not be allowed any form of residency in the Dominican Republic.

Some respondents, however, were keen to trade Dominican nationality for the perceived opportunities of US citizenship. The national flag was a popular metaphor during conversations. Clara del Castillo vociferously suggested: 'The United States is the only hope for our country. We're only missing the flag here!' Her friends expressed a strong conviction that the Dominican Republic should become a dependency of the United States like Puerto Rico, further enflaming a passionate discussion which traded national sovereignty for economic gain and allegiance to the United States. With thirteen aunts already working in the United States, a twenty-nine year-old David Marquez had no hesitation about migrating. He would burn the flag and never return to Santo Domingo if he had the chance: 'Here, there's no future for anyone.'

The influence of the United States

Despite emigration and travel by Dominicans to other parts of the world, the United States remains the focus of the transnational community. Among the Dominican population of Madrid, where over half of the estimated 50,000 Dominicans in Spain live, there is a marked reluctance to assimilate. Notwithstanding the historical lure of *la Madre Patria*, the Spanish motherland is not the chosen destination for the majority. During the 1970s, Dominican migrants to Spain were mainly students and members of the upper classes. They were more likely to settle than migrants today, who, according to a Dominican businessman in Madrid, are less attached to Spanish life and count their material success in dollars, the real mark of success:

> Each peseta they earn, they change into dollars... They don't give any value to the peseta, they think it's worthless. Their goal is the dollar. For this reason I don't think they'll ever integrate. It's as if they do not trust the country. (Piña Contreras 1995, 10)

Dominicans share a love-hate relationship with the United States in which Dominican culture and sovereignty is wagered against the materialism of American life. The latter pays a higher dividend for most aspirant migrants. The wealth of the United States compared with the

Caribbean region is an overriding factor of people's perception of the country: 'It's the biggest power (*potencia*) that there is—with the most money in the world.' The dominance of the United States is overpowering: 'The United States is *una potencia*. They do what they want.'

North American living standards and comparisons with Dominican society fuel the transnational flow. Many interviewees were desperate to migrate or travel to the United States. A repeated comment was that Dominican culture was worth little or nothing in comparison with the 'real' American or European culture. Alvarez (1991, 108-109) describes the rejection of the homeland by four Dominican women growing up near Boston in the 1960s:

We began to develop a taste for the American teenage good life, and soon, Island was old hat, man. Island was the hair-and-nails crowd, chaperones and icky boys with all their macho strutting and unbuttoned shirts and hairy chests with gold chains and teensy gold crucifixes. By the end of a couple of years away from home, we had *more* than adjusted.

The contradiction will always remain between devouring American popular culture, yet blaming the United States for the country's problems. A middle-aged farmer interviewed in Zambrana, participating in a United States-funded agricultural scheme, envisaged the vampire-like qualities of North American interests in the country: 'I don't see it as good. The United States has become fat on the countries of the Caribbean. It's sucked the blood of the people and discarded them.'

Concern over growing North American interests in the Dominican Republic has been evident since the nineteenth century. Many nineteenth-century critics were aware of the dangers of economic dependency. Persio C. Franco (in Calder 1981, 20) pointedly observed, 'If with the lands of the entire republic occurs what has occurred with those of San Pedro de Macorís, La Romana and Barahona, the Dominican Republic will be a myth.' Dominican sovereignty was lost to the United States at the start of the twentieth century. The United States government assumed formal control over the country's finances in 1907, occupying the country from 1916 to 1924. This first military occupation led to the consolidation of the process of capitalist expansion in the country, and tied the Dominican economy firmly to the North American market. By the 1920s, 95 percent of the sugar production was exported to the United States and twelve United States-owned companies controlled three-quarters of the sugar-producing land (Castor 1974). Since the 1920s, over a half of all Dominican imports have come from the United States.

The Dominican language changed during the eight years of occupation as anglicized words entered everyday speech. Baseball replaced cockfighting as the national sport. Urban elites began to follow North American music styles, but Moya Pons (1981) notes that some elements of society began to dance *merengue* more energetically as a sign of resistance to cultural infiltration by American styles. The occupation of 1965 reinforced growing trends of cultural and economic dependency.

Today, *bachata* and *merengue* retain their dominance, but only just under the challenge of widespread American rock and pop. A key aspect to the maintenance of *merengue* as the dominant sound is the Spanish language and the fact that many *merengueros/as* have a large Hispanic following in the United States, often living there. Transnational commercialization is maintaining the domestic and overseas strength of the national music, although the emergence of a pop-*merengue* fusion is evident.

Fifty-seven percent of the respondents in the present survey believed that the influence of the United States in the Dominican Republic was largely beneficial, with one fifth in opposition. The general reaction was one of passive acceptance of North American influence. A middle-aged salesman argued that Dominicans do not know their own island, 'We're always thinking about the other country.' Another interviewee enthusiastically suggested: 'There [in the United States], they have more peace. It's a blessed life. I would like to go one day—just imagine living there!' The dream of leaving the island and living in the United States is a potent force for reproduction of the transnational community. Alvarez, the Dominican novelist, describes Gladys, a Dominican maid dreaming of migrating to New York. Each icon on her small bedside altar represents a saint. A postcard of the Statue of Liberty, discarded by her employer, has special significance:

'This one is the powerful American Virgin.' Gladys handed me the card. 'She'll get me to New York, you'll see.'(Alvarez 1991, 260)

Capital is highly mobile, increasingly invested and accumulated on a world scale. The whole range of international relations, through migration, telecommunications, travel, business links, mass media and arts, provides an intense and frequent interchange of economic and cultural experiences. Returned migrants share family, friends and business contacts between two or more countries, whilst still maintaining strong social and cultural links with their country of origin.

Transnationalism is pulling Dominican society towards a United States-led global culture. The direction of change is predominantly outward looking. Monica Hernández, a 54 year-old female publicist living in Gazcue, remarked: 'We've lost much of our *dominicanidad*. We've lost our Dominican identity. No Dominican nowadays wants to be part of this country.' Transnationalism establishes new social, cultural and economic contexts, but its influence is not universal. The perception and awareness of race, the racial hearth of Dominican society, remains one of the few aspects yet to be transformed by the development of a transnational community.

6.
Race and *Negritud* in Dominican Literature

'All texts tell socially and culturally relevant truths about the period in which they were written, about the world in general and about human nature.'
—Belsey (1980, 16)

Introduction

What can contemporary literature tell us about Dominican attitudes to race? Poetry and prose, which deal with issues of race, reflect not only the style and character of the author, but also are intimately connected to the context in which they were written. The narrative is shaped as much by social and cultural surroundings as by the personal influences of the writers themselves. Despite the potential for fictional exploration, the author writes within the limits of his or her experience. However much the imagination is employed, the basis of literary creation is formed from the writer's particular experience of life.

The written text, prose fiction or poetry, adds an alternative dimension to social research. Literature reveals factors which orthodox sources of history cannot reveal; the writer's description of society allows the researcher to glean information from intimate details of social conduct. Any author's contribution may extend from the representation and description of social history and character to the literary production of popular cultural and political identities. Dominican writers have played an important part, particularly during the regime of Trujillo, in delimiting and outlining national and cultural values. Nationalist literature produced under the directive of the dictator made a significant contribution to the projection of *dominicanidad* as white, Hispanic and Catholic.

Race cannot be lifted from the text as an isolated factor; racial expression is dependent on the surrounding social, political and cultural structures that influence the narrative and the material world. Literary *negritud* focuses on social meaning and sentiment, and developed from the earlier forms of *negrismo*, which described physical characteristics and cultural attributes of the African Caribbean population (Candelier 1977). African Antillean poetry of the early twentieth century, despite its focus on African essentialism, did set an important precedent for Hispanic writers. Contemporary literature owes much to the *negrista* movement that was predominant during the 1920s and early 1930s. The political and literary vanguards of the 1960s established a wider interest in African Hispanic literature.

'Black literature' refers to writing which expresses the theme of black experience and which incorporates resistance to anti-black or anti-African sentiment. The use of generic categories such as black or African Hispanic literature is intended to suggest a type of literary output. Need black literature be written by black writers? The Dominican literary critic and author, Incháustegui Cabral (1976), preferred not to use the term when referring to Dominican poetry, arguing that the impact of black poetry in the Dominican Republic was limited. Many writers in the domain of African Hispanic literature are neither black nor mulatto, which arguably, 'compromises the formation of an Afro-Hispanic literary canon, at least one based on race as a guarantor of cultural authenticity' (Kutzinski 1996, 168). Black or African Hispanic literature, however, is defined more by content, specifically those works which aim to challenge racism and the white bias in Caribbean societies. Writers of black literature do not have to be *negro/a* or *mulata/o*, yet their work should address issues salient for a black or African community. Thus, African Hispanic literature refers to texts written about, and not just for and by, people of African descent.

Literature of *negritud* has not established a strong presence in the Dominican Republic. A progressive black literary movement failed to emerge in the Dominican Republic as a result of the negation of African descent and ongoing Hispanic bias among intellectuals. The opening for contemporary radical debate was limited, despite the death of Trujillo, by the accession to power and by the political repression of Balaguer.

Traditionally, most Dominican writers have originated from the lighter-skinned elite. Their work tended to reproduce romanticized, and often racist, stereotypes. Several Dominican *mulato* writers (most published authors have been male) maintain the traditional image of *negritud* in the Dominican Republic. Many modern Dominican writers reproduce idealized and misleading perceptions of the racial reality. Contemporary literature still reproduces stereotypical and biased images of Haiti and *negritud*. The history of antagonism with Haiti, and the constant Dominican fear of being absorbed into the neighboring country, is evident in the plethora of literary texts that emphatically differentiate the two nations.

An analysis of Dominican poetry and prose published after 1973 is the main focus of the following pages; this year marked the publication of two novels which address issues of anti-Haitianism and Black Power: *El presidente negro* (*The Black President*) by Manuel del Cabral and *El masacre se pasa a pie* (*You Can Cross the Massacre on Foot*) by Freddy Prestol Castillo. Both novels sold well, but failed to establish a black literary canon. The poetry of Blas Jiménez is discussed in detail as a leading contemporary 'black voice' in Dominican literary circles. He is one of the few contemporary writers to have produced a coherent body of literature which focuses on race.

My analysis of contemporary poetry and prose centers on seven themes in black literature. First, African essentialism and the metaphor of the drum are repeatedly woven into the construction of *negritud*. Secondly, Dominican writers frequently relate racial characteristics to the tropical environment; an emphasis on fertility also links the production and consumption of fruit to sexual imagery. Racialized images of the body are illustrated, and the importance of anti-Haitianism in Dominican literature is discussed with reference to selected poetry and *El masacre se pasa a pie*. The fifth topic addresses racial indecision and the difficulty of asserting a black identity within a society which rejects blackness. The limits of black awareness form the sixth theme, referring specifically to *El negro presidente*. The novel describes an imaginary black president of the United States and discusses issues of Black Power. The text, however, is littered with derogatory references to Haitian blacks. Finally, race is considered from a distanced perspective—that of the Dominican migrant.

Development of Dominican black writing

Dominican literature has often been excluded from general anthologies of Caribbean and Hispanic American prose or verse. This continues to be true despite the substantial increase in Dominican publications, especially poetry, since the 1980s. The limited prestige of Dominican literature beyond the national borders has been attributed to the reluctance of the country's intellectuals to assert a cultural affinity with the rest of the region (Torres-Saillant 1994). The Dominican intelligentsia suffers from an academic insularity of external and internal construction. Self-deprecation and pessimism has been the standard trait of many Hispanophile writers in the Dominican Republic.

Torres-Saillant (1994) posits a long-standing bifurcation of literature and criticism that has weakened Dominican literary impact outside the country. Nineteenth-century criticism, he argues, idealized the core of the Dominican population as culturally European, white and upper-class; the texts themselves, however, were more responsive to the social and cultural actuality. Even when the literature affirmed Dominican culture, critics followed a Eurocentric tradition. Such a clear disjuncture between text and criticism is difficult to believe. Many writers were both critics and authors. Torres-Saillant, however, is correct to draw attention to the cultural and racial bias in the Dominican literary scene. The pessimism inherent in the literature of the Dominican Republic was a result of a resolute historical devotion to Spain; the island's cultural losses were believed to outweigh the achievements following the end of Spanish colonialism. Local texts were evaluated through the lens of fashionable imported criticism. This continuing reliance on external literary and critical styles has provoked the call for critics to uphold the Dominican literary tradition as legitimate in its own right.

At the root of the pessimism and frustration concerning the future of the Dominican nation lies a restricted exploration of the racial complex. The Dominican nation is hailed and eulogized, but in terms of a light or white aesthetic. Black literature has consistently failed to gain acceptance in the Dominican Republic. While writers such as Aimé Césaire stirred the awakening of black literature in the twentieth-century Caribbean, a similar response in the Dominican Republic was not forthcoming. *Negritud* for Dominicans was a predicament to revoke rather than to herald. Coulthard (1962) explains that *négritude*, first introduced in print by Césaire (1994) in *Cahier d'un retour au pays natal* (*Notebook from a Return to the Country of Birth*, first published 1947), was a response by people of African ancestry to find a 'distinctive tonality' in the concert of world culture. The Dominican Republic plays out of tune with this global symphony.

The emergence of a black or African Dominican literature is difficult to discern. The 1920s black literary resurgence in the Caribbean and the United States, which also had its influence in Europe, failed to provoke a popular response in the Dominican Republic. Césaire's writings urged a revitalization and re-evaluation of black culture outside the white European literary tradition. An African conscience and the sense of a black cultural heritage were developed through an emphasis on new rhythms and metrics (Candelier 1974). The 1930s saw the appearance of black literature in the Spanish Caribbean that was tied to a folkloric revival. The Cuban, Nicolás Guillén, the Puerto Rican, Luis Palés Matos, and to an extent the Dominican, Manuel del Cabral, can be credited as founders of *poesía afrohispanoantillana*. The key criticism of del Cabral is that the *negros/as* about whom he writes were rarely Dominican. His black literature recounted the injustices of black oppression, but in a framework which continued to represent blacks as Haitian or African.

The popular late-nineteenth-century poet, Juan Antonio Alix, has been considered a forerunner of black literature in the Dominican Republic; his poems often criticized Dominicans who tried to pass themselves off as white. In general, however, a Dominican literature of *negritud* is more notable by its relative absence. Contemporary literature in the Dominican Republic has evolved from a historical background of physical insularity, slavery, colonialism, foreign occupation, authoritarianism and dependency. Anti-Haitianism motivates the preference for a white aesthetic, but literary styles have also developed as products of transculturation. European discourse was 'creolized' in the eighteenth- and nineteenth-century Caribbean, which created national versions of contemporary styles, such as neo-classicism, romanticism and Parnassianism.

The early nineteenth-century literary scene in the Dominican Republic celebrated the Arcadian forces of nature, which led to *costumbrismo*, the extolling of local culture, customs, flora and fauna. Local color and the bucolic evocation of a tropicalized Europe were the basis for literary exploration. In the latter part of the nineteenth century, indianist texts developed this rustic style. José Joaquín Pérez glorified the island's indigenous past in *Fantasías indígenas* (1877), whilst *Enriquillo* (1882) by Galván responded to the elite's desire to reject an African heritage in favor of a noble indigenous and Hispanic tradition. The end of the nineteenth century witnessed a growth of literature which focused on the Dominican nation.

Dominicanidad is dominated by a white or light aesthetic. Traditionally, the Dominican woman has been submissive, virginal and *blanca*, counterpoised with the potency of the *negra* or *mulata*, the antithesis of white purity (Cocco de Filippis 1988). The rejection of the African element is illustrated by the juxtaposition of the virginal *blanca* with the sinful, sensual *negra* or *mulata*. The latter were never explicitly Dominican, but represented African or Haitian traits; influences which diverted the Dominican (man) from the path of godliness. A poem written by Francisco Muñoz del Monte, 'La mulata' (1849), typifies this perception:

> Prayer is useless. She seduces and kills,
> opens and closes the tomb at her pleasure.
> When to the melody of a mournful bell
> the victim descends to the grave
> the cruel *mulata* lights her cigar
> and goes to sacrifice another man for her pleasure.[21]

La mulata is described in vampire-like terms as a sexual predator, callously devouring her lover through sexual passion. The sacrificial terms suggest that her prey is ensnared by an exotic sensuality, helpless to resist the raw terms of conquest dictated by the dark-skinned female. The exotic lure of *la mulata* fatally tempts the white male to sin; prayer is futile, and white Catholicism impotent. 'La mulata' outlines the potential threat of the dark-skinned woman who reverses her sexually and racially submissive role and challenges the dominant (white) patriarchal structure. The sexual predation and conquest of the dark-skinned temptress inverts colonial roles; the white man is now the powerless victim, who is used then cast aside. Male erotic fantasy becomes his deathbed, while *la mulata* gains pleasure from her false compliance, celebrating another conquest with the taste of a phallic cigar.

The image of *la mulata* as seductress remains potent in contemporary Dominican and Hispanic American writing. Miscegenation, the biological threat to white power, spawned fear among the ruling class who believed that the white male would be destroyed and civilization left ravaged by the overwhelming sexual savagery of *la mulata*. Early twentieth-century writing in the Dominican Republic edged in the direction of a more sophisticated, self-aware *criollismo*. However, greater acknowledgement of racial miscegenation did little to re-focus literature away from the positive connotations of the white aesthetic. Light skin color still suggested civilized behavior and 'classical' beauty. Darker skin projected images of raw emotion and sexuality.

European styles were refashioned for the tropics, accompanied by continued social and cultural dependency. The Dominican Republic could not break from the traditional, Catholic, Hispanic matrix imprinted during the previous century. Unlike other parts of the Spanish Caribbean, *modernista* angst and the search for meaning in contemporary affairs did not sever ties with favored metrics or lead to wide scale experimentation with differing rhythms. The expansion of the Dominican lexicon under *modernista* influences did, however, result in the creation of new styles in contemporary writing. Nevertheless, the evidence of a literary rejection of and revolt against Europe remains limited. The main foci of rejection suggested by Coulthard are not apparent in Dominican literature. Literature of rejection expressed the complaint that African Caribbean people were being constricted by the moulds of European thought, and claimed that European culture was failing. Traditional styles of Christianity were rejected, and direct attacks made upon the nature of European civilization (Coulthard 1962).

Francisco Domínguez Charro attempted to establish *la poesía trigueña* by focusing upon the process of *mulatización* (Icháustegui Cabral 1976). The euphemistic use of *trigueño/a*, 'wheat-colored', enhances the light aesthetic by promoting a literary framework with a light bias. *Poema del llanto trigueño* (*Poem of the Weeping Trigueño* 1969) by Pedro Mir and *Yelidá* (1942) by Tomás Hernández Franco, both prototypes for *la poesía trigueña*, focus away from the darker aesthetic. The latter, *Yelidá*, has been hailed as an epic narrative in the Dominican Republic. The verses recount the story of the poem's namesake, the son of a Norwegian man and a Haitian woman. This 'good' looking, but wayward, *blanco* is seduced by the magical potions and sensuality of the dark-skinned woman. After the birth of Yelidá, his father dies and the Norwegian's soul returns to his homeland. The Norse gods set out to reclaim the white soul of his offspring, but arrive too late, for it has already been 'tainted' by a sexual relationship with a black woman. Anti-Haitian sentiment frames the telling of the tale. The Haitian woman, and to some extent the errant Scandinavian, are portrayed as sinners, worshipping false gods and possessing weak morals. She is a destroyer of white souls, and thus, a threat to civilization. His mortal self has erred, but his white soul must be saved. White purity confronts, and is defeated by, the 'darker', immoral side of human behavior. Yelidá survives, but his *trigueño* soul is corrupted by the coarseness of Haiti, loitering across the border as an ever-present threat to the Dominican Republic.

The lack of a black literature in the Dominican Republic reflects societal mores and differs markedly from the situation elsewhere in the Caribbean. Black literary expression reveals its own insularities. A comparison of writing from Martinique, Jamaica, Cuba, Haiti and the Dominican Republic illustrates similar, but differing, historical experiences. Dominicans writing on a black theme rarely perceive themselves to be direct descendants of African slaves, but assimilate the feelings of oppression and resistance to prejudice or injustice. Manuel del Cabral, a light-skinned writer, refused the labels of *negrismo* or *poesía negra*. Coulthard (1962, 37) cites one of his comments during an interview: 'There is a Negro raggle-taggle going round these countries, a rhetoric of color resting on the physical basis of the word... Is there an American art? Is there a Negro poetry? I feel I must deny the existence of both.'

Del Cabral denies the existence of *negritud*, arguing: 'I am stirred by human feelings, not race... Poetry with a black theme is not about color, but about the human intensity which the poet is able to portray'(Anonymous 1980, 45). The ideal aim of literature, he argues, should be the rejection of all social and cultural inequalities. Postcolonial suffering and relations of dependency link texts of resistance which, at first glance, address spatially and racially divergent groups. *Poesía negra* has been equated with the literary movement of *indigenismo* as a reaffirmation of positive racial identities. Each evolved as a response to an oppressive situation of cultural domination, and both exhibit a tendency to relate back, or look forward, to an era of liberation. White bias is considered the determining factor of oppression, synonymous with discrimination, economic exploitation and an alleged racial superiority.

White writing black; black righting white

Can a white writer understand black experience? To an extent, yes, provided that the black theme does not take on a patronizing or racist quality. Nicolás Guillén, writing as a dark-skinned Cuban, experienced racism in a different manner from Manuel del Cabral or Luis Palés Matos, both of whom could be described as *blancos*. Guillén's writing is informed by a different knowledge, but that does not make his work any more authentic than that of the other two authors. Even Guillén traded stereotypes of African Caribbean culture and created nonsensical Africanized neologisms.

However, some critics have suggested that only black writers can understand or are culturally equipped to express the black experience. Alcántara Almánzar (1979, 167) argues that the externality of experience will always leave writers such as del Cabral outside an insight into *negritud*:

> ... despite the human understanding which the poems contain, it should be recognized that del Cabral observes the problems from outside: he cannot arrive at the intensity of a René Depestre (1926) or a Jacques Roumain (1908-1944), who have lived the drama of *negritud* for themselves.

Gayle (1971) proclaims that white writers are unable to portray or elucidate the black experience because they are culturally underdeveloped to do so. In this sense, black literature is left to re-write the white bias which misrepresents African Caribbean culture. The positionality of the author is reflected in the similar debate which questions the capacity of a male writer to write about female experience. The primary gift of a good writer, however, is imagination; the ability to think hypothetically and place himself or herself in the situation of others. A significant proportion of literature with a black theme by light-skinned Dominicans unfortunately reproduces negative racial stereotypes.

Joaquín Balaguer, a light-skinned President and writer, has produced several anthologies which reinforce prejudice, rather than react against it. In 'Venus negra' (1941), Balaguer describes a dark-skinned woman whose beauty matches that of the goddess Venus, entrancing men who are vulnerable to her devastating sensuality:

Your beautiful mahogany-colored body
holds the enchantment of a living statue,
which attracts and captivates us all
with its entrancing tropical perfume.

Always bewitching, stealing our hearts
your sensitive body of Cleopatra,
with its provocative sensuality,
Of a lounge and bedroom queen.

The delicate image of the God Helen,
from whose forms the sculpture arises,
fired in the flames of your dark skin,
appears more beautiful than its white form,
and you can occupy with full grace
a place at the side of the armless Venus.[22]

La negra is described sensitively, yet the poem reproduces her within a stereotypical framework; her sensuality is exotic, provocative and captivating. *Negritud* places her on the edge of a world of magic, an exotic primitivism that lures men to her side. Balaguer establishes the juxtaposition of light-skinned beauty with a darker, irrepressible aspect of sexual attraction. The poet makes several classical references, in part recognizing European beauty, but critically emphasizing the danger of sexual temptation. The dark-skinned Cleopatra lured Antony to a fateful end, while Helen was the cause of a war which led to the downfall of Trojan civilization.

The poetry of Balaguer is of interest given the overt racism of his politics as President of the Dominican Republic. 'Venus negra' was written only a few years after the massacre of thousands of Haitians and *negros/as* on the Dominican side of the border. Aspects of his poetry acknowledge the raw attraction of blackness, but the arousal of passion is a response to an allegedly primitive blackness, an overt threat to a susceptible white (male) civilization.

Héctor J. Díaz, another light-skinned Dominican poet, also writes on a black theme in the context of raw black sensuality. The poem entitled 'Morena' (1934) correlates exotic sensuality with sin. His other poems, 'Amor oculto' ('Hidden Love' 1940) and 'Beso imposible' ('Impossible Kiss' 1940), stress similar desire-guilt complexes. In 'Morena', the woman feeds the poet's pleasure, satiating his desire for her 'dark flesh' of sugar, cinnamon and clove hues:

> Sugar, cinnamon and clove
> her dark flesh tastes
> and idealizes the sin
> when surrendering to pleasure.
>
> That afternoon in her bedroom,
> lukewarm amphora of pleasure,
> I drank the red lust
> until my deep thirst was quenched...
>
> More... Oh, things in life
> that should not happen...
> since that afternoon, friend.
> We have not seen each other again.
> Where you will walk lost
> seller of pleasure.[23]

The poet consumes the women's sexuality; the first stanza portrays an image of eating and the second, that of drinking. The dark-skinned women is a prostitute selling pleasure, but leaving her client guilt-ridden. The eroticism of the poet's encounter is framed by the context of darkness, guilt, sin and illicit sensuality.

The descriptions of *la negra* or *la mulata* in the poetry of Balaguer and Díaz project similar racial-sexual stereotypes and connotations of a 'dark' sexuality. The poets' shared backgrounds are typical of upper-class Dominican society—a tradition of *blancura*, Catholicism and *Hispanidad*. Both poems are in the form of classical European sonnets, ignoring the Dominican style of *décima* or the black literary verse of *son*. Both reproduce the racist and sexist stereotypes of their cultural background, but this does not preclude all authors from writing 'outside' their own experience. Gates (1987) claims that not until he had stepped out of his experience as an African American into the second arena of western or white experience, could he evaluate black literature. The difference between these worlds enabled Gates to see the significance of black literature, but the difference has no resonance in the Dominican Republic.

The color aesthetic

The color aesthetic is a visual index, centered on the acceptance or renunciation of race and phenotype. Hoetink (1967) has developed a theory of the somatic norm image, a complex of physical characteristics that are accepted by a group as its norm and ideal. This image is the yardstick of aesthetic evaluation, and the visual standard for the somatic characteristics of group membership. Adherence to the group norm underlies the basis and strength of the color aesthetic. Solaún and Kronus (1970) agree that the main aesthetic preference usually corresponds with the physical characteristics of the dominant group.

The color aesthetic in the Dominican Republic incorporates a strong white bias of positive characteristics juxtaposed with the negative portrayal of blackness. This aesthetic is also found in Latin American literature, similarly characterized by black phobia and the white aesthetic:

> The association of the color black with ugliness, sin, darkness, immorality, Manichaean metaphor, with the inferior, the archetype of the lowest order, and the color white with the opposite of these qualities partly explains the racist preconceptions and negative images of the black man projected—at times despite the author's good intentions—in much of the literature of the area. (Jackson 1976, xiii)

Jackson adds that somatic ostracism of blacks in parts of Latin America is even more severe than generally imagined. The dominant cultural heritage is that of a white or light racial consciousness—transmitted by a collective sentiment where black is equated with negative qualities. Arredondo (1936) refers to the blight of color aesthetics in Cuba that projects self-disdain among *negros/as*, and forces them to adhere to a light concept of beauty.

Jackson describes *mestizaje* as a fact of 'black experience.' He elucidates the variation of color and phenotype not only in terms of racial and cultural fusion, but as the 'physical, spiritual, and cultural rape of black people' (Jackson 1976, 1). Jackson's thoughts originate from a dichotomized framework of race and the oppression of black by white. He discusses *mestizaje* or *mulatización* as a form of ethnic lynching whereby the white population attempts to dilute a black presence through racial inter-marriage. The immigration policy of *blanqueamiento* during the regime of Trujillo is similar. White immigration aimed to develop a pigmentocracy in which social status correlated with skin color and body aesthetics.

The process of *mulatización* embodies a troublesome connotation in the Dominican Republic. A history of racial mixing does not imply an easing of somatic barriers. Given the historically forced or unequal nature of sexual relations between racial groups, evidence of miscegenation is ultimately a misguided indicator of racial tolerance. It heralds the demise of *dominicanidad*, and draws Dominicans nearer to the historical experiences of slavery, *negritud* and the negative stigma attached to the dark aesthetic. The color spectrum of society is altered, but in a manner which simultaneously lightens dark skin and darkens light. Dominican authors fear a *mulato/a* future. The national fate is expressed by single-sided arguments which predict the extinction of the white population.

Contemporary poetry and prose

The contemporary analysis of verse and prose focuses upon work published during or after 1973. This year marked the publication of two texts which, given the right support, moment and time, could have established a burgeoning genre of black literature in the Dominican Republic. *El presidente negro* by Manuel del Cabral and *El masacre se pasa a pie* by Freddy Prestol Castillo both failed to ride the tide of Black Power which had created a surge of African Caribbean cultural self-awareness elsewhere in the region.

Both publications received critical acclaim and sold well; literacy rates in the Dominican Republic are relatively high by regional and world standards. However, the reading of prose fiction as a leisure pursuit tends to be restricted to the more educated and generally more affluent section of society.[24] Given that the most literate section of society tends to be lighter and more affluent, it is perhaps unsurprising that this group failed to support radical black politics.

The potential for the rise of a Dominican literature that expressed a reactive and positive racial aesthetic was nullified. Much of the so-called black literature in the Dominican Republic remains locked in the gridiron of racial stereotype and stamped with a mimetic or patronizing quality. The leitmotif of *negritud* in Dominican literature suggests that *negras/os* tend not to be Dominican. Thus, black literature is a marginal, almost exotic, literary branch in the Dominican Republic. Blas Jiménez, perhaps the leading and most expressive writer on racial themes in the Dominican Republic, argues that he can only afford to produce black literature because he does not ~~d on~~ writing for a living.[25] His established social status, in ____ to write without fear of ostracism from the ____tural circles.

____minican literature reproduces an established range ____ and images. Conceptions of *negritud*, beauty and ____ changed little from the earlier work of Balaguer and ____ g section outlines a series of themes expressed in ____ and prose which have been published since 1973 and ____ e.

The innate rhythm of the drum

____literary critic, Candelier (1974), portrays the beating of ____ sential icon of African Dominican identity. He reduces ____ ninican Republic to the level of the fallacious triumvirate ____ *gros*, Hispanic *blancos* and indigenous *indios*, while co____ ____ological characteristics with cultural traits. In the same critiqu____ *esía negra*, Candelier (1974, 42) emphasizes the tambour, an often-u__d metaphor suggesting the primitive essentialism and natural rhythm of *negritud*:

Bantu culture arrived in America with the drum of the black slaves, and that rural instrument was used not only to produce dance and rhythm—the ultimate expression of *negritud*—but would reproduce—perhaps unnoticed by the colonizers—the emotive language of black African lyrics. Many of the traditional creole poems attempted to discover its significance and to imitate that expressive sound.

Fanon (1986, 124) also states the importance of the drumbeat: 'Only the Negro has the capacity to convey it, to decipher its meaning, its import.' Its resonance is a symbol of inner black strength and resistance; a prelude to revolution and liberation from racist oppression. Blas Jiménez employs the pounding of the tambour to conjure up a supposedly inherent African lyricism, echoing the chant of resistance and emancipation. 'Canto al abuelo desconocido' ('Song to the Unknown Grandfather') celebrates the *cimarrones*, the runaway slaves who established their own communities in the highlands of the Dominican Republic:

Tam-tam tam-tam tam-tam
I can hear your drum
sounding through the mountains
tam-tam tam-tam tam-tam
as if it were your voice

A tam-tam a tam-tam
as words
as symbols
as a language of peace
as a sign of liberty.[26]

The sound of the tambour vibrates through the mountains, echoing the animated cry for freedom of *el negro cimarrón*, who broke his chains and fled from slavery. Jiménez urges contemporary Dominicans to beat off racism and celebrate *negritud*. Dominicans, despite breaking the chains of slavery, remain bonded by color.

Depestre (1970) outlines *cimarronaje cultural* in Caribbean literature, which he describes as an escape from dominant culture in order to construct a minority culture. It represents 'a form of resistance, and legitimate defense against the legacies and racist discourse of slavery, colonialism and imperialism' (Depestre 1970, 347). The Dominican experience after emancipation rejects this form of cultural upheaval. Dominicans did not want to flee from an Hispanic identity. Instead, their vehemence and energy were directed towards resisting Haitian influence.

Alfonso Torres combines sexuality, *cimarronaje* and this rhythmic force in a series of poems entitled 'Amor cimarrón' (*'Cimarrón Love'* 1994). The tambour becomes a symbol for the 'synthesis of races', infusing vitality and passion through the veins of Antillean lovers:

I

Cimarrón love has the virtue
of carrying the blood of the tambour
love in the Antilles is *cimarrón*
synthesis of races.
...

III

...

Oh...!*Cimarrón* love in our veins
cause of this inexhaustible passion
keeper of islands and hurricanes
hotchpotch of flesh and skeletons.[27]

Torres's poetry, written in the 1990s is laden with racial stereotypes akin to those of the nineteenth- and early twentieth-century romantics. His collected poems reinforce the image of the sensual, dark-skinned woman as an object of desire and aesthetic adoration. Alternatively, his verse espouses an essentialist vision of African Caribbean identity. The raw essence of *cimarronaje* permeates Dominican territory, as vital and irrepressible as the forces of nature.

Tony Pichardo (1992) produces a grittier drumbeat. His collection of poetry is presented in bilingual format—Spanish and Haitian creole translations—and emphasizes the shared history of Dominicans and Haitians. For both, he argues, the fiery beat of the tambour, (*el sonido del fuego vital*), symbolizes an inner strength and passion which could fuel the co-development of both countries. Pichardo suggests that the fire of resistance burns within every Dominican and Haitian who faces oppression, whether racial, cultural or economic. The ignition of this fire sparked the end of Haitian and Dominican dictatorships, and must now be rekindled for continued social and political change. Pichardo employs the well-worn symbol of the tambour, yet he re-directs his verse away from the romanticism that engulfs many contemporary Dominican writers, towards a pithy social realism.

Consuming tropical fertility

While the drum is as a metaphor for an African past, *negritud* and the tropical climate of the Caribbean are often related by fake concepts of environmental determinism in Dominican literature. Writers correlate the heat, sun and characteristics of the physical environment with racial traits. The fertility of the tropics conditions the female character in 'Mulata' (1994), a poem by Torres. A fruitful earthiness and the omnipresent rhythm of the tambour represent her fecundity:

> A *cimarrón* spell
> shakes her
> beads of sweat
> running off her body
> like showers of fire
> scorching the West.
>
> *mulata* fruit of the earth
> cry of the tambour in my ears
> give a little of your rhythm
> to my words
> fertilize with your dreams
> my destiny.[28]

The humidity and moisture of the Caribbean is expressed by the perspiring body. The poet juxtaposes the ripeness of her sexuality with the sinful side of desire. *La mulata* is skilled in witchcraft; African spirituality has the power to scald the economically developed, but culturally bereft, western world.

A poem by Carlos Lebrón Saviñón, also titled 'Mulata' (1980), similarly portrays dark-skinned women as fruit to be consumed. Coulthard (1962) has remarked upon the tendency of Caribbean writers to compare women with fruit and vegetables. He suggests that this tendency parallels nineteenth-century European lyricism which sought to make comparisons between the physical attributes of women and flowers. European writers, though, arguably also employ food metaphors to convey desire or beauty. The substitution of foreign flora for local fruits or vegetables is not only an obvious literary ploy, but addresses an important symbolic difference. Flowers are generally looked at and appreciated, whereas fruit or vegetables are devoured to satiate a hunger or need. *La mulata* was an object to satisfy sensual and sexual gratification. Lebrón Saviñón (1985) combines this image with animalistic, predatory metaphors:

Your fever which intoxicates me more than
the sweet bitterness
of alcohol.
But the drum resounds in your skin
Your rumba is a music which cries
in the mad torrent of your rivers.

But your tropical flesh devours
the ancestral stillness of my loathing.
Mulata of desire: when you pass,
you are the first
you are the loveable synthesis of races
frenzy of the panther,
night and day merengue and restless-rumba...[29]

The *mulata* is described in terms of the stealth and physicality of a (black) panther, whose animal-like passions can turn to the frenzy of debauched sexual lust. Her body becomes a dangerous object of desire, devoured and drunk by the eyes of the poet-voyeur, yet her 'tropical flesh' holds the 'sweet bitterness' of guilt-ridden revelry.

Body aesthetics

Ideals of beauty and color dominate Dominican literature with the theme of racial heritage. Jiménez, however, argues for the appreciation of African Dominican phenotype and color in 'Pelo-pelo-pelo' ('Hair-hair-hair' 1987). The poem attempts to reverse the dominant attitude which prescribes that certain physical features such as tight curly hair should be considered as ugly or 'bad'. The poet stresses pride in every strand of his hair, and asserts contentment with his skin color:

...
my hair
grows in my skin

like the skin of my grandfather
skin which gives pride
hair and skin
hair
my hair
curly strand
strand + strand + strand
creates my good hair
a curly hair
an Afro hair
a hair of a *negro*
my hair [30]

Repetition and the use of a dominant personal pronoun underline the hereditary nature of blackness, stressing the poet's pride in his familial ancestry. The racial aesthetic expressed in Dominican literature, however, is not usually that of radical Black Pride. More commonly, the metaphors construct color within a traditional framework of racial perception.

Jiménez, one of the most radical of Dominican writers, produces work, which seen as a parody of reality, mimics the socio-sexual construction of race and existing stereotypes. This is clearest in a poem from his first collection, 'Negra No. 1' (1980); employing a repetitive and simple rhythm which suggests the beat of a drum:

Negra with the large breasts
negra with the firm buttocks
negra who cuts the cane
negra you really are sexy
negra with the large breasts
negra with the firm buttocks
negra who washes clothes
negra who fries the food
negra who bears many children
negra you really are sexy
negra with the large breasts
negra with the firm buttocks
when you walk slowly

one sees all the sweetness
of the cane which you have cut
in your bitter life
negra with the large breasts
negra with the firm buttocks.[31]

The large-breasted, firm-buttocked *negra* is imbued with the earthiness, fertility and raw sex appeal that is the trademark of much contemporary Dominican poetry. The bitterness of her racial oppression is only hinted at, in contrast to the sweet sugar cane which she cuts. Cutting cane, frying snacks and washing clothes are the stereotypical chores of the poor, dark-skinned woman. Jiménez conveys an aspect of social reality, but veils it with heavily worn sexual and racial clichés. Alternatively, one could argue that the poet employs ironic exaggeration in order to criticize these stereotypes in a subversive manner.

Haitians and Haiti

Dominican literature on *negritud* inevitably focuses on the neighboring population of Haiti. Jiménez often ridicules the Dominican attitude which suggests that only Haitians are 'real' or quintessential *negras/os*. Dark-skinned Dominicans are frequently teased or insulted by being called Haitian. 'Haitiano' (1980) derides this discrimination:

You are Haitian
you are Haitian by being *negro*
you are *negro*
that makes you Haitian
not by birth
By being *negro*
You are *negro*
Negro is bad
Bad is Haitian
Negro is ugly
Ugly is Haitian
You are Haitian
By being *negro* you are Haitian [32]

The poet taunts those Dominicans who equate *negritud* with Haitian nationality, and he challenges the commonly espoused insult that Haitians and blackness are the epitome of ugliness. Dominicans, he argues, are black, so by that reason they must be all ugly as well.

Sherezada (Chiqui) Vicioso is a contemporary Dominican author who directly challenges traditional Dominican animosity towards Haiti. Her poem, entitled 'Haití' (1981), addresses the plight of the Haitian state. The black, virginal nation was violated, sexually and environmentally, by slavery and colonialism. A humiliated nascent state, left open to the vagaries of abuse by political powers, parallels the rape of black women in the context of (white) male sexual hegemony:

Haiti
I imagine you virginal
before pirate predecessors
removed your clothes of mahogany
and left you thus
with your breasts in the air
and your torn grass skirt
scarcely green,
timid brown.[33]

Dominican writers' attacks on anti-Haitianism have become more vocal and politicized during the last fifty years, particularly since the massacre of 1937. *El masacre se pasa a pie,* by Freddy Prestol Castillo, is an eyewitness account of the Haitian massacre, written from notes made in the late 1930s, but not published until 1973. The book was received well within the Dominican Republic, although the subject matter was judged controversial enough for the author to wait over three decades before publication. *El masacre se pasa a pie* has sold over 34,000 copies, a substantial amount, given that the majority of publications in the Dominican Republic do not exceed an initial print run of 1,000 copies.

The narrator-protagonist works in a Dominican border town, sent there by the government to preside as a provincial judge. Prestol Castillo was himself sent to Dajabón as a federal magistrate during Trujillo's regime. The story recounts the moral dilemma and ultimate cowardice of the young magistrate during the massacre of thousands of

Haitian and dark-skinned Dominicans along the border region in 1937. The narrator is unable to face up to his responsibility to humanity and fails to react against the campaign of racial murder, although he knows that he should do so.

El masacre presents the tragedy of extreme nationalism and the atrocities of genocide. Prestol Castillo, though a potential political critic of Trujillo, expresses a strong anti-Haitian undertone and racist sentiment. Haitians are described consistently as primitive, savage, and alien to Dominican civilization, an ironic reversal of the barbarity of the Dominican-led massacre. Several characters in the novel refer to previous Haitian invasions and barbarity in order to legitimize the massacre.

The author makes the tacit assumption of white supremacy, and presumes that the expulsion of Haitians from Dominican territory by some means was a self-evident necessity. Prestol Castillo suggests in an interview that though he considered the killings abhorrent, the outcome was a reassertion of Dominican nationality along the border region (Sommer 1983). The massacre was a justifiable assertion of nationalism—it is argued that violent racism is more correctly a characteristic trait of Haitian history.

Haitians were deemed worthless, their humanity carried no weight in the profit and loss of Dominican agriculture. The narrator records the paltry sum offered by the Dominican government as compensation for Haitians killed in the massacre: 'A cow is worth more than a prisoner and a Haitian is worth less than a mango' (Prestol Castillo 1973, 73). The massacre destroyed a source of cheap labor, some of who would work even for a sack of potatoes as payment. The reader suspects that Prestol Castillo harbors similar sentiments. Haitian labor was an unfortunate, but economically valid, requirement. He adopts a biological racism, characteristic of nineteenth- and early twentieth-century European thought:

The Haitian is the stalker of the night. And the best guide is the breeze. The noses of the Haitians appear to grasp the breeze in order to lead them to the stockyards, given away by their smell of dung, in the night... This primitive race reads an alphabet of smells. (Prestol Castillo 1973, 75)

Haitians are described as a primitive race, prone to theft and guided by their sense of smell. Basic sensations govern their blunt, dangerous and animalistic tendencies: 'Haiti signifies hunger. Hunger knows no limits' (Prestol Castillo 1973, 78). The Haitians raided Dominican territory at night to steal or reclaim livestock and agricultural produce, but their stealth and thieving is seen as implicit, as natural and as dangerous as the night. Haitians belonged to the dark, and the darkness to Haiti: 'Haiti came at night... It was, night. It was, Haiti' (Prestol Castillo 1973, 126).

The narrator reproduces the long-standing fear of the Haitian revolutionary tradition, a delirious nightmare of Haitian revenge on whites. A Haitian laborer, facing death at the hands of drunken Dominican soldiers, screams:

'I want to drink blood! Blood! More blood...! The desire to drink with rum. Blood of white Spaniards! ... Give me blood, I want to wash my face with blood, in honor of the *negro* gods of Haiti.' (Prestol Castillo 1973, 137-138)

In contrast to the brutality of the massacre and heathen lives of the Haitian population, the narrative describes the beauty and intelligence of the young Dominican teacher, Angela Vargas. The surrounding class of Haitian and Haitian-Dominican pupils stands in stark opposition to her virtues:

In this parish of ugliness the teacher was the contrast: she was beautiful. Here there was danger for a woman: to be a teacher, which is like saying that she was miserably poor, and to possess a beauty that could incite the sadism of any one of the savages who populated this distant territory. The girl was from the South and was barely twenty years old. She was the color of cinnamon and had greenish eyes, beautiful black braids and the figure of a model in an aristocratic salon of a big city.

... she is also the only person here who knows that the *Dominican Republic* exists. 'What's that?...' the surprised residents of the place would say. They have only their miserable lives, like the lives of pigs, and lack any notion of the fatherland.[34]

The assumed innocence and purity of the teacher is threatened by the Haitian presence. Prestol Castillo again posits his great fear of Haitian invasion, sexual and cultural, of all that is Dominican. Her beauty is enhanced by a faithful duty to *dominicanidad*. She reacts against the barbarity, whereas the protagonist, guilt-stricken and helplessly in love with her, is too weak to confront his cowardice. Her fortitude comes from that of the Dominican nation, her loyalty to *dominicanidad*. She survives, and he crumbles to nothing. Prestol Castillo fails to challenge racism just as the protagonist is unable to confront the realities of genocide and his own confused state of mind.

Identity and indecision

Black identity is seldom asserted in Dominican literature. The affirmation of *negritud* challenges the prevalent racial norms of *blancura* or the concept of *indio/a* and leads an element of self-doubt. Indecision, fear and the uncertainty about one's self are aptly expressed by Jiménez in 'Aquí' ('Here' 1980):

> What am I?
> *negro, mulato*, thick-lipped.
> What am I?
> Dominican, American, Antillean,
> black African who feels the beat
> a mad *negro* in a white world, a Spanish world.
> I search,
> search for the tam-tam of my ancestors
> I want to leave.[35]

The poet seeks escape from a society in which his race is denied or deemed abnormal; yet the search for identity still refers to the essentialism of an African drum beat. 'Identidad' ('Identity' 1980), also by Jiménez, explodes the myth of indigenous ancestry as a racial smoke screen. All *indios/as* in the Dominican Republic share a variety of racial ancestries; African descent, however, is dominant:

> *Indio* with the green eyes
> son of Arab-*negro*
> son of *blanco-negro*

tercerón, cuarterón, mulato.

Indio with the green eyes
son of Spaniard
son of Taino
son of *negro cimarrón.*[36]

Jiménez challenges the concept of the light aesthetic and the *indio*-myth throughout his three collections of poetry. 'Indio claro', published in 1987, mocks those who try to 'lighten' their race through false terminology and challenges the weakness of their ill-founded prejudice. The rhetorical voice of the poet questions why anyone would want to be *negro/a*. If one Dominican asserts her or his *negritud*, then all Dominicans would have to follow:

Why do you want to be *negro?*
you are *indio*
indio claro
...
why do you want to be *negro?*
I cannot let you be it
because if you are *negro*
they will be *negros*
because if you are *negro*
I will be *negro*[37]

The Dominican literature of *negritud* presents a portrait of self-denial and exclusion of reality. The Black Pride movement has failed to gain literary roots in the Dominican Republic; only Blas Jiménez has created a coherent body of work in recent times which addresses racial issues. His verse holds an optimistic outlook for a racially equitable future, but much hope remains shrouded in pessimism. He returns to the complexity of the Dominican racial matrix in 'Otra vez... aquí' ('Once Again... Here' 1984):

Among this Spanish people,
the *negro* dies
like the *indio*, by wanting to be *blanco*.

Among this Spanish people,
the *negro* civilizes himself
with tones of various colors.

Among this Spanish people,
tears of the old *negro*
for the infant people: '*the negrito was born dead*'

Among this Spanish people,
people of suffering
one kills the *negro* on the outside, but he is born again within.[38]

Jiménez suggests that the vitality of black rebirth is irrepressible, even through the living nightmare of racial 'death.' The final stanza points to the failed awakening of political and social energy.

Black awareness?

Manuel del Cabral, perhaps the best known of Dominican writers of black literature, awakened a limited response with a novel that combined *negritud* and politics. *El presidente negro* was first published in 1973. The subject of the novel was unthinkable—a black president governing the United States. It is significant that del Cabral locates the novel in the United States; Black Power had no place in Dominican politics. Despite the focus on radical politics, *El presidente negro* breaks few of the moulds of Dominican literary style. Del Cabral uses well-established stereotypes and themes which do little to promote a reappraisal of black literature in the Dominican Republic. Instead, the narrative, while ostensibly addressing race relations and Black Liberation in the United States, employs a range of minor characters to provide derogatory images of Haiti.

The *negros/as* about whom del Cabral writes are seldom Dominican; yet critics have generously portrayed del Cabral as a spokesperson for literary *negritud* in Dominican society:

...the *negro* of Manuel del Cabral is a *negro* with tears who thinks, with sadness which demands reflection, with smiles which nourish our firm hope for social redemption, for human equality and the elimination of the injustices which torment

humankind at all latitudes and among all races. (Lantigua
1989, 113)

This type of criticism supports the whimsical, and at times patronizing,
rendition of black stereotypes which characterizes Dominican literature.
El presidente negro sustains this belief in a false and essentialist *negritud*.
    The novel charts the rise and assassination of William Smith, the
first black president of the United States, who supports the oppressed,
the poor and the black population, in their struggle against capitalism
and unsympathetic modernizing forces. Del Cabral includes numerous
racial stereotypes and clichés in his writing. In the early stages of the
novel he reverts to the environmental racism of the nineteenth century,
describing how the black population of Harlem has been fortunate to
overcome the cold New York climate, not their original 'geographical'
climate, enabling them to sing and dance in the streets (del Cabral
1990, 35).
    The protagonist is presented as a messianic figure. He sacrifices his
own son, who has been kidnapped by the business mafia, to the causes
of socialism and racial equality. His trustworthy and faithful assistant is
Peter, a rock of consistency—the only white man who has his full
confidence (del Cabral 1990, 91). Peter himself is the son of an Irish
immigrant and provides an obvious inversion of the white-benevolent-
master and dutiful-black-servant tradition. Joe, the ill-fated mulatto son
of the president and his former white girlfriend, is portrayed as the
brilliant synthesis of two races, black and white. His father proposes a
federal policy of racial inter-marriage to forge a new American nation;
this, however, would contradict the narrator's earlier bizarre claim that:

the mulatto complex is more complicated than that of the pure
white and the pure black; he does not like being in between,
perhaps so that he is not confused with being homosexual.[39]

Among the background characters, two elderly black sages, Tic and
Papá-Ciego, each possess spiritual powers which produce an
otherworldliness. Perhaps the most wooden characterization is reserved
for the president's parents, Tom and Jane. Both are described as
overwhelmed by the splendor of the White House, which offends their
simple and humble spiritual beliefs. They continually express their

unease to their son: 'Imagine now two savages out of control in this palace. We move like animals in a cage of luxury...'⁴⁰ The primitive nature of the parents' mentality is consistently described in the first sixty pages of the novel. Tom refuses to brush his teeth with toothpaste, since they, he argues, have always been white and that will remain the limit of his whiteness (del Cabral 1990, 55). Jane, the blackness of her skin compared to the night and her teeth compared to the lightness of day, maintains a fatalistic view of their lives (del Cabral 1990, 53). She argues that despite avoiding politics, her skin will always be political. The black population is, thus, fated to be subordinate to the whites. William promises, however, that class relations will one day transcend racial discrimination. Notwithstanding his attempts to institute a black state, the president then reverses his theory of self-imposed apartheid to claim: 'The word black... that's already a thing of the past.'⁴¹ The confusion of the novel is exacerbated on the following page by the president's next statement to his mother: 'The black shouldn't let a white see him crying, he enjoys our pain, our skin nourishes his sadism.'⁴²

William, while travelling as a young man, was wrongly imprisoned in a Dominican jail by Trujillo. The Dominican dictator makes several appearances during the novel in which he is portrayed as an evil simpleton. The narrative briefly criticizes Dominican attitudes towards Haiti, but concentrates on describing the overt sexuality and immense fecundity of Haitian women. A barman recounts:

'Here in Haiti... the women have sons under the trees, under the donkeys, in the corners, on the road, there is no place overlooked... If the rhythm of proliferation continues out of control like this in this country, the Haitian drama will return in several years with international significance.'⁴³

Del Cabral uses an indirect voice to repeat the perceived demographic and cultural threat of Haiti to the Dominican nation. Haitians, it is argued, survive their misery only through drug abuse and the omnipresent malignancy of *vodoun*. Whilst *El presidente negro* addresses themes of black awareness, it does little to revoke existing prejudices against *negros/as* and Haitians in the Dominican Republic.

A view from outside
The appraisal so far points to the failure to establish a creditable literary tradition of *negritud* within the Dominican Republic. Dominican writers living outside the Dominican Republic over the last three decades, such as Julia Alvarez, Chiqui Vicioso and Daisy Cocco de Filippis, have more directly addressed the racial prejudice of their compatriots. The external viewpoint and the experience of contemporary race relations in the United States have produced subtle assessments of the Dominican racial complex. The novel by Julia Alvarez, *How the Garcia Girls Lost Their Accents* (1991), is one such example that directly focuses on the influence of the migratory experience.

The story recounts the history of four Dominican girls growing up with their family near Boston in the 1960s, describing their reactions to exile in the United States. Alvarez comments upon their return during summer vacations to the complexities of Dominican ethnicity, in stark contrast to the black-white dichotomy of North American society. Before their enforced political exile, the Garcia family were part of the lighter-skinned Dominican elite. On their arrival in the United States they became black immigrants who spoke Spanish. This was a catastrophic shock to the father who had indoctrinated his daughters with the importance of *hispanidad*, playfully holding them upside down and asking if they had the blood of the *Conquistadors* in their veins: 'Then he puts her right side up and laughs a great big *Conquistador* laugh that comes all the way from the green, motherland hills of Spain' (Alvarez 1991, 197). The father, later, expresses his racial prejudice after the birth of his grandson, which Alvarez recounts with subtle irony and ridicule:

> During his two visits, the grandfather had stood guard by the crib all day, speaking to little Carlos. 'Charles the Fifth; Charles Dickens; Prince Charles.' He enumerated the names of famous Charleses in order to stir up genetic ambition in the boy. 'Charlemagne,' he cooed at him also, for the baby was large and big-boned with blond fuzz on his pale pink skin, and blue eyes just like his German father's. All the grandfather's Caribbean fondness for a male heir and for fair Nordic looks had surfaced. There was now good blood in the family against a future bad choice by one of its women. (Alvarez 1991, 26-27)

After an initial reluctance to see his Dominican daughter marry an unknown German from outside the traditional elite, the father warms to the union. 'Good blood' transcends his class-based fears.

Alvarez describes a Haitian servant, known as Chucha, who formerly worked for the family whilst they lived in the Dominican Republic. The author describes her from the viewpoint of one of the young sisters:

> There was this old lady, Chucha, who had worked in Mami's family forever and who had this face like someone had wrung it out after washing to get some of the black out of it. I mean, Chucha was super-wrinkled and Haitian blue-black, not Dominican *café-con-leche* black. She was real Haitian too and that's why she couldn't say certain words like the word for parsley... (Alvarez 1991, 218)

Alvarez projects an patronizing image of the Haitian woman, loyal to her employers. She casts spells to protect them, her mysticism accepted as a benevolent form of *brujería*. Another maid, Pila, is also Haitian, but remains set-apart from the others: 'The light-skinned Dominican maids feared her, for Haiti was synonymous with voodoo' (Alvarez 1991, 279). Through the voice of the young sister, the farce of racially-constructed images of beauty are guilefully chided:

> Nivea, the latest of our laundry maids, was 'black-black': my mother always said it twice to darken the color to full, matching strength. She'd been nicknamed Nivea after an American face cream her mother used to rub on her, hoping the milky white applications would lighten her baby's black skin. (Alvarez 1991, 260)

Literature alone cannot pre-empt a radical re-evaluation of race in Dominican society, nevertheless the foundations of African Hispanic writing in the Dominican Republic are weak and offer limited support for such a reappraisal. Among contemporary authors, even the more sympathetic and enlightened writers maintain certain racial stereotypes which impede ambitions for a more equitable representation of race. The literature of *negritud* in Dominican Republic has failed to contribute to a process of reducing racial discrimination. Can such a goal be achieved within the bounds of a racially or ethnically oriented literary canon?

Expressing *negritud*

It is difficult to equate Dominican literature about *negritud* with that of the region as a whole. Braithwaite (1993) has suggested four kinds of written tradition in the Caribbean: the rhetorical, the literature of African survival, the expression of Africa, and those works that seek a reconnection with Africa. Few of these categories seem to fit the Dominican tradition. Black literature has been longer lasting in the territories of the former British and French Caribbean, largely due to the stronger reaction to white colonialism. A key factor for the lackluster response to *negritud* in the Dominican Republic has been the officially accepted and pervasive anti-Haitian ideology in society.

Negritud has not had the revitalizing literary impact so often described in other parts of the Americas. Lewis (1983, 4) laconically attributes the limited impact of black literature in some instances to the 'positive emphasis upon the African cultural heritage in societies that quite often denied its value.' The Dominican Republic is such an example. Lewis adds that when blackness at both the main social and linguistic levels becomes imbued with negativity, a tremendous amount of pressure to conform is exerted. Why write black, when white is right?

Writers in the Dominican Republic found no intellectual or popular space for a black aesthetic, neither was the audience color-blind. Acceptance would have meant acquiescence to the *négritude* and barbarity of Haiti, the natural antithesis to *dominicanidad*. Lewis (1983) describes an African Hispanic literary dichotomy that welds Hispanic language, style and technique on to an African conception of *negritud* and black Latin American culture. This fusion joins the legacy of slavery with that of contemporary racial prejudice. Dominican society has avoided this literary synthesis.

The rejection of Hispanic culture in the Dominican Republic has been limited. Socially and culturally-engineered ignorance supports the myth of a benevolent Spanish colonial regime, outlined sardonically by Jiménez in 'Discriminación a la dominicana' (Discrimination Dominican-style 1984):

> But
> but slavery
> slavery was not bad here. [44]

Sarcastic disbelief is expressed that Hispanic civilization could be associated with a barbarity similar to that experienced in Haiti.

Anti-Haitian feeling promoted the romance of an imagined European and indigenous history for the Dominican nation. Any foothold for an ensuing Afrocentric construction of the past was removed, in sharp contrast to the success of Jean Price-Mars's commentaries on Haiti and the work of Marcus Garvey in Harlem and Jamaica. *Ainsi parla l'oncle* (1927/1973) by Mars was a direct revaluation and rehabilitation of African elements in Haitian life. In the same vein as the writings of Garvey, Mars deemed African civilization superior to the cultural barbarity of European societies. Reminiscences of a similar Black Arcadia in the Dominican Republic would have been tantamount to treason.

The literature of *negritud* fronts a cosmetic myth, rather than addressing the prevalent racial hypocrisy and sham of ethnic tolerance. The racial, cultural and historical realities of black experience in the Dominican Republic are generally shrouded by racial mysticism and essentialism. *Negritud* still represents a cult of the dark exotic and glorifies a false innocent primitivism, which has been fashionable in European culture since the Renaissance, and notable among Latin American authors since the First World War.

Dominican literature with a black theme veers towards *africanización perpetua*, a phrase used first by Gastón Baquero, and repeated by Jackson (1976), to describe the continuing representation of Africa as exotic; celebrating the crude physicality of the primitive. The excessive focus on Africanness, echoed by the beat of the drum or fed by the fruits of plantation labor, tends to minimize the role of racism in maintaining an essentialist view of African culture. A tradition of caricature 'has made the black a literary buffoon, a bongo-beating idiot mindlessly singing and dancing his way down through the centuries, all the while speaking a 'broken tongue" (Jackson 1976, 42). Alternatively, the black female is represented as the bar temptress or salon seducer, an unintellectual sexual animal. Whilst many authors are no doubt well-meaning, most Dominican texts are apologetic, patronizing or condescending. Manuel del Cabral described the character in 'Este negro' ('This *Negro*' 1942) as a simpleton, a folkloric object in verse form:

Simple *negro*
you who have
your life and the world
within your amulet.

From you,
arises only
the smoke of your pipe.

Neither the children,
nor the ass,
have your simplicity.[45]

Black literature need not provoke a radical process of liberation or self-assertion nor appear as a confessional for white racism or black essentialism. Literature of *negritud* in the Dominican Republic has been largely the preserve of light-skinned intellectuals, a game of stylization and mimicry, and a reaction against Haitian cultural influences. Jiménez's call for an appropriate black literature in his second collection of poems, *Caribe africano en despertar* (African Caribbean Awakening) has yet to arouse sufficient writers or readers.

7.
Race and Nation in Dominican Politics

'The homeland is the most inviolable of property rights.'
—Pedro Mir (1993), *Concerto of Hope for the Left Hand*

A fortnight before the second round of the Dominican presidential elections in June 1996, an opinion poll claimed that 9 percent of the electorate would not vote for the candidate of the Partido Revolucionario Dominicano (PRD), Dr José Francisco Peña Gómez, because they believed that he was Haitian.[46] Eleven percent also said that race or color would influence their vote. Over a fifth of Dominicans interviewed affirmed that racial characteristics played an important part in their electoral choice. Peña Gómez, born black in the Dominican Republic and despite popular support, could not escape the prejudiced politics that surrounded him. Blackness in Dominican politics ultimately loses elections.

Anti-Haitianism has a long history as the ideology of national cohesion and domination for the ruling Dominican elite, but, significantly, during the 1990s, racism and nationalism became the basis for a racist agenda in internal Dominican politics. Peña Gómez, an active force in Dominican politics since the 1960s, died suddenly in May 1998. He was dark-skinned and allegedly had Haitian ancestry. In 1994, he was the main challenger to the long-standing white president, Dr Joaquín Balaguer. The latter, as a close aide to Trujillo, had had a major position in Dominican politics for over sixty years.[47] During the previous elections, in 1990, with the PRD in disarray, the presidential campaign of Peña Gómez was marginalized. The real battle was then fought between President Balaguer and Professor Juan Bosch. Victory fell to the former, amid the customary accusations of serious fraud.

Nationalism and racism
Nationalism is often a potent form of racism. Asserting and protecting a community, nationalist sentiment manufactures confrontation and

alienation as by-products of claimed cohesion. The racialization of politics relates closely to the concept of nationalism. Race is first and foremost a political concept (Solomos and Black 1995). In Dominican politics, race and nation cannot be considered as isolated, unitary terms. Dominicans rarely speak of the *nación dominicana*, they are far more likely to mention *raza dominicana*. Race and nation are effectively entwined, *nación* is a term seldom used in everyday language. The national territory is racial territory; national belonging denotes racial belonging.

Unlike political discourse in the United States, race in the Dominican Republic incorporates overwhelming nationalist overtones. Dominican nationalism is politicized and racialized; nation and state form a political unity where state politics legitimize the politics of race. Despite highly racialized politics in the 1990s, there has been a lack of black or *negro/a* political mobilization compared to the United States, which experienced the civil rights movements and urban uprisings of the 1960s and the emergence during the 1980s and 1990s of black and minority mobilization. Black political consciousness was unlikely to take off in a country that ignored racism at the official level, and where racial identification generally negated an African heritage. Instead, racial political mobilization in the Dominican Republic focused on the rejection of Haiti and *negritud*, which were personified for many by the presidential candidacy of Peña Gómez.

Racism plays a fundamental part in Dominican politics, but does race transcend class influence? Writing about the Haitian political experience, James (1994, 104) states:

> The race question is subsidiary to the class question in politics, and to think of imperialism in terms of race is disastrous. But to neglect the racial factor as merely incidental is an error only less grave than to make it fundamental.

Rex (1973) also believes that class is the major motivation for political action. Racial discrimination and conflict, he argues, can be explained by inequalities in the 'market situations' which fuel conflicts between indigenous workers and immigrants. Rex considers the special case of immigrants in society, placing their experience in terms of an underclass, rather than as a working class. Rex considers class from a Weberian standpoint focusing upon relative access to resources. From a Marxist rather than Weberian perspective, Miles (1982) opposes race as a useful category since he views racism as integral to capital accumulation. Race, he argues, is always a component of the class dynamic, and is thus, an indirect medium for political action—it is an ideological effect, a mask hiding reality. Politics focused on ethnicity misjudges the central problematic of the class struggle.

Balibar and Wallerstein (1991) describe the class system and nationalism as complexity reducers for political action, suggesting that the latter is now the principal complexity reducer in modern history. Nationalism is formed in opposition to class struggle, which is then repressed by the former—the two do not compensate one another under these terms. If nationalism opposes class struggle, then racism cannot be a class-based ideology. Neither does nationalism automatically repress class struggle, and it is false to equate racism with the latter. Racism, and thus nationalism, are expressions formed through ethnicity. By recognizing the importance of race and nation for political action, the significance of ethnicity is inadvertently emphasized. Anderson (1991), too, gives racism a basis in class relations. He separates nationalism from racism by associating the latter with class, bloodlines and aristocracy. The emphasis on racial lineage is, however, an important aspect which unites nationalism as a form of racism.

Race and nation were the leading influences in Dominican political discourse during the 1990s, a marked transition from the class politics of the 1960s, the decade of the April Revolution. What initiated this racialization of electoral discourse? The key factor, coupled to economic stagnation, was the presidential candidacy of Peña Gómez in a society primed for the explosion of anti-Haitianism. The 1980s and 1990s witnessed growing concern about Haitian immigration, the 'silent invasion', threatening the demise of *la raza dominicana.*

Fanon (1970, 42) describes the defense of a racialized nation as 'cultural racism.' Gilroy (1987, 43) similarly regards new racism as a definition of race in terms of identity and culture, an attempt at legitimization. Race becomes coded in the language of nation and culture, aimed at deflecting the negative accusations of racism. Nationalism in popular terms is admirable, but the censure of racism leaves a social scar. However, the language of nation invokes a hidden racial narrative. The issue of sovereignty, a key component in Dominican electoral campaigning, is a powerful weapon in the armory of racial politics. Barker (1981, 65) describes sovereignty as a 'kinship illusion', a sentiment of national homogeneity, or a national character, which implies a lineage of inheritance—nation and culture gain a pseudo-biological importance, a dangerous vestige of nineteenth-century European racism.

The existence of extremist right-wing parties allows conservative parties to oppose them, implying their own anti-racism, while espousing similar policies in more palatable language. This more acceptable, yet racist, polity uses the facade of a legitimized xenophobia:

> The form of theory into which such words as 'alien' have been placed, giving them wider and more explicit meaning, is a theory of xenophobia. The wish to exclude foreigners has been built into a theory capable of operating at different levels. At one level... the theory inhabits the language of political arguments. In those arguments ideas about the naturalness of xenophobia allow politicians to move between (selected) evidence and policy conclusions. The implicit concept acts as a 'bridge', allowing individual experiences, particular bits of information and evidence, to be theorized, given status and significance. Emotional responses now seem justified by their very 'naturalness.' (Barker 1981, 4)

Racist political mobilization is a response to the fear of social and economic change, the inadequacy of a section of the population to compete legitimately in a changing society. The politicization of race and the scapegoating of racial groups provide a platform for the articulation of fears and the rejection of existing social and economic relations to emphasize the need to protect the interests of the nation. In a context of social and economic uncertainty, race and nation are potent myths in political discourse.

Twentieth-century anti-Haitianism: a political history

The context of Dominican elections during the 1990s was one of anti-Haitianism, fuelled by a growing concern over Haitian immigration and the demographic threat of a politically unstable neighbor. The border with Haiti has always been a highly contested and emotive physical entity in Dominican history. Policies similar to Trujillo's *dominicanización* of the borderlands have been consistently reproduced since the 1930s.

In the mid-1930s, Trujillo aimed to establish Dominican claims to border territory by blocking further Haitian occupation of the region and by fostering a stronger sense of Dominican identity. For over a century and a half before the Trujillo-Vincent agreement in 1936, there had been no mutually recognized border between the Dominican Republic and Haiti. The border population consisted of many *rayanos/as*, people of mixed Haitian and Dominican ethnicity. Many Dominicans in the border area spoke creole as their first language, were followers of *vodú*, adopted Haitian settlement and kinship patterns, and used the Haitian *gourde* as the unit of currency (Augelli 1980). Of great concern, was a purported 'darkening' of the population as more Haitians migrated to settle in the border provinces.

Trujillo feared the growing influence of Haitian culture in Dominican territory. The boundary agreement in 1936 established the foundation for a program of *dominicanización*, but the most brutal example of this policy to reclaim the nation came a year later in the form of the previously mentioned massacre of around 18,000 Haitians, and dark-skinned Dominicans, resident in the border zone. Continuing expulsions of Haitians were carried out by the Dominican military during the following decades, and an intense religious and educational campaign was pursued in the border areas. A select corps of Frontier Cultural Agents disseminated Dominican propaganda, and a network of highways was constructed to reduce physical and economic isolation from the rest of the country. Houses were constructed in traditional Dominican styles, and agricultural colonies promoted. To 'lighten' the population, Trujillo attempted to encourage the resettlement of refugees from Eastern Europe, Italy and Japan in the Dominican borderlands.

The concerted program of *dominicanización* lost momentum with the demise of Trujillo and the relative improvement of relations with Haiti at an official level. However, Haitians and Haitian-Dominicans are regularly deported from Dominican territory by the military, regardless of the legitimacy of their presence, and the concept of *dominicanización* remains a popular nationalist platform. Luis Julián Pérez, the leader of a small, extreme right-wing party, the Unión Nacionalista, published a book at the start of the 1990s, defending the Haitian massacre in 1937 and advocating a contemporary campaign to defend the Dominican nation. His implicit agenda supported a strategy of ethnic cleansing not far removed from that of the *trujillato*. Pérez (1990) undermines the legitimacy of Haiti as a state that evolved from a French colony founded on piracy and barbarity, suggesting that the island is intrinsically Spanish. The uncivilized and savage origins of the Haitian nation are repeated in the sexual and racist overtones of the threat of Haitian migration to the Dominican Republic: the 'passive penetration, repetitive and incessant,' and the implied rape of a virginal, pure and blameless Dominican nation (Pérez 1990, 11).

The romantic idyll of a Spanish past is resurrected in contrast to the brutality of the Haitian revolution. Pérez classes the latter as one of the most barbaric and sadistic crimes in American history, though he disregards the preceding two centuries of slavery. Despite errant Spanish colonial rule, Dominicans have always opposed Haitians to defend and assert their *hispanidad*. Dominican society is:

> ... above all a community of Hispanic origin... its centuries old culture in a constant relation with European civilization. [Dominicans] recovered their old status and became Spanish again, in spite of Spain... loyal to the sentiment of *hispanidad*. (Pérez 1990, 29).

The racism of Haitians towards *mulatos/as* dictates that co-operation between the two countries will always be impossible, especially, in Pérez' opinion, given the situation of complete incompatibility. He regurgitates a string of stereotypes which associate Haitians with witchcraft, AIDS, promiscuity, unemployment and an inability to understand birth control. Pérez' text recommends the expulsion of all Haitians from Dominican territory, while failing to acknowledge that the Dominican government encouraged the majority of Haitians to migrate in the first place, and suggests that a temporary wall or fence should be erected to seal the border more effectively. Far from dissociating his plans for *dominicanización* from those of Trujillo, he praises the regime's functionaries for their patriotism, arguing that the 1937 massacre was a repugnant but necessary action, and an inevitable consequence of Haitian aggression.

Despite such bigotry, Pérez attempts to separate his brand of nationalism from racism by suggesting that the racial, or aesthetic, differences between Haitians and Dominicans are not great enough to typify racial prejudice. Besides, he argues, racism is a Haitian problem resulting from the predominance of African heritage in Haiti and the ensuing 'lower level of culture' (Pérez 1990, 132). While the opinions of Pérez are extreme, it should be noted that he is the leader of a relatively well known nationalist party which receives noticeable political coverage in the media, and the person to whom Balaguer dedicated a recent edition of his poetry. The reason for the dedication is explained by reference to Balaguer's best-selling book, which shares a similar concern for the destiny of the Dominican nation.

In 1983, Balaguer published *La isla al revés*, now in its seventh edition, in which he outlines the demographic threat from an expanding Haitian population, the echo of an imperialism which sought to subjugate the Hispanic population—'a plan directed against the independence of Santo Domingo and against the American population of Hispanic origin' (Balaguer 1993, 33). Balaguer relies upon the scientific racism of the nineteenth century to explain the demographic explosion of the neighboring country, listing three key factors:

a) the characteristic fecundity of the *negro*; b) the primitive conditions which single out the low social standard of a considerable part of the Haitian population, and c) the resistance to illnesses due to the strong physique of the *negro*. (Balaguer 1993, 35)

Using a Malthusian framework, Balaguer then elucidates the biological threat of Haiti on the basis of race:

... the *negro*, left to his instincts and without the limiting brake on reproduction that a relatively high standard of living imposes on all countries, multiplies at a speed almost comparable to that of plants. (Balaguer 1993, 36)

Nearly half of the books listed in the bibliography were published in the nineteenth century, a third were published between 1900 and 1950, and none after 1979. *La isla al revés* is based heavily on an earlier work, *La realidad dominicana* (1947), written when Balaguer was Foreign Minister to Trujillo, in order to explain the 1937 Haitian massacre. Doré Cabral (1985) describes *La isla al revés* as a 'book of the past', but it contains the sentiments of a man who until recently was president of a modern Caribbean state. At the time of publication, *La realidad dominicana* was an impressive text— original, coherent and representative of contemporary intellectual thought in the Dominican Republic (Cassá 1984). *La isla al revés* is weaker, and less coherent. It is not just another edition of an historical text, but was published to confront present day issues within the context of a nationalist agenda.

The nation that Balaguer wishes to defend faces racial, cultural and moral peril from a the passive invasion by darker-skinned Haitians, who will destroy the roots of *hispanidad*:

The immense wave of color that daily invades Dominican territory, not only exposes Santo Domingo to the loss of its national character, but also corrupts its customs and lowers moral standards. (Balaguer 1993, 74)

... the Hispanic language and tradition, for more than a century, were the only defensive barriers against the terrifying wave of color and disintegrating force which had been invading Dominican territory in an interrupted, yet systematic manner, since 1795. (Balaguer 1993, 63)

Haitians put Dominican morality at risk. Both Pérez and Balaguer are concerned about the fatal attraction of Dominicans to Haitian dissolution, undermining traditional kinship, Christian values and irreversibly altering the ethnic make-up of the Dominican nation. The powerful stereotype of sexual promiscuity reiterated by Pérez, is employed by Balaguer to separate the two nations and to outline the pervasive menace of racial and cultural contamination: 'The clandestine penetration across land boundaries threatens to disintegrate the moral and ethnic values of Dominican families' (Balaguer 1993, 156).

Regardless of a nationalist discourse, which focuses upon the alleged traumatic consequences of the growth of *la raza negra*, Balaguer denies, with Pérez, that racism ever existed in the Dominican Republic. The only prejudice to which he concedes is religious, the defense of Catholicism. Fennema and Loewenthal (1987) observe that while the Haitian is always identified by the color of his or her skin, and blackness is equated to Haitian origins, Dominicans are seldom referred to by Balaguer in racial terms, but are defined as Spanish, and by implication white. He admits, however, that the majority are *mestizo/a*. The town of Baní, situated in the south-west of the Dominican Republic, is selected as the 'flower of the Republic', because the population is 'somatically least blended' and the Spanish tradition supposedly remains intact.

Balaguer believes that the savagery of Haitian culture is at least in part due to economic distress and underdevelopment, which gives some credence to his surprising proposition, at the end of *La isla al revés*, that a federation on economic grounds might be established between the two countries for practical reasons of development. This federation could extend, with restricted conditions, to the granting of dual citizenship. This single, unexpanded statement would initially seem to undermine the previous two hundred pages of nationalist discourse, but the elusiveness of Balaguer's statement seeks merely to provoke discussion, aimed at reasserting the strength and dominance of the Dominican nation. The granting of severely limited rights of citizenship would be a calculated measure for political or economic development of greater benefit to the Dominican economy. The subordinate role of Haiti in the confederation remains implicit (Cassá 1984).

Nationality, in Balaguer's terms, can never be granted or exchanged, only inherited. Paradoxically, while Balaguer's writing points towards a tentative integration between the two states, the opponents of Peña Gómez castigated him for allegedly favoring the fusion of the island, an accusation which he vehemently denied. Anti-Haitianism is a virulent component of Dominican intellectual history, and Haiti lies at the foundation of Dominican nationalism.

Dominican electioneering in the 1990s: the politics of race

Electoral politics have had a controversial history in the Dominican Republic since the 1960s, after three decades of authoritarian rule under

Rafael Leónidas Trujillo. The 1980s and 1990s witnessed a series of closely fought, or more accurately fraudulent, election results (Table 3).

Table 3. Election results in the Dominican Republic, 1986-1996

			% vote		
Political Party	1986	1990	1994	1996	1996
PRD	36.5	23.2	41.4	46.1	48.75
PRSC	41.6	35.5	42.4	15.3	-
PLD	18.4	33.8	13.2	38.4	51.25

Source: Junta Central Electoral

PRD—Partido Revolucionario Dominicano; PRSC—Partido Reformista Social Cristiano; PLD—Partido de la Liberación Dominicana

Dr Joaquín Balaguer maintained power through fraudulent elections for thirty years, letting go of control, only after international pressure, for two terms between 1978 and 1986. The PRSC again accepted defeat in the 1996 presidential elections, which were heralded as the first non-fraudulent elections in the country's history.

The key to understanding election campaigns in recent years is the development of an intensely racialized political discourse. This occurred most noticeably during the 1990s, when Peña Gómez became the presidential candidate for the PRD and leader of the main opposition party. Political campaigning developed tones of overt racism, and was fueled by anti-Haitianism and racist attitudes among the electorate. Peña Gómez had suffered racist slurs during the elections in 1982 as candidate to be mayor of Santo Domingo, but not to the same extent as he did in the 1994 and 1996 presidential election campaigns.

Race is politicized in the Dominican Republic, coded in the evocative language of culture and nation. The attack against Peña Gómez suggested that his Haitian ancestry made him an unsuitable, and potentially disloyal, candidate for the presidency of the Republic. A Gallup poll stated that 25 percent of those interviewed would not vote for Peña Gómez because he was 'violent and uncontrollable', his aggressive nature usually being linked to the assumed savagery of his Haitian heritage. Thirty-one percent of respondents, from another poll ten days before the second-round vote, believed that national sovereignty could be at risk if Peña Gómez became president.[48] The main complaint against Peña Gómez' Haitian origins was that he would support a fusion of Haiti and the Dominican Republic to create a single state, resurrecting fears of nineteenth-century Haitian plans to make the island *une et indivisible*. Electoral campaigns indirectly, or overtly, insulted the *negritud* of Peña Gómez. Anti-Haitianism, legitimized by popular opinion, acts as a respectable nationalist shield for the racism which pervades Dominican society, and rejects *negros/as* as suitable candidates for the presidency. Enrique Serrano, an ardent supporter of the PRD and Peña Gómez, was forced to lament, 'Here, nobody, ever, will want a black president.'

The stance of Peña Gómez in the face of the racist political agenda must be analyzed and questioned. Many would argue that he failed to challenge the racist accusations of his opponents, frequently responding to blatant prejudice in a defensive manner, thus failing to tackle the 'legitimacy' of racism as a platform for party and personal politics. At times, his defensive, almost apologetic, response to racial antagonism suggested that he, too, was trapped in an anti-Haitian mentality, strengthening his *dominicanidad* by rejecting Haiti.

Threats to sovereignty have been a major issue in the Dominican Republic. The country has been occupied by foreign powers for a total of 35 years since 1822—by Haiti between 1822 and 1844, Spain between 1861 and 1865, and twice by the United States, from 1916 to 1924 and 1965 to 1966. International agencies and foreign governments had a significant input into Dominican affairs for most of the twentieth century. As late as 1940, the Dominican customs administrator was an American nominated by the United States president, a hangover from the 1910 American-Dominican Convention.

Fraudulent mandates and the exclusion of the majority of the population from state politics has meant that the Dominican political system has lacked credibility and legitimacy. Maríñez suggests that democratic transition in the Dominican Republic occurred with the election of the PRD government in 1978, yet every presidential election, except the most recent in 1996 and 2000, has been accompanied by complaints of fraudulent practice being lodged with the Junta Central Electoral. Espinal (1991) suggests that democratic development faced particular problems in the Dominican Republic, not only from a strong authoritarian political history, but also as a monocultural economy with a heavy dependence on the external market, combined with a low level of industrialization and high unemployment. Insularity and the fear of United States' intervention also placed pressures upon incipient democratic regimes.

The presidential elections in 1996 and 2000 broke the mould of fraudulent elections following the widespread condemnation and political fiasco of the 1994 elections. In 1994, the main contenders for the presidency were Balaguer and Peña Gómez. Balaguer was adjudged to have won, but accusations of fraud threatened to paralyze the country amid popular discontent. An agreement was signed between the political parties which limited Balaguer's term of office to eighteen months, later extended to two years after political maneuvering by the PRSC, with the proviso that the veteran *caudillo* could not stand for re-election.

Although the presidential mandate was changed, the results of the elections in May 1994 stood as calculated by the electoral board, the Junta Central Electoral, despite notable reservations among international observers at the elections and active opposition by non-governmental political groups. The scale of the fraud received international media coverage.[49] The PRD claimed that 150,000 opposition supporters were unable to vote, the deception being committed by the Junta Central Electoral in favor of the PRSC. The electoral board, three fifths of whom were appointed by Balaguer, gave victory to the PRSC, several weeks after the day of the election, by a marginal 22,000 votes. International observers from the Organization of American States, the International Foundation for Electoral Systems and the National Democratic Institute for International Affairs agreed that opposition parties were disenfranchised, supporting the credibility of the claims to fraud. Under a fortnight before the elections, observers were excluded from the offices of the electoral register for three days; one observer was expelled from the country without explanation. During those days the electronic archives of the voting lists were allegedly altered in the government's favor. Government supporters were given multiple voting rights, and opponents excluded from the electoral lists or intimidated. In several areas, dark-skinned Dominicans or Haitian-Dominicans with legitimate voting rights were prevented from entering ballot station by the police or military, on the supposition that they would vote against the government. Similar intimidation allegedly occurred during the 1996 elections, but to a lesser degree.

The examples of fraudulent practice were many and varied in 1994. First, the Junta Central Electoral failed to display, publicly, electoral lists as required by law, and refused access to them for over a month after the elections. Secondly, due to the exclusion of thousands of voters, the electoral board agreed to extend voting hours from six o'clock to nine o'clock on the night of the election, but delayed issuing news of the extension until 10 minutes after the polls had closed. Few ballot stations re-opened, and many stations were kept closed by armed government supporters or by the police. Thirdly, the creation of a new electoral register fourteen months before the elections created a surplus 225,000 *cédulas* which were still unaccounted for at the time of the elections. Fourthly, abstention at presidential elections in the Dominican Republic is usually between 27 and 30 percent. In 1990, the abstention was 44 percent. In 1994, the Junta Central Electoral reported an abstention rate of 6.3 percent for the whole country, down to 4.5 percent in the interior. Finally, in eight of the twenty-nine provinces, more votes were cast than were registered on the electoral lists. Excess votes amounted to 23,135 in Espaillat, 4,700 in Montecristi, and 4,225 in Monte Plata, giving a total of 36,553 votes. This amounted to over 14,000 votes more than the stated margin of victory. Despite this contradiction in the electoral board's own calculations, the election results were confirmed.

Presidential elections were held next in May 1996, involving a three-way battle between Jacinto Peynado of the PRSC, Peña Gómez of the PRD, and Leonel Fernández of the Partido de la Liberación Dominicana (PLD). Balaguer, barred from re-election, refused to support his party's candidate or to vote in the elections. Peña Gómez, despite gaining the greatest number of votes, failed to obtain a sufficient majority for outright victory under the revised constitution, and so entered a second round of elections with the runner-up, Leonel Fernández, in the following month. A pact between the PLD and the PRSC, sealed by a remarkable political reconciliation between Bosch and Balaguer, the respective party patriarchs and long-term opponents, gave victory to Leonel Fernández. International observers upheld the legitimacy of both rounds of elections. Whereas fraud was not reported during the recent elections, racialized politics remained prevalent during both periods of electoral campaigning in 1994 and 1996. Racism during 1994 was perhaps more virulent, if only because the PRSC, without Balaguer in 1996, was never a major contender and failed to orchestrate a campaign on the same scale as during the previous election. Balaguer returned as presidential candidate in 2000, but failed to gain office, losing to the PRD candidate, Hipólito Mejía.

The political motives for Bosch and Balaguer to form the Frente Patriótico are easy to understand at the party level, but as an individual, Bosch had to overcome considerable personal grievances against Balaguer to accept any form of political contract. Political maneuvering establishes neither true friends, nor real enemies. Fierce antagonists for over fifty years, Bosch was exiled while Balaguer governed through the years of the *trujillato*, then denied non-fraudulent elections by Balaguer for the greater part of three decades. In 1990, Bosch failed to gain the presidency from Balaguer by a margin of 24,000 votes, a result of blatant electoral corruption. Peña Gómez and Bosch, the latter now 92 years old and suffering from Parkinson's disease, were close allies within the PRD until Bosch left and formed the PLD in 1973. It could be suggested that Bosch held a personal grudge against Peña Gómez and therefore wished to preclude him from the presidency. Perhaps Bosch was racially prejudiced against his former colleague. The latter remains unlikely, however, since Bosch (1965, preface) dedicated his autobiographical account of the early 1960s to the young Peña Gómez:

> To José Francisco Peña Gómez,
> and through him,
> to the youth of the people,
> the seed of hope
> for the Dominican nation.

Nevertheless, Bosch's writing shows seeds of anti-Haitian sentiment. As president of the republic following the death of Trujillo, before being ousted after barely seven months by the military coup, Bosch was involved in bitter brinkmanship with François Duvalier, the Haitian dictator. Whilst Bosch's opposition to the Haitian dictatorship is understandable, his writing at times exhibits a derogatory view of the neighboring country:

> Haiti's presence on the western part of the island represents an amputation of the Dominican future... We Dominicans know that because Haiti is there, on the same island, we can never realize

our full potential. We know that inevitably, because of the Haitian revolution, we will sooner or later be dragged down to our neighbor's level. (Bosch 1965, 179-180)

While political adversaries, Balaguer and Bosch seemed to have shared a mutual distrust of Haiti. The fear of Haitian influence, and the possible fusion of the island under Haitian dominance, prompted the formation of a Patriotic Front to block Peña Gómez from gaining the presidency. An editorial in *The New York Times* criticized the racist campaign of the PRSC, also arguing that the pact with Bosch was based on misguided anti-Haitianism.[50] The two *caudillos* joined forces to defend the Dominican nation. The name of the political union itself assumed an aggressive defense of *la Patria*. As *blancos*, both suggested, and feared as inevitable, the fate that would befall a light-skinned minority on an island where the first successful slave revolution occurred. Both, undoubtedly, were active participants in racialized politics.

The motives for the political alliance between Balaguer and Bosch may be questioned, but the outcome was clear. Peña Gómez would never be the president of the Dominican Republic in a political and social climate where racism is legitimized, and where Haitian influence remains the prime political scapegoat for Dominican politicians.

The Haitian context in contemporary politics

During 1994, the political crisis in Haiti became a major issue in the Dominican elections. Anti-Haitian sentiment was fueled by fears of an exodus from a politically unstable neighbor, heightened at the time of United States military intervention. Dominican sovereignty was deemed to be under threat. An imminent invasion of Haiti by the United States provoked fears of a Haitian 'avalanche.'[51] Jacinto Peynado, then vice-president, voiced his concerns over health risks and the spread of AIDS if Haitians were allowed to flee to the Dominican Republic *en masse*.[52] The media reacted to a tense, expectant atmosphere at the border, describing as a stampede the relocation of several Dominican families who feared an influx of refugees.[53]

The sovereignty issue was effectively used by opponents of Peña Gómez during the 1994 electoral campaign. His alleged sympathies for Haiti and a pact with the exiled Haitian president, Jean-Bertrand Aristide, were questioned, amid claims of an international conspiracy

and foreign meddling in Dominican affairs. To vote for Peña Gómez, a
woman in Gazcue argued, was effectively to hand over her
dominicanidad to a Haitian president. A reputed plot existed to unite
the island under a single government, and allegations of potential
political treason by Peña Gómez received wide coverage in the
Dominican media during the elections.[54] Balaguer's support for
ongoing trade with Haiti, breaking an international embargo, gained
limited attention until an editorial in *The New York Times* challenged
the Dominican government.[55] International concern over the failure of
the Haitian embargo, and the role of foreign observers during the 1994
elections, created the basis for Dominican claims of covert foreign
interference in domestic affairs.

The economic and political embargo against the Haitian military
government was decreed initially by the Organization of American
States in 1991. It was ratified and strengthened later that year by the
United Nations after the September *coup d'état* in Haiti. The embargo
terminated three years later, towards the end of the period of electoral
crisis in the Dominican Republic, when United States troops occupied
Haitian territory on 18 September, 1994. Corten (1994) supports the
suggestion of a secret pact between Balaguer and the United States
government—Balaguer's assistance with enforcing the embargo, in
return for recognition of his fraudulent election victory. The Dominican
government, fully aware of the lucrative nature of embargo breaking,
had previously ignored the international sanctions against trading with
Haiti. According to Corten, vigorous international condemnation of the
fraud was muted because the international community needed to solicit
Dominican support for the Haitian embargo. By the end of May, the
Dominican government, which always claimed that the embargo was
inhumane, began to respect the sanctions, and attempted to restrict
illicit trade across the border.

The Haitian embargo was imposed at sea by the United States. An
agreement with the Haitian government of Jean-Claude Duvalier in
1981, allowed the United States Coast Guard to intercept Haitians who
fled the country by sea. Since October 1993, the aim of the newly
imposed naval blockade was to restrict trade, but also to prevent
thousands of Haitian refugees arriving on North American shores. In
May 1994, the United States President, Bill Clinton, ordered the
summary repatriation of all Haitian 'boat people.' At the same time as

the Haitian exodus, hundreds of Cubans were fleeing from Havana by boat, unimpeded by the government of Fidel Castro as part of a Cuban effort to pressure the United States government into lifting trade restrictions.

The two situations differed in that the Cuban refugees were at first granted automatic political asylum, as had been customary for any Cuban who arrived in the United States as a refugee. This was in stark contrast to the thousands of Haitian refugees who faced immediate repatriation or internment in military camps, while their applications for asylum were processed. Immigration policy clearly favored the lighter-skinned, and usually more wealthy, Cuban migrants. The privileged status of Cuban refugees was changed in August 1994, but only after forceful lobbying by the human and civil rights lobby in the United States.

Following the demise of apartheid in South Africa, and with an active exiled Haitian president and community in New York, Corten (1994) argues that the Congressional Black Caucus in the United States adopted the Haitian political crisis as a symbolic weapon. A hunger strike by the United States congressman Randall Robinson in May 1994, focused attention on Haiti and on Haitian-Dominican relations. The exploitation of Haitian contract workers in the Dominican Republic, which had already been brought to worldwide notice in 1979 by the Anti-Slavery Society in London, was re-emphasized by Americas Watch and the National Coalition for Haitian Refugees and Caribbean Rights in the United States. The Dominican government had carefully avoided commenting on the Haitian situation; it certainly did not welcome a revival of international interest.

Foreign accusations that the Dominican authorities were ignoring the international embargo elucidated an angry response from the government, who had so far made few comments about the political crisis of its neighbor. Peynado's retort to criticism in *The New York Times* that the land border with Haiti was an open trade route, which was blatantly obvious, was one of indignation. Nothing, he assured, could be further from the truth; such a statement was akin to accusing the United States of allowing Mexicans to migrate freely across its borders. The Dominican response equated products with people, deflecting the issue of economic sanctions to one of immigration policy. The editorial in *The New York Times* added further insult by undermining the legitimacy of Balaguer's election victory. Peynado rejected such carping, and criticized international observers for openly supporting Peña Gómez during the election.

Peña Gómez sidelined himself from the debate stirred up by the North American media. Potentially, it could be used to attack the Balaguer administration and to gain the open support of the foreign human and civil rights lobby. He was, however, aware of the pitfalls, both economic and political. He could neither offend the powerful Dominican business interests who had operated during the embargo, nor could he become associated with the radicalism of Haitian or African American movements. Without an adequate response, he would be seen simply as an agent of the United States government. Several Dominicans interviewed in the study areas claimed that the United States favored the candidacy of Peña Gómez for president because he shared similar political beliefs to Clinton. He would be, thus, more amenable to an internationally backed fusion of Hispaniola.

There is little doubt that the United States has been a strong influence in Dominican society, increasingly playing the role of *patrón*—a source of inspiration and consternation eliciting attitudes of love and hate (Wiarda and Kryzanek 1992, 134). Bell describes the relationship thus:

> ... friendship toward the United States as a nation is nepotic-avuncular in character; and while Dominican 'nephews' are happy enough when Uncle Sam gives them expensive Christmas and birthday presents, they do not like it when he talks to them like a Dutch uncle.(Bell 1981, 250)

The United States embassy in Santo Domingo has been described as the major hub of Dominican politics (Wiarda and Kryzanek 1992, 75). A Dominican newspaper suggested sarcastically that Clinton should have signed the Pact for Democracy between Balaguer and Peña Gómez, the electoral compromise that ended the 1994 crisis.[56] North American influence is generally regarded as inevitable, yet fears surrounding the issue of sovereignty had been heightened since the Haitian intervention. In 1996, the United States government felt it necessary to assure the Dominican public of its strict neutrality in the election process. Most governments, however, would be alarmed by the comments of a former Assistant Secretary of State for Inter-American Affairs in the Reagan administration who argued that Caribbean states have little more to offer than sand, and 'little to export but their populations... While a reversal to full colonial status may be a non-starter... a beneficial erosion of sovereignty should not be.' The countries of the Caribbean, he added, 'may well be best off accepting and trying to regularize American intervention—as several have now done with regard to the United States Coast Guard and Navy—in exchange for certain trade benefits.'[57]

In the acceptance speech at the beginning of his eighth presidency in 1994, on the Day of Restoration, the day that marked the final withdrawal of Spanish rule 129 years earlier, Balaguer warned of foreign interference.[58] The ceremony in the National Assembly ended with the unusual singing of the Dominican national anthem. The dialogue of conspiracy and international meddling in the Dominican polity, was already in full flow. Foreign influence was verbally challenged. The next day, the Department of Migration published a warning in the national newspapers that all foreigners living in the Dominican Republic must have legal residency papers by the end of the month, or face deportation.[59] A flurry of complaints in the media that foreign guides were overrunning Dominican tourism without legal permits was further evidence of anti-interventionist hysteria.[60]

Nationalism and the international conspiracy

The nationalist dialogue supported by the PRSC aimed to deflect attention away from the feeling of unrest following the electoral fraud. Nationalism, the protagonists argued, would unite the electorate and humiliate Peña Gómez. A few days after the elections in 1994 the Unión Nacionalista was launched. Peña Gómez, as one of the vice-presidents of the Socialist International, had just sought foreign support for the PRD's accusations of disenfranchisement through fraud. The Unión Nacionalista is a small political group, but with influential access to the media, including a regular television program, *La Hora de Consuelo*, which champions nationalist doctrine. The group backed Balaguer, but demanded a stronger defense of the nation and the rebuttal of foreign antagonism. The Haitian embargo, it was argued, was an attempt to force an exodus of refugees across the Dominican border, making the fusion of the two countries inevitable.

Why did the nationalists consider foreign powers to have conspiratorial interests in internal Dominican affairs? First, as mentioned above, the nationalist debate diverted attention away from political corruption. Secondly, there was genuine concern over the increasing influence of the United States in Dominican politics and society. Thirdly, most nationalists were fervent anti-Haitianists. Overt racism, thus, could hide behind the shield of respectable nationalism.

Fennema (1995, 13-14) notes that conspiracy theory is a fundamental element in far-right ideologies: 'In the extreme right discourse, however, the conspiracy is not just related to an acute danger, but to a perceived decadence, a decline of the nation.' A belief in ethnic superiority or domination would arguably strengthen the nation, coagulating popular conviction:

> ... conspiracy theory is the poor man's [sic] social science: it replaces the invisible hand by a visible one, it replaces the counterintuitive law of unintended effects by plots and purposes of friends and foes, of heroes and scoundrels. (Fennema 1995, 17)

The Unión Nacionalista is composed of a nucleus of right-wing intellectuals and business people who aim to provoke popular nationalist support. Their political agenda responds to the belief that the Dominican Republic is about to be overwhelmed by Haitian migrants and North American politicians. The leader of the party, Pérez, outlined his political agenda in the previously mentioned work, *Santo Domingo frente al destino* (1990). Pérez claimed that the Dominican Republic was highly susceptible to external and internal forces that sought to take advantage and to unite Haiti and the Dominican Republic, or to annex them to the United States. Conspiracy was afoot. He went on to lament the lack of a strong leader similar to Trujillo to defend *la raza dominicana*. Dominican democracy had already failed, he argued, and popular democracy merely misplaced power in wasteful, incapable hands. Another leading nationalist, Pedro Manuel Casals Victoria, backed the argument for autocratic leadership in the Dominican Republic.[61] He warned that the Unión Nacionalista could take a combative role in Dominican politics, where democracy was clearly a lost cause. Both individuals, paradoxically, share a similar idea with Bosch, who projected the concept of a dictatorship with popular support. Developing states required direction and strong decision-making. In many ways, Balaguer had already filled this role for the previous three decades.

The Unión Nacionalista has an implicit anti-Haitian stance. Pérez deplores what he calls the 'suicidal tolerance' of the Dominican government to Haitian immigration. Haitians were bleeding the nation dry, sapping the vitality of the nation like vampires. Haitians, he described, arrive looking ashen gray in the *bateyes*, but despite the harsh conditions, they have sufficiently better lives in the Dominican Republic which restores them to their natural color, '*negro brillante*' (Pérez 1990, 81).

A newspaper headline in August 1994 claimed that over a million Haitians were living in the Dominican Republic.[62] Most, including their children, were allegedly seeking Dominican citizenship, in the face of which Dominican government passivity was deemed inexplicable. The estimated resident Haitian population and citizenship claims were exaggerated. The Dominican military had been, and still does, round up Haitians and deport them, on frequent, if random, occasions. The newspaper article gave evidence of anti-Dominican violence in Haiti, whilst castigating the Haitian ambassador for his ostensibly inappropriate comments on state-sponsored brutality against Haitians in the Dominican Republic.

Following the 1994 election, another publication concurred with the Unión Nacionalista's version of the fraud and the role of foreign intervention (Velázquez-Mainardi 1994). North American aid, it argued, had established a state of dependency in which Dominicans had absolutely no faith in their country. The nation was increasingly impotent and without destiny, unless the nationalist vanguard could vanquish the degenerate forces. Behind this upbeat nationalist front lay a new pessimism which suggested the inevitable and constant threat of alien insurgency.

A few days after the election, the Unión Nacionalista made an immediate call for a show of national unity to reclaim respect for Dominican sovereignty. Each household was asked to fly the Dominican flag outside their home. The proposal received popular support across all class and race categories, with a greater show in the urban areas, most likely due to the supply and affordability of flags. Skeptics have argued that the flags had been bought in advance to celebrate Balaguer's victory; as a result of the electoral confusion a new cause had to be found, one that would also build support and credibility for the PRSC. The nationalist demonstration was a ploy to sell off unused merchandise. Sales of flags and nationalist paraphernalia boomed, making nationalism a highly profitable enterprise. Victor Grimaldi, a media specialist and spokesperson for the Frente Nacional Progresista, a nationalist group not unlike the Unión Nacionalista, supported the display of *dominicanidad*.[63] He denied that the campaign was directed against Peña Gómez, whose problems, he argued, were genetic. Peña Gómez could not, he suggested, escape the Haitian origins which dictated his mannerisms and volatile character, a sign of mental instability and psychosis. Grimaldi distributed nationalist baseball caps, which on closer inspection were 'Made in the USA'— somewhat of a paradox for a campaign sponsoring Dominican economic and political independence.

The nationalist rhetoric is riddled with contradictions. Nationalists stated that the invasion of Haiti by the United States showed monstrous disregard for 'our' Haitian allies. The nationalists, however, vehemently refused any assistance for the tens of thousands of Haitian refugees who might try to cross the border, spreading their social and economic ills in the Dominican Republic. Pérez blamed the United States as the root cause of national decline; in particular with respect to the recruitment of Haitian labor by North American sugar mills in the Dominican Republic. His prejudiced discourse, however, refused to condemn the exploitative recruitment of *braceros* by the Dominican authorities, while repeatedly blaming the Haitian presence as the basis for Dominican problems. Dominicans are forced to migrate to the United States, he alleged, because Haitians take up employment opportunities and lower wage levels in the Dominican Republic. Hypocrisy binds the nationalist thesis. The United States is criticized for the harsh repatriation of Dominicans, compelled to live at the margins of the law, and whose deportation increases Dominican unemployment and takes away crucial remittances.

Although less vitriolic, with no foreign intervention in Haiti or condemnation of electoral practices on which to concentrate, the 1996 elections were witness to further nationalist debate, again undermining

Peña Gómez' suitability to be president. A few days after Peña Gómez polled the most votes in the first round, opponents called for the creation of a national front to preserve Dominican sovereignty.

Leonel Fernández criticized *The New York Times* for suggesting that the PLD-PRSC pact was an attempt to defeat a presidential candidate of Haitian origin. The Frente Nacional Progresista condemned such accusations as a mark of desperation among foreign supporters of Peña Gómez, and the Secretary General of the PRSC claimed that the editorial itself was part of an international campaign to discredit the Dominican Republic. Dominican newspapers ran a series of articles voicing fears that the nation was in peril. Between the election rounds, Leonel Fernández campaigned for the creation of a nationalist program, the Proyecto Nacional Dominicano. The ongoing nationalist crusade, however, could not match the overt racism exhibited against Peña Gómez during the 1994 elections.

Peña Gómez: the failure to confront racism

The presidential elections of 1994 marked a watershed in the history of racialized politics in the Dominican Republic, but the signals had been evident since the first attempt by Peña Gómez to win the presidency. A newspaper article stated that race was a major handicap for Peña Gómez' political career; no Dominican could ignore that Haitian aggression and savagery have been confirmed by history.[64] Haitians made up more than 10 percent of the Dominican population. Peña Gómez was himself an example of the current Haitian infiltration and usurpation at the very heart of the political system.

The 1994 defamatory campaign against Peña Gómez concentrated on his suspected Haitian parentage, emphasizing the negatively perceived stereotypes of Haiti. A series of videos were shown on state-controlled television networks illustrating Peña Gómez as a hot-headed, irrational man, shouting and arguing at political meetings—alluding to his savagery and uncivilized behavior. He was closely linked with *vodú*, alleging his irrationality and faith in the occult and non-Christian ways. One video showed him attending a faith-healing ceremony for the treatment of his bodyguard's tumor in 1983. A direct link was made to Haitian *vodú* and its perceived evils. This tack was maintained in the run-up to the following elections. A newspaper printed that Peña Gómez feared the ghost of Trujillo which allegedly stalks the National

Palace, while the souls of Trujillo's political victims haunt those who enter.[65] Peña Gómez is linked in the same article to the witches of San Juan de la Maguana, an area renowned for the influence of *brujería*.

Faxes which were sent anonymously on 5 May, 1994 to every fax machine in Santo Domingo depicted Peña Gómez as a blood-thirsty and power-hungry Haitian savage. A series of eight racist cartoons stressed his desire to unite the island under Haitian control, his complicity with the evil powers of *vodú* and the exaggerated claim that his followers would burn the country if he failed to gain power. Overtly racist political fliers and posters were not acknowledged by the opposition parties, though the funding of aerial leaflet drops and printing costs would have been paid for from official coffers and by business interests. One set of leaflets, dropped by airplane over central Santo Domingo on the eve of the election, divided the island into two colors; the red of the PRSC in the Dominican Republic, versus the black, PRD-supporting Haiti. The threat of Haiti was made clear by the slogan underneath the map which implied that if Peña Gómez and the PRD won, Dominican sovereignty would be handed over to the Haitians: 'Your vote makes frontiers! It's nothing to do with skin color, but simply due to those who want to deceive you again. Vote PRSC.'

Other leaflets were posted by PRSC party activists throughout Santo Domingo—the election message was blunt. One flier suggested that although Balaguer is effectively blind, he was the only candidate who can see ahead in political terms. Jacobo Majluta, the candidate for the marginal Partido Revolucionario Independiente, received abuse for his Lebanese origins, and Peña Gómez was berated as ugly and Haitian. Many interviewees framed their aversion to Peña Gómez in racist aesthetic terms, he was too dark and too ugly to be president. A middle-class woman said that the Haitian blood of Peña Gómez made him ugly. Additional posters claimed that a vote for Peña Gómez represented a vote against the Dominican nation, Christianity and civilization.

Few Dominicans clearly differentiated between Peña Gómez as a Haitian or *negro*. For the majority, the issues of *haitianidad* and *negritud* were inseparable, re-emphasizing the fusion of race and nation in the concept of *la raza*. Seventy percent of interviewees believed that racism presented a problem for Peña Gómez' election as president. Ten percent of the sample, predominantly from the lower classes, were unsure or declined to comment on the influence of racism on Peña Gómez' political career. There is little variation of opinion between class groups or self-defined racial categories when the distribution of these characteristics is compared with the total sample. Individual responses, however, illustrate a pervasive racism, at the individual and societal level.

Many who described themselves as lighter skinned were more negative about the suitability of a president whom they perceive as Haitian. Armando de la Cruz, a black accountant living in Gazcue, suggested that Dominicans were *negros claros*, and Haitians *negros oscuros*. Peña Gómez was evidently *negro oscuro*, and so could not be president. Sara Figueras, commenting on a poster of Peña Gómez nailed to a telegraph pole outside her house in Los Guandules, emphasized her skin color as *india* and argued pointedly that not even black Dominicans supported Peña Gómez, 'You can't have a *negro* governing the *blancos*.' Across town in Gazcue, wealthy white resident Maria Romeu Poviña added, 'He thinks like a Haitian and will bring them all over here'; her sister agreed, 'He wants to bring the island together; we don't want him here because he's *negro*.' The conspiracy theory was proving fruitful for Peña Gómez' opponents. Such comments represented the popular undertone of interviewees' responses. Flérida Hierro was more lenient towards Peña Gómez's motives, however, at the same time expressed thoughtless racial prejudice: 'He is a *negro*, but in my mind, I think he is as human as us.' In Gazcue, Jose Torres-Subero described himself as *mestizo*, suggested that there were problems with Peña Gómez's Haitian descent, but that overall his heart was in the right, white place: 'Yes, there are problems, but he has a 'white soul' (*una alma blanca*).'

Peña Gómez himself was denounced as a racist. Some saw his three marriages to *blancas* as an expression of his own racial bias, but such an argument is itself based on racist sentiment. An interviewee who described his race as *mulato*, suggested that Peña Gómez was racist because he tried to change his color, through marriage and by denying his own heritage. This has been an important line of argument among opponents of Peña Gómez and among those who have noticed his consistent reluctance to confront allegations of racism.

Zaiter (1993), illustrating an almost fanatical dislike for Peña Gómez, published a small volume that used newspaper articles to portray his racism. He attempts to show that Peña Gómez aimed to divide the country into *negro/a* and *blanco/a* racial groups, creating apartheid as an extension of his own racial inferiority complex. Peña Gómez, he argued, always surrounded himself with lighter-skinned colleagues and relatives. Peña Gómez lived in a personal world of racial contradiction; while rejecting his own race, he predicted election victory on the basis of race, 'because I understand that the Dominican has black behind the ears (*el negro detrás de las orejas*)' (Zaiter 1993, 8). Peña Gómez criticized the white elite for having never done anything for the majority of Dominicans.

The impassioned denials of Haitian parentage resulted in Peña Gómez commissioning a biography, which painstakingly reconstructed his origins, repeatedly refuting any Haitian ancestry. The publication did little to convince the reader that Peña Gómez was himself not trapped in a framework of anti-Haitian phobia. Salmador (1990), the biographer, reiterated the importance *ad nauseam* of Peña Gómez' real surname, Zarzuela. As a baby, Peña Gómez was separated from his dark-skinned Dominican parents during the family's flight from the massacre of 1937. The family surname originates from descendants who served a Spanish landowner, Don Felipe Zarzuela Díez, during the seventeenth century. On emancipation it was common for favored former slaves or employees to take the surname of their former master. Salmador (1990, 14) stresses that Peña Gómez' beginnings were firmly rooted on the Spanish half of the island:

> ... the scandalous story that Peña Gómez has Haitian origins is untenable today... It is proven and documented... that he was born in La Loma del Flaco; that means his *dominicanidad* is without doubt, and that his *dominicanidad* is integral and global, not only physically by the known fact of his birth on Dominican soil, but also intellectually and innately.

He was brought up as an orphan by a Spaniard, Don Regino, 'of pure Castillian stock', and his Dominican wife, Doña Fermina. It was under their influence that Peña Gómez grew up as, 'a man spiritually saturated with Europe.'

Salmador, not content to emphasize only the Hispanic element of Peña Gómez' heritage, imbued his birthplace with important indigenous links. La Loma, 'in pre-Columbian times possessed rare splendor, since there was found one of the most important indigenous populations' (Salmador 1990, 15). It was also allegedly located on the original route of Columbus' arrival. A subsequent historical work by Salmador (1994), implied by its title that Peña Gómez was destined to assume his rightful place as president, following the lineage of the indigenous habitants—*La isla de Santo Domingo: desde los indios tainos hasta Peña Gómez*.

The reiteration of Peña Gómez' *dominicanidad* was usually defensive. The political campaigning of the PRD was criticized in the same manner. Peña Gómez defended racist accusations with indignant personal histories, and rarely attacked the illegitimate core of racist party politics. Peña Gómez typically vindicated himself, thus:

> 'I am a passionate devotee of my party; a lover of my country; I carry the flag of my homeland and my *dominicanidad* etched on my heart and my innermost feelings... Nobody, absolutely nobody, is going to surpass me in my total, absolute and complete commitment to the service of my country and of my people. Likewise, nobody, absolutely nobody, will be able to accuse me to my face that the color of my skin lessened the level of my commitment to *dominicanidad*, in which I am enveloped, in which I am saturated; and which in reality, when one feels like I feel, is more than skin color or blood, since it is all the same skin and the same blood.' (Salmador 1990, 227)

During an interview with a journalist, Peña Gómez seemed ashamed by the 'vulgar' lies which suggest that he, or his family, have Haitian origins, yet he denied that racial discrimination has affected him:

> 'One of the biggest lies which has been said about me is that I was born in Haiti. This is a vulgar lie... I do not consider that racial discrimination, as some believe, has been a major obstacle for me. I believe that there is another type of discrimination, more than discrimination, a type of social fear.'[66]

Peña Gómez asserted that it was not racism, but fear which placed barriers between people. Perhaps he was implying a class bias which prevents social mobility, regardless of race. While some believed that the color of his skin and his socio-economic origins could have been a source of electoral strength since his experience showed that a *negro* from outside the traditional elite circles could achieve political success, few mentioned this aspect of social and political accomplishment. A middle-class, *blanco* interviewee respected Peña Gómez for his rise from a difficult and poor background, but would not vote for him because of his color. Another lower-middle-class respondent pointed out that Peña Gómez was not from the 'right' background to be president. Class played a limited role in the rejection of Peña Gómez. Racial perception visibly governed the electoral space.

Why did Peña Gómez not challenge racism directly? First, personal defamation is part of the art of politics. Within the matrix of a racist society, it would be unlikely that Peña Gómez could have expected to avoid racist abuse. He acknowledged that even members of his own party were racists. Presidential battles are fought at the personal level and Peña Gómez' background presented an easy target for Dominican racial prejudices. It would have been impossible for him to reverse a century of anti-Haitianism, yet he made no attempt to demolish racist discourse as a legitimate basis for political practice.

Secondly, the PRD misjudged the political arena and failed to create a convincing anti-racist platform in the 1990s. Peña Gómez, too, was naïve in his assessment of electoral campaigning. A comment that he made in 1992 proved to be woefully wrong: '... it would not be easy to orchestrate and bring to a successful conclusion a political campaign based on race in the Dominican Republic.'[67]

Thirdly, the emphasis on personalistic politics gave no political space for an effective and thorough anti-racism policy to flourish at the party level. No parties have displayed clear policies concerning citizenship or immigration, despite the key issue of anti-Haitianism. Would such policies be too rigid or controversial, given the importance of Haitian labor for the economy? Any policy would be difficult to implement successfully and fairly, and therefore, could be a potential vote loser.

Beyond racialized politics?
Would anti-Haitianism have been challenged under the presidency of Peña Gómez? The vehement denial of Haitian origins, and the need for Peña Gómez to distance himself politically from alleged Haitian sympathies, arguably could have encouraged a harsher anti-Haitian policy and an even less sympathetic approach. The *mulato*, 43 year-

old Leonel Fernández, presented a more acceptable and less controversial figurehead.

Without Peña Gómez's presence, will the political scene, with a lighter-skinned president of *la nueva generación*, leave behind almost a decade of racialized politics? An opportunity has arisen to deracialize the personalism of Dominican politics. Toward the end of his life, following his final election defeat, allegations connected Peña Gómez with the acceptance of drug money for campaign funds.[68] No mention of his Haitian origins was made. Perhaps these accusations indicated a move to deracialized attacks. Such a transition, however, seems unlikely. Leonel Fernández appointed two key figures in his new government from the nationalist movement. First, Marino Vincio Castillo was controversially nominated as president of the National Drug Control Council. He had previously initiated the allegations of Peña Gómez's links with drug money, but he also assisted the author of a previously mentioned nationalist text (Velázquez-Mainardi 1994). Second, Victor Grimaldi, a leading nationalist, was designated as Permanent Ambassador to the Organization of American States.

Shortly before death, Peña Gómez made two of his most frank comments concerning racialized politics. He remarked that racism had succeeded in Dominican politics as a result of the Dominican belief that Haitians were the only true *negros,* despite the fact that 70 percent of Dominicans are *mulatos.*[69] He had earlier claimed that the Dominican Republic was not ready for a black president. Even if he had been elected, he argued, the traditional elites would have reacted with violence: 'The country would be bathed in blood. Of this, I am convinced.'[70] Racism will endure as a key text of Dominican political discourse, in which the Haitian context can never be underestimated. It remains ironic that the slogan adorning Peña Gómez's political posters was '*Vota Blanco.*' Vote white, the traditional color of the PRD.

8.
Conclusion: Race and Ethnicity in the Dominican Republic

'How do you name the fistful of earth in which your roots were nourished?'
—Incháustegui Cabral (1969, 23)

Racial ancestry and the proximity to Haiti underlie a pervasive racial prejudice that devalues the African influence in Dominican society. I have argued that racism is prevalent at all levels of Dominican society. Baud (1996, 145) has recently surmised that 'popular anti-Haitianism in the Dominican Republic might well be a great deal less virulent than the Dominican elite and many foreign observers have wanted us to believe.' The results of my research and fieldwork suggest otherwise; anti-Haitian feeling remains a malignant form of racism that is reproduced across all class groups and in every location. A national poll of 1,200 Dominicans undertaken at the time of my field research confirmed the prevalence of this sentiment: 51.2 percent of respondents did not want a close family member to marry a Haitian (Doré Cabral 1995).

The Dominican Republic is a class-stratified society in which cultural pluralism exists. Cultural differences are expressed through the diversity of race, religious affiliation, household formation, nationality and gender roles. The impact of international migration differentiates families and individuals within a transnational household, in economic and cultural terms, from the non-migrant population. The majority of Dominicans are Catholic, yet Afro-syncretic beliefs extend across all class groups. Lower-class Dominicans born of Haitian parentage in the Dominican Republic participate in the dominant culture, yet, like Haitians, they are differentially incorporated into Dominican society on the basis of citizenship and race. A greater part of the Dominican population could be described as *mulato/a*, but a variety of racial identities exist within this broad color ascription.

Torres-Saillant (1995) has argued that *negro/a* and *mulato/a* Dominicans passively tolerate the Eurocentrism of historical and contemporary Dominican discourse; African Dominicans do not see blackness as central to their racial awareness. Other racial terms are employed instead to describe racial identity. *Indio/a* is by far the most common and adaptable; flexible descriptions of color and phenotype allow familial and social variations of race to be incorporated within a society where the light racial aesthetic is paramount. Despite the malleable nature of racial definition, everyday instances of prejudice and discrimination are evident and often overt. My research illustrated the pervasiveness of anti-Haitian and anti-*negro/a* attitudes among Dominicans. Derogatory images of *negritud* are common, as are racial myths that, for example, still urge mothers to drink milk of magnesia during pregnancy in order to lighten the color of their offspring.

The second chapter illustrated the close historical association of the Dominican Republic with Haiti, and emphasized the use of *indio/a* as a racial category that avoids the direct association of *dominicanidad* with *negritud*. The background for contemporary anti-Haitianism originated from the Haitian invasions and the subsequent occupation of Dominican territory in the first half of the nineteenth century. The regime of Trujillo did much to reinvigorate antagonism between the two countries and popularized the notion of a European and false indigenous ancestry, at the expense of African influence, among the Dominican population.

Haiti has been fundamental to the construction of Dominican nationality. The creation of a nation is often synonymous with the destruction, at least metaphorically, of its rivals (Smith 1992). *Dominicanidad* is nourished by the negative portrayal of its neighboring nation. The Dominican economy was dependent on Haiti in more tangible terms; as a trading partner since the colonial period, but more specifically to fulfil the labor requirements on Dominican sugar plantations from the beginning of the twentieth century. Similar to other societies reliant on an immigrant labor force, the presence of Haitian labor has produced two distinct strata of citizens and immigrants. The lower stratum of Haitians and Dominican-Haitians performs the function of a reserve army of labor, marginalized and ostracized from the rest of society. Race sometimes strengthens class relations, at other times racial issues are antagonistic to class issues.

Relations of race, class and gender are in constant flux and depend on the context of their influence. Rapid changes are re-shaping these variables at local and global levels. With estimates of up to ten percent of the Dominican population living in the United States, international migration has transformed Dominican society. Transnationalism establishes new social, cultural and economic relations among Dominicans. Remittances usurp traditional patterns of class, which has led to the rapid creation of a new 'class' of migrants—the *dominicanyorks*—among whom the successful may trade low status employment in New York for the most comfortable material well-being on their return to the Dominican Republic. Race, however, remains one of the few aspects yet to be transformed by transnationalism. Race relations in the United States have had little impact on the formation of racial identity in the Dominican Republic. Dominicans migrants are categorized as Black Hispanics in the United States; a marked inversion of racial identity for those migrants who had considered themselves as *blanco/a* or *indio/a* while living in the Dominican Republic. Migrants, however, have not adopted North American racial terminology. On return to the Dominican Republic, the migrant's racial identification is re-established in the Dominican context. The influence of the migratory experience on perceptions of race, thus, appears to be limited.

Race and nation were the dominant issues on the agenda for the elections of the 1990s. Dominican antagonism towards Haiti, and the reluctance by many Dominicans to elect a black president, twice combined to stall the election campaign of Peña Gómez. The long-standing *blanco* president, Joaquín Balaguer, was replaced by a younger *mulato*, Leonel Fernández. The presidential candidacy of Peña Gómez undoubtedly enhanced the virulence of racist politics. Racialized politics are likely to dominate during moments when it becomes politically expedient to resurrect traditional racial and national rivalries.

The Dominican Republic has changed dramatically during the last four decades, since the end of the *trujillato* and the opening up of Dominican society to external cultural and economic influences. Frederico Liscano, a 16 year-old from Los Guandules, found it difficult to push aside his desire to up and leave: 'I don't like being Dominican [*mi raza como ser dominicano*]. It's not much fun for me. I want to get out.' Dominicans are attempting to consolidate their identity with an outward glance towards the United States, which has replaced Spain as the new metropole. The traditional antagonism towards Haiti, however, remains intact. Both countries are weak states on the global stage; political antagonism and confrontation only weakens them further (Corten 1989). In a context of increasing globalization, local and regional conflict are severe drawbacks to external confidence, and hence, investment or development opportunities. A re-evaluation of race and ethnicity is a key step towards the maturation of more progressive intra-island relations.

Race
Previous conceptions of race have employed definitions that grouped people according to an alleged common biological origin, stressing the importance of descent. Given the Darwinian evolutionary law which states that no racial classification can be permanent, it has been recognized that a meaningful taxonomy of human beings is impossible. However, terms such as Negroid and Caucasoid still appear at times in text. Race has been defined biologically as a subspecies or species, culturally as a nation, or socially as a group sharing similar phenotypical features.

Contemporary discussions recognize that races do not exist as scientific entities. Races are formed subjectively by the translation of phenotypical variation into objective systems of differentiation (Gilroy 1987, 38). The objectivity of race centers on phenotype and color, both of which act as subjective signs for racial identification. Skin color variation is the basis of the formation of racial categories:

Skin color is a feature which varies along a continuous scale when measured by a light meter, but in social life it is used either as a discontinuous scale or a continuous variable in ordering social relations. (Banton 1991, 118)

The categorization of infinite phenotypical variation forms the basis for the aesthetic construction of race. Racial formation is not static. Phenotype and color remain constant for the individual, but the interpretation and meaning of color can vary. Therefore, a plurality of role signs creates various forms of racism, which differ according to the social and historical context. Rex (1983, 159) has produced several accounts of what he calls 'race relations situations':

> Race relations situations and problems... refer to situations in which one or more groups with distinct identities and recognisable characteristics are forced by economic and political circumstances to live together in a society.

The situation, according to the interpretation of Rex, is marked by a high degree of conflict and hostility between groups bounded by ascriptive criteria. This conflictual concept of race centers on the competition between racial groups to gain access to status and power in society. Banton (1992) proposes that competition is the critical process shaping patterns of ethnic and racial relations. Consequently, *la raza dominicana* has developed as a result, rather than in spite of, the Haitian presence. Defining racial groups by the 'presence or absence of certain socially relevant abilities or characteristics', immediately associates race with a false binary concept of 'haves' and 'have-nots' (van den Berghe 1979, 11).

Racism has frequently been defined with respect to the dual notion of winners and losers, the fortunate and the ill fated. Jackson (1987, 12) defines racism as 'the attempt by a dominant group to exclude a subordinate group from the material and symbolic rewards of status and power.' He adds that 'racism need not have recourse to purely physical distinctions but can rest on the recognition of certain 'cultural' traits where these are thought to be an inherent and inviolable characteristic of particular social groups.' An individual is thus 'possessed' by her or his race as a matter of circumstance.

Racialization describes the political and ideological processes by which people are identified by reference to their real or imagined phenotypical characteristics. Miles (1989) suggests that racialization should be considered as a process, and racism more properly as the underlying ideology. Racialization focuses on the conditions that cause social, economic and political processes to be racialized. Racism on the other hand was used only as an ideology after the start of the twentieth century. An ideology, he argues, is any discourse that represents a people or a society in a misleading or distorted way. Racist ideology attributes social meaning to phenotypical and/or genetic difference, and negatively evaluates characteristics of a group allegedly constituted by descent.

Racial discrimination, alternatively described as racialism, is the active expression of racism, aiming to deny members of certain groups equal access to limited and valued resources (Cashmore 1995). Prejudice, the motivation to discriminate against an individual or group, is the maintaining of derogatory attitudes about the members of a section of society. It has been proposed that people are prejudiced because their biases meet certain needs associated with their personalities (Adorno et al 1950). High levels of prejudice may be the result of an authoritarian personality, holding rigid beliefs and being intolerant of other racial or ethnic groups.

Tajfel (1978) suggested that social behavior, and thus prejudice, fall somewhere along a continuum between behavioral extremes. He outlines the importance of distinguishing between inter-personal and inter-group behavior; the former involving action as an individual person, the latter as a group member. There is general agreement that contact between social groups, without some form of co-operation or shared aims, will not reduce and may exacerbate inter-group prejudice (Hewstone and Brown 1986). Sherif (1966) analyzed inter-group behavior as a reflection of the objective interests of the in-group *vis-à-vis* out-groups. His research showed that distinctiveness is often valued positively for the in-group, but negatively for the out-group. Individual identity is defined in terms of group affiliations; thus, the analysis of the in-group will be biased to favor a positive self-concept.

Racial prejudice, argues Parsons, has been concentrated more among the lower social classes. In the context of North American society, Parsons (1975) suggests that the concept of black inferiority fuels white working-class prejudice, providing 'a floor below which they cannot fall, that is, they cannot be identified with the lowest group of all, the blacks.' While dark-skinned Dominicans, tend to be located among the lower status group in Dominican society, their position is somewhat relieved by the presence of the Haitian and Haitian-Dominican groups. However, my research suggests that racial prejudice exists to a similar extent throughout all social classes in the Dominican Republic. Haitians and Dominican *negros/as* experience racist abuse from groups at all socio-economic levels.

Color and phenotype, from a racist perspective, are both visible and indelible marks of an individual's level of superiority or inferiority. The definition of racism in terms of relative inferiority or superiority, however, is not satisfactory. The dichotomy simplifies the complexity of everyday interaction. In what spheres do these power relations apply? It is often unclear whether inferior status refers to social, economic, political, or cultural relations, and with respect to which other individuals or groups in society.

Barker (1981) challenges the superiority/inferiority construction of race, and argues that those definitions that focus on this context of racism are misleading. Racism, he believes, may take many forms in which biological or pseudo-biological groupings are designated as the outcome of social and historical processes. This inflation of the definition of racism by Barker causes some problems. Under these rubrics, sexism and gender bias could also be termed as forms of racism. Nevertheless, he makes an important contribution by claiming that racist emotions are frequently justified by an assumed 'naturalness.' Racism has become increasingly 'naturalized' and disguised in discussions of alleged cultural and national norms. Dominican antagonism towards Haiti is, thus, legitimized as a form of patriotism. Blaut (1992) comments on this sanitization of racism in society, whereby general consensus suggests that racism abounds; yet few people are labeled as racists. Cohen (1993) describes the 'perversions of inheritance' which establish the significance of race and nation through common myths of descent and breeding codes. These common myths cleanse popular racist beliefs and assumptions.

The potency of racism lies in its embeddedness as a perceived natural phenomenon. The seeming naturalness of race has given it a translatable, pseudo-scientific status. Those who suffer racist abuse tend ultimately to be perceived as the cause of the problem. Haitians bear the brunt of Dominican aggression, but dark-skinned Dominicans suffer similar racist insults or are treated as lower status citizens, somatically sidelined from authentic *dominicanidad*. Racist ideology portrays Haitians and dark-skinned Dominicans as victims of their own racial fate; both are trapped by the color of their skin and their genetic history. Sympathy for the victim, however, is muted by the racist argument that Haitians induce antipathy towards themselves via allegedly innate cultural practices, such as *vodoun*, which are incompatible with Dominican society.

Gilroy (1987) comments on the oscillation between black as problem and black as victim. Race is de-historicized, removed from the context of contemporary discrimination, and established as an immutable biological and cultural standard. Hall (1980) suggests how racism is able to articulate with other ideologies in society, de-historicizing its influence. Social relationships consequently become interpreted in racial terms; racism, removed from its specific historical context, perpetuates the deception.

Ethnicity

An ethnic group relates to a collectivity of people who are conscious of having common origins, interests and shared experiences. This research has been concerned with race, that aspect of ethnicity informed by socially constructed issues of color and phenotype. Race forms a subset of Dominican ethnicity; the two are not synonymous. Anthias (1990, 20) separates the concepts of race and ethnicity, focusing on the former term as a means of discriminating against social groups on the basis of biological or cultural immutability:

The racial categorization is often, although not always, a mode of pursuing a project of inferiorisation, oppression and at times class subordination and exploitation. Ethnicity, on the other hand, relates to the identification of particular cultures, of ways of life or identity which are based on a historical notion of origin or fate, whether mythical or 'real.'

Racist discourse uses ethnic categories (which might be constructed around cultural, linguistic, territorial or supposed biological differences) to signify deterministic differences between individuals and groups.

Ethnicity is the feeling of belonging to a shared group linked to common grounds of race, territory, religion, language, aesthetics and kinship. It cannot be desegregated from its constituent components; the individual labeling of social categories falsely suggests the independence of their nature and effect, since their influences crosscut and interact in the creation of ethnic identity. Van den Berghe (1979) suggests that race is socially defined on the basis of physical criteria, whereas definitions of ethnicity are informed by cultural criteria. The significance of physical characteristics, however, is culturally defined. Banton (1992) argues that the traditional separation of race relating to physical or biological traits and of ethnicity describing cultural characteristics oversimplifies social analysis. A racial group may possess cultural institutions that shape its boundaries as well as race. Goldberg (1992) similarly stresses the close relationship between the two forms, suggesting that the term *ethnorace* is appropriate for instances where race takes on significance in terms of ethnic identity. The Haitian population in the Dominican Republic is discriminated against on the grounds of its allegedly different racial ancestry, nationality and cultural traits. To separate race and ethnicity through rigid frameworks is to miss the point of their inter-relations.

All people share a feeling of ethnicity, which should not be restricted to terms of minority status or marginality. It is misleading to assert that 'whereas 'race' stands for the attributions of one group, ethnic group stands for the creative response of a people who feel somehow marginal to the mainstream of society' (Cashmore 1995, 102). Moreover, it is incorrect to formulate a conception of ethnicity and race where the former is deemed to reflect positive notions of inclusion while latter stresses dissociation and exclusion. The strict separation of positive/negative and inclusive/exclusive forces imposes a false dichotomy upon both concepts. Ethnic inclusivity/exclusivity establishes feelings of us and them, or 'we-ness' and 'they-ness' (Ringer and Lawless 1989). The strength of ethnicity lies at source in the subjective relevance it creates for group members.

Ethnicity can be a reactive concept, elicited and shaped by constraints on the social, economic and political opportunities for members of certain ethnic groups. Thus, some believe that ethnicity or race should be more politicized, to be used as a political instrument for anti-racism rather than being perceived as a cultural or social phenomenon. The effectiveness of an ethnic basis for political mobilization comes from the premise that at its most general level, ethnicity involves belonging to a particular group and sharing its conditions of existence. Anthias and Yuval-Davis (1992) suggest that ethnicity crosscuts gender and class divisions, but at the same time involves the positing of a similarity (on the inside) and a difference (from the outside) that may transcend these divisions.

Parsons (1975) also considers that the black-white dichotomy in the United States will be beneficial in the long run, by radicalizing issues of race and more effectively promoting concepts of racial equality.

Emphasizing black politics, for example, implies the adoption of a strategic essentialism, by recognizing the social construction of race, but using that essence or blackness as a political lever to campaign for equality in society. The inherent contradiction of appropriating racial myths to dispel prejudice, however, is troublesome. The study of race relations or the adoption of strategic essentialism leads along a dangerous path that ultimately perpetuates racial falsehoods.

Rather than perceive ethnic assertion solely with the attainment of equality, ethnicity is often expressed as an affirmation of achieved status. Ethnic status can become a symbol of middle-class affordability, exhibited when the ethnic group members are less vulnerable in social, cultural and economic terms. In this manner, the visibility of ethnicity is a cultural and social response to the material conditions of group members. The middle-class residents of Gazcue were relatively more willing to describe themselves as *mulato/a*, given their secure socio-economic position.

Nevertheless, across a wide range of changing economic and social conditions, ethnicity has grown as a term of reference and basis for identity and conflict. Some authors would pronounce the demise of class, believing ethnicity to be a more fundamental form of stratification:

> Ethnicity has become more salient because it can combine an interest with an affective tie. Ethnicity provides a tangible set of common identifications, for example, through language, food, music, names, when other social roles become more abstract and impersonal. (Bell 1975, 169)

Bell (1975) emphasizes the strategic salience of ethnic mobilization, and gives three main reasons for the assertion of ethnicity. First, he credits its importance to an innate desire for primordial anchorage. Secondly, he cites the break-up of traditional authority structure, and thirdly, expresses the greater political need for group organization.

Will ethnic affiliation weaken or become more flexible if greater syncretism and ethnic mixing occurs as societies evolve? Increasing social status or access to power in society may provide the security to emphasize ethnic group membership without fear of provoking discrimination. Parsons (1975) concurs with the desocialization theory of ethnic groups, initially proposed by Schneider. The theory suggests that the growing homogeneity of ethnic groups, encourages exaggeration of the smaller, immutable differences in order to emphasize variations in-group status. Although the cultural content of ethnic groups has become increasingly similar, the emotional significance of belonging to an ethnic group remains important.

It is useful to expand upon Tajfel's concept of a behavioral continuum to explain ethnicity in relation to the various forms of racism. Figure 1 illustrates how this continuum incorporates notions of ethnicity. Nationalism expresses a collective sentiment specifically belonging to a territory. The nation is the collective term for a population delimited by territorial claims, or an imagined community with an attachment to place. The work of Anderson has opened up new intellectual space for theories of nationalism, as has Smith's (1986) concept of *ethnie*, the 'myth-symbol complex' that surrounds and creates the ethnic origins of nations. These ideas are juxtaposed to the belief that nations develop primarily from the prior establishment of centralized governments and state systems.

Figure 1. The equality-racism behavioral continuum

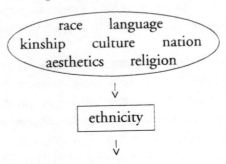

Ethnicity is a product of culture, an integral term which represents a shared set of meanings and meaningful activities experienced at the individual and group level. The work of M. G. Smith (1984, 140) stresses the importance of cultural practice in shaping the relations of race and ethnicity:

...personal status, relations and conduct are always significantly qualified by race; and likewise, whatever the racial identity or difference among them, personal status and conduct are always heavily qualified—some might even say determined—by cultural practice.

Ethnicity is the expression of the overall affiliation to the shared set of social meanings, frequently considered separately in racial, national, religious, aesthetic, kin or linguistic terms, through which individual and group identities are created. Anthias and Yuval-Davis (1992, 155) emphasize the variation of ethnic associations that are subverted and manipulated to become signifiers of racism. Racist prejudice and discrimination:

> ... can be directed against any ethnic collectivity that undergoes a process of racialization. Therefore it is not just physical appearance, but also language, religion, clothing or any other cultural project which can be used as racist signifiers, as long as they come to be perceived as the identification of a separate human stock with an immutable heritage.

The distinction made by Hall (1990) between overt and inferential racism is salient for the Dominican racial context. The latter form of racism is expressed by the nationalist terms of difference between Haitian or Dominican, terms which refer to apparently naturalized racial divisions, but inevitably are placed in a prejudicial framework. The former is a more openly racist statement that emphasizes race above person. Emphasis on the word order of *dominicano/a negro/a* or *negro/a dominicano/a* subtly reflects this difference when the phrases are used derogatively. The first phrase refers to a Dominican who is dark-skinned; the second reverses the role of adjective and noun to stress the racial identity of someone who is also Dominican.

Racism in the Dominican Republic, as elsewhere, is often tied to specific issues of immigration, which are perceived through the prism of a racist ideology. Racism in the Dominican Republic castigates the presence of Haitian labor and devalues darker phenotypes, but also operates within itself. The ambiguity of race can turn the abuser into victim and *vice versa*.

Raza unites, race divides

Two processes have operated historically at popular and governmental level with respect to immigration policy. Firstly, one of *blanqueamiento* or whitening, either by encouraging European immigration, for example during the 1930s, or by maintaining a social and cultural light bias. Secondly, the propagation of the idea of the Haitian population as a threat to the Dominican nation.

The concept of *la raza dominicana* unites Dominicans against Haitians, but when perceived in terms of race, the same concept relegates dark-skinned Dominicans to the margins of an imaginary racial heartland. *La raza* inclusively combines race and nation, and the prejudices of overt and inferential racism. All forms of racism create societal division in synthesis or discordant with socio-economic differentiation, which together foment individual and group status. The impact of social cleavage varies between societies, groups and individuals; the levels of bias vary by degree rather by than nature. Despite the amalgam of motivations that serve to enlighten or occlude racial and class awareness, the universality of their influence can only be derived by independent analysis:

> At the risk of being tritely eclectic, we must conclude that class, race, and ethnicity are all types of social cleavage; that no matter how much they might overlap empirically, their analysis is impoverished by lumping them together; and that there is no *a priori* reason to expect one type to be more basic, more important, or more salient than the others. (van den Berghe 1979, xiv-xv)

Omi and Winant (1994) outline three clear paradigms in the literature on race: ethnicity-based, class-based and nation-based. This proposal is, however, treated with caution. Race formation is not reducible to class formation, even when they become mutually entangled. Neither can class factors be dismissed in instances of overt racism, though its inclusion makes life difficult for the theorist (Gilroy 1987).

Writers, such as Miles, insist that the essential relations in society are those of class, which have been overlaid by the distortions of racism as a historical complex, generated within and by capitalism. Race under this rubric should be banished as a false construction, nothing more than an ideological effect. Racism, it argues, is a product of particular struggles between capital and labor, an obvious example being migrant labor. An approach such as this, however, ignores the effects of popular and institutional racisms that draw together groups with different histories. Gilroy (1987, 28) contests the reductionism of Miles by arguing:

... 'race' can no longer be reduced to an effect of the economic antagonism arising from production, and class must be understood in terms qualified by the vitality of struggles articulated through 'race.'

It is from this stance that the Dominican racial complex is most profitably addressed. Hall (1980) adopts a class paradigm approach to race: social divisions based on race can be explained largely by economic processes, yet, the importance of race is incorporated as the 'modality' through which class relations are experienced. The study of race must be considered as historically specific, since each racism is reorganized and rearticulated with the changing relations of production. What conditions make the ethnic or racial grouping of people socially pertinent? Why is racism articulated at certain historical disjunctures or stages of capitalism? In the case of colonialism, Hall views plantation slavery as the specific product of labor shortage which necessitated judicial racism, though he criticizes a straightforward articulation between racism and capitalism.

Class relations alone cannot design the center stage for societal dynamics. Populist politics of race and nation in the Dominican Republic emphasize the fact that class is not something created through economic friction alone. Class relations alone do not account for a political arena in which racism shadows much of the discourse. As Gilroy (1987, 34) insists, class 'no longer has a monopoly of the political stage, if indeed it ever had one.'

Can anti-racist politics rouse a Dominican social order, not only founded on racist pretences, but also grounded in class relations and a culture of patriarchy? The lack of anti-racist policy and grassroots organizations suggests not. Attempts to assert rights and claims for justice have been muted by the deeply embedded racism in Dominican society. These claims, however, do not challenge traditional hegemonies, but evoke a reappraisal of past and present anti-Haitianism.

Racism is continually denied at official and personal levels in the Dominican Republic. The government is able to legitimate the forceful repatriations of Haitians on economic grounds. The threat of Haitian immigration, implicitly assumed to be poor and *negro/a*, is exaggerated to mobilize political support. Claims of a crumbling social order and the defense of national character are common forms of anti-immigration rhetoric. The interests of the nation must be protected from without and within—immigrants are deemed potentially malignant additions to the national body.

Right and left wing politicians in the Dominican Republic cultivate an established basis of 'us' and 'them', in order to protect the national community. The recent and continued rhetoric and discrimination against Haitians suggests that the Dominican government is unwilling or unable to quell racist political discourse in the Dominican Republic. Dominican politics fit the agenda outlined by Solomos (1989, 132):

In neo-fascist-political discourses about race common sense images resonate with references to racial purity, cultural superiority or difference and the defense of the nation from the threat posed by immigration and racial mixing. The alien, the stranger, or the subhuman are the themes struck repeatedly.

Unlike the ebb and flow of support for racist political parties in western Europe, mainstream parties in the Dominican Republic have issued racist rhetoric as a consistent component of their manifestos for over four decades. All parties reject Haitian immigration, yet support the contracting of Haitian labor for the Dominican economy. Political and ideological discourses about race are entrenched in Dominican society, and therefore limit the possibility of radical reforms. Omi and Winant (1994) perceive all states to be inherently racial. Every state sector, they argue, acts as a racial institution, although the impact of racism varies between these institutions over time. A comparison with other countries further reveals the discriminatory nature of race in Dominican society.

The hindrance of racial democracy
Dominican experience of race and ethnicity show similarities with other countries in the Caribbean and South America that are described as

racial democracies. In countries such as Brazil and Venezuela, the predominance of populations, which could be described as *mulato/a*, has led to these societies being summarized as virtually free of racial prejudice or discrimination. Freyre (1946) portrayed Brazilian society in this way during the 1940s. His analysis of plantation society emphasized the positive contribution of Africans to the formation of Brazil, but argued that *mesticismo* symbolized a racial democracy which transcended class and provided an integrated Brazilian race. Conversely, but still employing the concept of *mestizaje* or racial democracy, political discourse in Venezuela has focused on class antagonism during the twentieth century, deflecting attention from racially discriminatory practices (Wright 1990).

The myth of racial democracy, however, has been more a source of racial delusion than harmony. First, it relegates racism to a side issue. State ideologies in racial democracies fail to acknowledge racial discrimination, maintaining an official myth of racial equality. To discuss concepts of prejudice is paramount to admitting that color bias exists. Accusations of racial discrimination are often greeted with dismay or superficial hurt pride. In reality, the integral terms of *mulato/a*, *mestizo/a* and *indio/a* hide a racial hierarchy based on color and phenotype in Brazilian, Venezuelan and Dominican societies. A vast array of color terminology has currency in everyday language. Harris (1970) has outlined the referential ambiguity of the hundreds of terms used to describe color and phenotype in Brazil. Despite the considerable number and flexibility of terms, Sanjek (1971) notes that a proportion is recognizable as the most frequently used. He proceeds to demonstrate that skin color and hair types are the primary variables enlisted for racial identification. However, the different histories of Caribbean countries have encouraged a multiplicity of racial interpretations. A similar term may correspond to a markedly different racial identity from that expected by the observer. Contemporary theorists such as Sollors (1989, xi) have pointed to the context-dependent nature of race and ethnicity, describing them as 'collective fictions that are continually reinvented.' These inventions or social constructions, nevertheless, are salient and active factors in modern societies. Racial and ethnic identities are more than just imagination, but the outcome of human interaction and historical reality.

The importance of color aesthetics is illustrated by examples from Colombia and Nicaragua. Following field work in the Chocó region,

Wade shows how race acts as an identifier through which Colombians distinguish an individual, and attach the appropriate social and cultural traits of his or her racial group. Race, as a social marker, is consequently more ambiguous in the middle ranges of the color continuum (Wade 1993). Lancaster (1992, 216) similarly attributes much importance to color signs in Nicaraguan society:

> ... in everyday usage and for most purposes, color terms are *relational* terms. The relativity of this sort of usage turns on the intention of the speaker, comparative assessments, and shifting contexts.

Lancaster ultimately relates color relations to power relations in society, where color signs are used to naturalize inequalities within a social hierarchy in which race equates with class. A similar situation exists in the Dominican Republic.

There is a misleading tendency, outlined by Booth (1976) for the case of Cuba, to consider racism in *mulato* societies as being much less prevalent and milder than in North American countries. This myth suggests that higher levels of social and cultural interaction in everyday life are more likely to create inter-racial friendship and marriage, thus, reducing levels of prejudice. The fallacy of racial democracy, however, is revealed when it is realized that Brazilian society, for example, also sustains high levels of racial inequality and persistent racism. Telles (1995) discusses the social transformations during the 1980s in Brazil, which point to increasing segregation by race and by class whereby greater class segregation produces greater racial segregation. Social interaction, he adds, is generally limited to low-income neighborhoods, between the minority of poor *brancos/as* and the majority of poor *negros/as* and *mulatos/as*.

The limited official recognition of racial prejudice has meant a corresponding lack of anti-racist legislation and mobilization. Whereas Agier (1995) recounts a growing African-Brazilian movement in Bahia, similar activities are not evident in the Dominican Republic; nor can the incremental change in racial conceptions in the Dominican Republic be heralded to the extent that Winant (1992) suggests for the Brazilian context. He proposes that ethnic issues are being re-evaluated in the context of shifting national, regional and global identities.

The incipient global process of cultural homogenization and the exposure of local or national cultures to new ethnicities have been the focus of increasing attention within the 'shifting frontier' of Latin American identities (Wilson 1995). The poet, playwright and social commentator, Rueda (1985) argues that the Dominican Republic, like many small states, faces a technological and cultural invasion that threatens to usurp the national 'essence.' The development of ethnicity as a combination of local, regional and global influences arises from the more frequent and more expansive interaction of populations and ideas. Transnationalism, however, has yet to expand racial attitudes in Dominican society beyond those of the established norms. Zaiter (1987) suggests that Dominicans should face up to the racial reality of their African ancestry, focus away from historical antagonism towards Haiti, and incorporate themselves more actively in a collective Third World opposition to cultural dependency on the First World. Rational policy intervention by the state, however, is the primary method by which to address racism at the national level.

Anti-racist policy and legislation in the Dominican Republic is virtually non-existent (other than in respect of employment), and never practiced. The lack of anti-discrimination policies is partly due to the myth of racial democracy, which suggests that the most pressing needs are for economic or political reform. The subjectivity of race and the universality of racial prejudice in the Dominican Republic additionally hinder effective policy-making; Brazilian anti-racism movements face a similar challenge due to the lack of consensus as to what constitutes an act of racism (Winddance Twine 1997). Anti-racist policy is necessary, but racial prejudice cannot be quickly washed away as a societal stain... 'nor can it be overcome, as a general virus in the social body, by a heavy dose of liberal inoculation (Hall 1980, 341).

Multicoloring the nation: common-sense policy

Given the Dominican political climate, it is unlikely that a major reappraisal of the legislature incorporating racially sensitive policy reform will occur in the near future. There remains no clear basis for political action against racism, and neither is it deemed politically necessary to change policies in order to counter racial discrimination. Racism is central to social and political realities, but marginal to any notion of policy reform. Racist politics have been functional to the political system during recent election campaigns, although in the long run this may be playing with fire.

The instability and societal discord inherent in a racialized political and social system warrants an implicit recognition that racial equality is a common good. The most appropriate course to achieve this is to popularize anti-racism and to incorporate it as 'common sense' (Hall 1990, 8). Popular democratic ideology and rational state intervention are the means by which anti-racist policy is disseminated. Hall (1992) describes the change from a struggle over the relations of representation (the absence, marginalization and simplification of ethnic experience) to the politics of representation itself. Once race is politicized from a positive anti-racist platform, as part of a government policy of multiculturalism, possibilities then exist for the common sense promotion of racial harmony.

Anti-racism should be common sense, but it is not. This is unsurprising, given the pervasive myth of the Dominican Republic as a racial democracy. However, the evidence suggesting that darker-skinned Dominicans face discrimination in the workplace, and at all social levels, needs to be recognized and addressed at policy level. Banton (1985) suggests that racial prejudice derives from the pressure felt by individuals to conform to the prevalent social standards. Thus, group norms need to be challenged. A re-representation of the country's history in the media and via education could remove the sheen from the image of a noble indigenous and European heritage. Attempts are only slowly being made to remove derogatory images of Haitians and to rewrite the light bias in school history textbooks.

A popular democratic ideology of multiculturalism or multiracialism could provide the basis for effective anti-racist policy in the Dominican Republic. The former term is preferred since it addresses a range of cultural institutions and ethnic identities. *Mestizaje* is a form of multiculturalism, popularized yet not incorporated into government policy. Multiculturalism promotes policies acknowledging 'racial diversity while at the same time disavowing divisive social realities' (Kutzinski 1993, 5). The celebration of *mestizaje* as the cornerstone of a broad-based government agenda could lay the foundation for the equal recognition of various ancestries and ethnicities in Dominican society.

Recognition at the governmental level of racial difference and its contribution to *dominicanidad* is a crucial beginning to the promotion of multiculturalism. Kallendorf (1995) suggests that Dominicans are beginning to challenge previous European-oriented histories of the country in favor of non-romanticized accounts of the indigenous past. Competent multicultural policy, however, requires a more radical reappraisal of the island's history, emphasizing indigenous, European, Asian and African influences. Given that African Dominicans have not been excluded by law from a full participation in society, their situation is somewhat similar to that experienced by the population of African descent in Central America (Minority Rights Group 1996). African Dominicans, however, do not form a minority of the population.

Dominican-Haitians and Haitians in the Dominican Republic are discriminated against racially as a result of their, or their parents', nationality. Clear and fair guidelines are needed to establish their status as Dominican citizens or legal residents. A more constructive and documented approach would remove the stigma of Haitian illegality. The granting of citizenship to the offspring of legally resident Haitians in the Dominican Republic, and establishing the legal status of legitimate migrants, are important issues. The more efficient regulation of immigration would weaken the perception of an incessant Haitian flow. The forceful repatriation of Haitian cane cutters reproduces the image of the Haitian as the usurper or the unwelcome invader. Revised contracting is required to ascertain the number of laborers required and to put an end to random expulsions. Above all, effective legislation to establish a multicultural framework is fundamentally lacking.

Racial harmony works for the common and public good. Anti-racism aims, thus, to exchange the negative presence of racism, for its positive absence. Racism devalues human relations: 'If racism brutalises and dehumanises its object, it also brutalises and dehumanises those who articulate it' (Miles 1989, 10). Banton's (1985, ix) critique of the success of the 'race relations industry' in the United Kingdom suggests that while many supported the governmental goal of 'equal opportunity accompanied by cultural diversity, in an atmosphere of mutual tolerance', there existed a substantial amount of vagueness and uncertainty 'about the best means to the end.' This is just as true in the

Dominican Republic where cursory agreement on the basic premises of anti-racism has failed to result in practical governmental action. As Blaut (1992) succinctly infers, the removal of the roots of racism will not eradicate prejudice. Dominicans must do even more than dig up the vine, but also disempower the hegemonic position of 'white bias', which legitimizes racism and reproduces the legacy of racial discrimination in society.

Notes

1. For example, Logan (1968)

2. Padre Juan Vázquez, quoted in Franco (1989, 74)

3. Fernández Rocha (1975); Deive (1973); Rodríguez Demorizi (1975)

4. *Listín Diario* 7 September 1994

5. *Listín Diario* 12 September 1994

6. The number of Haitians and Haitian-Dominicans murdered has been the subject of some debate. Estimated death tolls have ranged up to 30,000. A figure of 12,000 is suggested by Roorda (1996).

7. *Listín Diario* 22 December 1987

8. *Última Hora* 28 July 1992

9. *Listín USA* 11 May 1994

10. *Hoy* 24 July 1992

11. *Listín Diario* July-August, 1992

12. *Listín Diario* 15 July 1995

13. *El Siglo* 26 September 1994

14. *Listín Diario* 3 August 1994

15. Advertised in *Rumbo* 8 August 1995

16. 'En la playa.' In *El Siglo*

17. *El Nacional* 22 September 1994

18. *New York Times* 16 September 1991

19. *El Siglo* 2 September 1994; *El Siglo* 11 August 1995

20. Blas R. Jiménez interview 24 September 1995

21. In Morales (1976, 109-110):
    Plegaria inutíl. Ella goza y mata,
    abre y cerra la tumba a su querer.
    Cuando al son de la lúgubre campana
    a la fosa su víctima desciende
    la cruel mulata su cigarro enciende
    y a inmolar va otro hombre a su placer.

22. In Bisonó (1994, 5-6):
    Tu hermoso cuerpo de color caoba
    tiene el encanto de una estatua viva,
    que a todos nos atrae y nos cautiva
    con su perfume tropical que arroba.

    Siempre hechizante, el corazón nos roba
    tu cuerpo de Cleopatra sensitiva,
    con su sensualidad provocativa,
    de reina del salón y del alcoba.

    La fina imagen de la diosa Helena,
    de cuyas formas la escultura arranca,
    fundida al fuego de tu piel morena,
    surge más bella que en su forma blanca,
    y puedes ocupar con gracia plena
    un sitio al lado de la Venus manca.

23. In Bisonó (1994, 38):
    Azúcar, canela y clavo
    sabe su carne morena
    y se idealiza el pecado
    cuando al placer se entrega.

    Aquella tarde en su alcoba,
    tibia ánfora de placer,
    bebí la lascivia roja
    hasta saciar mi honda sed...

    Mas... Oh cosas de la vida
    que no deben suceder...
    desde aquella tarde, amiga.
    No nos hemos vuelto a ver.
    Por donde andarás perdida
    vendedora de placer.

24. 21 percent of interviewees listed reading as a favorite past time; four-fifths of these respondents were from the upper and middle classes.

25. Blas Jiménez, interview with the author, 14 September 1995

26. Jiménez (1987, 56-57):
> Tam-tam tam-tam tam-tam
> puedo escuchar tu tambor
> repicando entre los montes
> tam-tam tam-tam tam-tam
> como si fuera tu voz
>
> Un tam-tam un tam-tam
> como palabras
> como símbolos
> como lengua de paz
> como señal de libertad

27. Torres (1994, 33-36):
> I
> El amor cimarrón tiene la virtud
> de portar sangre de tambor
> es cimarrón el amor en las Antillas
> síntesis de razas.
> ...
> III
> ...
> ¡Oh...! amor cimarrón en nuestras venas
> origen de esta pasión inagotable
> dueño de islas y huracanes
> amasijo de piernas y esqueletos.

28. Torres (1994, 53-54):
> Un hechizo cimarrón
> la estremece
> gotas de sudor
> desprendidas de su cuerpo
> como lluvia de fuego
> queman el Occidente.
>
> mulata fruto de la tierra
> grito de tambor en mis oídos
> dale un poco de tu ritmo
> a mis palabras
> fecundiza con tus sueños

mi destino.

29. Lebrón Saviñón (1985, 20-21):
    Que me emborracha más tu calentura
    que la dulce amargura
    del alcohol.
    Pero en tu piel retumba la tambora.
    Tu rumba es una música que llora
    en el loco torrente de tus ríos.

    Pero tu carne tropical devora
    la quietud ancestral de mis hastíos.
    Mulata del deseo: cuando pasas,
    eres tú la primera
    Eres amable síntesis de razas
    frenesí de pantera
    noche y diá-merengue y rumba-inquieta...

30. Jiménez (1987, 63-64):
    mi pelo
    crece en mi piel
    como en la piel del abuelo
    piel que da orgullo
    pelo y piel
    pelo
    mi pelo
    filamento crespo
    filamento + filamento + filamento
    crea mi buen pelo
    un pelo crespo
    un pelo en afro
    un pelo de negro
    mi pelo

31. Jiménez (1980, 23):
    Negra de las tetas grandes
    negra de las nalgas duras
    negra que corta la caña
    negra tú sí que eres chula
    negra de las tetas grandes
    negra de las nalgas duras
    negra que lava la ropa
    negra que hace la fritura
    negra que da muchos hijos
    negra tú sí que eres chula

negra de las tetas grandes
negra de las nalgas duras
cuando despacio caminas
se ve toda la dulzura
de la caña que a cortao
en tu vida de amargura
negra de las tetas grandes
negra de las nalgas duras.

32. Jiménez (1980, 65-66):
Eres Haitiano
eres haitiano por ser negro
eres negro
eso te hace haitiano
no por nacimiento
Por ser negro
Eres negro
Eres haitiano por ser negro
Negro es lo malo
Malo es lo haitiano
Negro es feo
Feo es haitiano
Eres haitiano
Por ser negro eres haitiano.

33. In Cocco de Filippis (1988, 111-112):
Haití
te imagino virgen
antes de que piratas precursores
te quitaran tus vestidos de caoba
y te dejaran así
con tus senos redondos al aire
y tu falda de yerba desgarrada
apenas verde, marrón tímida.

34. Prestol Castillo (1973, 64):
En aquel paraje de fealdades la maestra era el contraste: era bonita. Aquí
estaba el peligro por una mujer: ser maestra, que equivale casi a decir que es
miserable, y poseer una belleza que incita el sadismo de cualquier bárbaro
de los que pueblan esta tierra lejana. La muchacha era del Sur, con veinte
años apenas. Tenía el color canela y ojos verdosos. Bellas trenzas negras y un
cuerpo propio para modelo en una sala aristocrática de modas de una
grande ciudad.
    ... es la única persona que sabe eso de que hay una *República
Dominicana*. ¿Qué es eso... dirían los asombrados habitantes del paraje, que

sólo tienen una vida mísera como la de los cerdos, sin noción de patria.

35. Jiménez (1980, 19-21):
¿Qué soy?
Negro, Mulato, Bembón.
¿Qué soy?
Dominicano, americano, antillano,
negro africano que siento el bongó
un negro loco en un mundo blanco, mundo español.
Busco,
busco el tam-tam de mis antepasados
quiero salir.

36. Jiménez (1980, 59):
Indio de los ojos verdes
hijo de árabe-negro
hijo de blanco-negro
tercerón, cuarterón, mulato.

Indio de los ojos verdes
hijo de español
hijo de taíno
hijo de negro cimarrón.

37. Jiménez (1987, 100-101):
¿Por qué quieres ser negro?
eres indio
indio claro
...
¿por qué quieres ser negro?
no puedo dejarte serlo
porque si eres negro
ellos serán negros
porque si eres negro
yo seré negro
porque si eres negro.

38. Jiménez (1984, 54):
En este pueblo español,
muere el negro
como indio, en querer ser blanco.

En este pueblo español,
civilízase el negro
con tonos de varios colores.

En este pueblo español,
lágrimas del viejo negro
por el pueblo bebé; '*el negrito nació muerto*'

En este pueblo español,
pueblo de los sufrimientos
se mata al negro por fuera, nace de nuevo por dentro.

39. del Cabral (1990, 23):
   ... el complejo del mulato es más complicado que el del puro blanco y del negro puro; no le gusta estar entre dos aguas, quizá para que no lo confundan con el homosexual.

40. del Cabral (1990, 43):
   'Imagínate ahora dos salvajes sin control en este palacio. Nos movemos como animales en una jaula de lujo...'

41. del Cabral (1990, 97):
   'La palabra negro... ya es cosa del pasado'

42. del Cabral (1990, 98):
   'Que el negro no debiera mostrarle las lágrimas al blanco, él goza con nuestro dolor, nuestra piel alimenta su sadismo.'

43. del Cabral (1990, 111-112):
   'Aquí en Haití...las mujeres tienen hijos debajo los árboles, sobre los burros, en las esquinas, en el camino, no hay sitio previsto... Si el ritmo de proliferación se mantiene así desorbitado, en este país a la vuelta de algunos años el drama haitiano tomará proporciones de transcendencia internacional.'

44. Jiménez (1984, 45):
   Pero
   pero la esclavitud
   la esclavitud no fue mala aquí.

45. del Cabral (1976, 221):
   Negro simple,
   tú que tienes
   a tu vida y al mundo
   dentro de un amuleto.

   De ti,
   sólo asciende

el humo de tu cachimbo.

Ni los niños,
ni el asno,
tienen tu sencillez.

46. *Rumbo*-Gallup 11 June 1996

47. Balaguer, born in 1907, has been elected president seven times as leader of the PRSC from 1966 to 1978, and 1986 to 1996.

48. *Rumbo*-Gallup 19 June 1996

49. *New York Times* 20 May 1994, editorial 'Mr Balaguer's Dubious Victory'; *New York Times* 6 August 1994

50. *New York Times* 12 June 1996

51. *Listín Diario* 1 August 1994

52. *Hoy* 15 September 1994

53. *Hoy* 17 September 1994

54. *Listín Diario* 14 September 1994

55. *New York Times* 24 May 1994

56. *Ultima Hora* 11 August 1994

57. PeaceNet 1 July 1996 peacenet-info@igc.apc.org

58. *Listín Diario* 17 August 1994

59. *Última Hora* 11 August 1994

60. *Última Hora* 15 May 1994

61. Pedro Manual Casals Victoria, interview with the author, 29 September 1994

62. *El Siglo* 26 January 1996

63. Victor Grimaldi, interview with the author, 27 September 1994

64. *Hoy* 17 July 1992

65. *El Siglo* 26 July 1995

66. *Última Hora* 15 May 1994

67. *Ultima Hora* 28 July 1992

68. *Listín Diario* 3 July 1996

69. *El Nacional* 26 August 1996

70. *Hoy* 5 July 1996

Bibliography

Adorno, T. S., E. Frenkel-Brunswick, D. J. Levine, and R. N. Sanforo. 1950. *The Authoritarian Personality*. London: Harper and Row.

Agier, M. 1995. 'Racism, culture and black identity in Brazil.' *Bulletin of Latin American Research* 14:245-264.

Aizpun, I. 1994. 'Como pinta la vida para las jefes de familia.' *Rumbo* 31.

Albert-Batista, C. 1993. *Mujer y esclavitud en Santo Domingo*. Santo Domingo: CEDEE.

Alcántara-Almánzar, J. 1975. 'Encuesta sociológica de la ciudad de Santo Domingo.' *Ciencia* 2:5-30.

Almánzar, J. Alcántara. 1979. *Estudios de poesía dominicana*. Santo Domingo: Editora Alfa y Omega.

Alvarez, Julia. 1991. *How the Garcia Girls Lost Their Accents*. New York: Penguin.

Alvarez Perelló, J. de J. 1973. 'La mezcla de razas en Santo Domingo y los factores sanguineos.' *Eme-Eme* 2:67-98.

Anderson, B. 1991. *Imagined Communities: reflections on the origin and spread of nationalism*. London: Verso.

Andújar, C. 1992. 'El proceso de conformación de la identidad cultural dominicana.' in *Día del Mulato*. Centro de Trabajo Popular, Santiago.

Anonymous. 1980. 'Entrevista con Manuel del Cabral: poesía negra y metafísica.' *Letra Grande* 1:44-49.

Anthias, F. 1990. 'Race and class revisited: conceptualising race and racisms.' *The Sociological Review* 38:19-42.

Anthias, F., and N. Yuval-Davis. 1992. *Racialized Boundaries: race, nation, gender, color and class and the anti-racist struggle*. London: Routledge.

Anwar, M. 1979. *The Myth of Return: Pakistanis in Britain*. London: Heinemann.

Arredondo, A. 1936. *El Negro en Cuba*. Havana: Editorial Alfa.

Augelli, J. P. 1980. 'Nationalisation of the Dominican borderlands.' *Geographical Review* 70:19-35.

Balaguer, J. 1947. *La realidad dominicana: semblanza de un país y de un régimen*. Buenos Aires: Imprenta Hermanos Ferrari.

Balaguer, J. 1993. *La isla al revés: Haití y el destino dominicano*. Santo Domingo: Editora Corripio.

Banton, M. 1985. *Promoting Racial Harmony*. Cambridge: Cambridge University Press.

Banton, M. 1991. 'The race relations problematic.' *British Journal of Sociology* 42:115-130.

Banton, M. 1992. *Racial and Ethnic Competition*. Aldershot: Gregg Revivals.

Barker, M. 1981. *The New Racism: conservatives and the ideology of the tribe*. London: Junction Books.

Bastide, R. 1961. 'Dusky Venus, Black Apollo.' *Race* 3:10-18.

Baud, M. 1987. 'The origins of capitalist agriculture in the Dominican Republic.' *Latin American Research Review* 22:135-153.

Baud, M. 1996. '"Constitutionally white": the forging of an identity in the Dominican Republic.' Pp. 121-151 in *Ethnicity in the Caribbean*, edited by G. Oostindie. London: Macmillan.

Báez, C., and G. Taulé. 1993. 'Posición socio-cultural y economía de la mujer en la República Dominicana.' *Género y Sociedad* 1.

Bell, I. 1981. *The Dominican Republic*. Boulder: Westview Press.

Belsey, C. 1980. *Critical Practice*. London: Methuen.

Benítez-Rojo, A. 1992. *The Repeating Island: the Caribbean and the post-modern perspective*. London: Duke University Press.

Berghe, P. L. van den. 1967. *Race and Racism: a comparative perspective*. New York: Wiley.

Betances, Emelio. 1995. *State and Society in the Dominican Republic*. Boulder: Westview.

Bisonó, P. 1994. *Lo mejor de la poesía amorosa dominicana*. Santo Domingo: Ediciones Cultural de Santo Domingo.

Blaut, J. M. 1992. 'The theory of cultural racism.' *Antipode* 24:289-299.

Booth, D. 1976. 'Cuba, color and the revolution.' *Science and Society* 11:129-172.

Bosch, J. 1965. *The Unfinished Experiment: democracy in the Dominican Republic*. London: Pall Mall Press.

Bosch, J. 1992. *Clases sociales en la República Dominicana*. Santo Domingo: Editora Corripio.

Braithwaite, E. 1993. *Roots*. Ann Arbor: University of Michigan Press.

Bray, D. B. 1984. 'Economic development: the middle class and international migration in the Dominican Republic.' *International Migration Review* 18:217-236.

Brittan, A., and M. Maynard. 1984. *Sexism, Racism and Oppression*. Oxford: Basil Blackwell.

Bueno, R. A. 1992. 'Estudio del prejuicio hacia los haitianos en tres escuelas intermedias con diferentes niveles de interacción social.' in *Department of Social Studies*. Santiago: Universidad Católica de Madre y Maestra.

Bueno, L. 1995. 'Experiencias de migración de retorno de mujeres dominicanas: historias e vida de cinco mujeres.' *Género y Sociedad* 2:1-52.

Calder, B. J. 1981. 'The Dominican turn toward sugar.' *Caribbean Review* 10:18-21, 44-45.

Candelier, B. R. 1974. 'Los valores negros en la poesía dominicana.' *Eme-Eme* 15:29-66.

Candelier, B. R. 1977. *Lo popular y lo culto en la poesía dominicana*. Santiago: Universidad Católica de Madre y Maestra.

Cashmore, E. (Ed.). 1995. *Dictionary of Race and Ethnic Relations*. London: Routledge.

Cassá, R. 1982. *Historia social y económica de la República Dominicana*. Santo

Domingo: Punto y Aparte Editores.

Cassá, R. 1984. '*La Isla al Revés*: entre la cuestión nacional y la cuestión social.' Santo Domingo: Department of History and Anthropology, Universidad Autónoma de Santo Domingo.

Cassá, R. 1994. 'La verdad del nacionalismo.' Unpublished paper.

Castor, S. 1983. *Migraciones y relaciones internacionales: el caso haitiano-dominicano*. Mexico City: Universidad Nacional Autónoma de México.

Castro, Max. 1993. 'Hispanics in the 1990s: on our way.' *Vista* 8:6-8, 30.

Césaire, A. 1994. *Cahier d'un retour au pays natal*. Ibadan: New Horn Press.

Chant, S. 1996. 'Gender, urbanisation and housing: issues and challenges for the 1990s.' *Environmental and Spatial Analysis (London School of Economics)* 32.

Chodorow, N. 1978. *The Reproduction of Mothering: psychoanalysis and the sociology of gender*. Berkeley: University of California Press.

Clarke, C. G. 1984. "Pluralism and plural societies: Caribbean perspectives." Pp. 51-86 in *Geography and Ethnic Pluralism*, edited by C. G. Clarke, D. Ley, and C. Peach. London: Allen and Unwin.

Cohen, P. S. 1969. 'Theories of myth.' *Man* 4:337-353.

Cohen, P. 1993. 'The perversions of inheritance: studies in the making of multi-racist Britain.' Pp. 9-113 in *Multi-Racist Britain*, edited by P. Cohen and H. S. Bains. London: Macmillan.

Collado, L. 1992. *El tiguere dominicano*. Santo Domingo: Editora Panamerica.

Contreras, A. M. 1991. 'Dinámica urbana en la década de los 80s: concentración del ingreso, segregación especial y exclusión social.' *Estudios Sociales* 83:37-59.

Corcino, D. A. 1988. *Identidad nacional*. Santo Domingo: Editora Panamerica.

Cordones, H. Omos. 1980. 'Tres rasgos géneticos en una población dominicana.' *Boletín del Museo del Hombre Dominicano* 15:89-102.

Cornielle, C. 1980. *Proceso histórico dominicano-haitiano: una advertencia a la juventud dominicana*. Santo Domingo: Publicaciones América.

Corten, A., and A. Corten. 1968. *Cambio social en Santo Domingo*. Río Piedras: Universidad de Puerto Rico.

Corten, A. 1989. *El estado débil: Haití y la Repúblic Dominicana*. Santo Domingo: Editora Taller.

Corten, A. 1994. 'The Dominican Republic elections and the United Nations embargo against Haiti.' *Institute of Latin American Studies Occasional Papers* 6:3-20.

Corten, A., and I. Duarte. 1995. 'Five hundred thousand Haitians in the Dominican Republic.' *Latin American Perspectives* 22:94-110.

Cosgrove, J. 1992. 'Remigration: the Dominican experience.' *Social Development Issues* 14:101-120.

Coulthard, G. R. 1962. *Race and Color in Caribbean Literature*. New York: Oxford University Press.

Cox, O. C. 1970. *Caste, Class and Race*. New York: Monthly Review Press.

Daly, M. 1975. *The Church and the Second Sex*. New York: Harper and Row.

David, D. 1992. 'Dominican Republic Country Report.' *The Courier* 131:10-46.

Davis, M. E. 1987. *La otra ciencia: el vodú dominicano como religión y medicina populares.* Santo Domingo: Editoria Universitaria.

Davis, M. 1999. 'Magical urbanism: Latinos reinvent the US big city.' *New Left Review* 234:3-43.

De la Cruz, C. 1978. 'El radicalismo izquierdista en barrios marginados.' *Estudios Sociales* 42:59-126.

Degler, C. N. 1971. *Neither White nor Black: slavery and race relations in Brazil and the United States.* New York: Macmillan.

Deive, C. E. 1973. 'El prejuicio racial en el folkore dominicano.' *Boletín del Museo del Hombre Dominicano* 8:75-96.

Del Cabral, M. 1976. *Obra poética completa.* Santo Domingo: Editora Alfa y Omega.

Del Cabral, M. 1990. *El presidente negro.* Santo Domingo: Editora Corripio.

Del Castillo, J., and M. F. Murphy. 1987. 'Migration, national identity and cultural policy in the Dominican Republic.' *Journal of Ethnic Studies* 15:49-69.

Derby, Lauren. 1994. 'Haitians, magic and money: *raza* and society in Haitian-Dominican borderlands 1900-1937.' *Comparative Studies in Society and History* 36:488-526.

Despradel Batista, G. 1936. *Las raíces de nuestro espíritu.* Ciudad Trujillo: Sección de Publicaciones.

Depestre, R. 1970. 'Problemas de la identidad del hombre negro en las literaturas antillanas.' *Casa de las Américas* 31:51-59.

Doré Cabral, C. 1985. 'La inmigración haitiana y el componente racista de la cultura dominicana (apuntes para una critica a *La isla al revés*).' *Ciencia y Sociedad* 10:61-69.

Doré Cabral, C. 1995. 'Los descendientes de haitianos no son picadores de caña.' *Rumbo* 62.

Duany, J. 1994. *Quisqueya on the Hudson: the transnational identity of Dominicans in Washington Heights.* New York: Dominican Studies Institute, City University of New York.

Duany, J. 1996. 'Transnational migration from the Dominican Republic: the cultural redefinition of racial identity.' *Caribbean Studies* 29:253-282.

Duany, J. 1998. 'Ethnicity, color, and class among Dominicans in the United States and Puerto Rico.' *Latin American Perspectives* 25:147-172.

Duarte, I. 1989. 'Household workers in the Dominican Republic: a question for the feminist movement.' Pp. 197-219 in *Muchachas No More: household workers in Latin America and the Caribbean*, edited by E. M. Chaney and M. Garcia. Philadelphia: Temple University Press.

Ducoudray, F. S. 1975. 'El vudú nuestro no llego de Haiti: es Dominicano.' *¡Ahora!* :16-19.

Espinal, R. 1991. 'Between authoritarianism and crisis-prone democracy: the Dominican Republic after Trujillo.' Pp. 145-165 in *Society and Politics in* the *Caribbean*, edited by C. G. Clarke. London: St Antony's-Macmillan.

Evertsz, F. Báez, and F. d'Oleo Ramírez. 1986. *La emigración de dominicanos a Estados Unidos: determinantes socio-económicos y consecuencias*. Santo Domingo: Fundación Friedrich Ebert.

Fanon, F. 1970. *Toward the African Revolution*. Harmondsworth: Penguin.

Fanon, F. 1986. *Black Skin, White Masks*. London: Pluto Press.

Fennema, M., and T. Loewenthal. 1987. *La construcción de raza y nación en la República Dominicana*. Santo Domingo: Editora Universitaria.

Fennema, M. 1995. 'Hispanidad and the construction of national identity in Santo Domingo.' Unpublished paper .

Fernández-Rocha, C. 1975. 'El refranero popular dominicano: apuntes sobre el blasón popular negro en la República Dominicana.' *Eme-Eme* 8:53-62.

Fiehrer, T. 1990. 'Political violence in the periphery: the Haitian massacre of 1937.' *Race and Class* 32:1-20.

Cocco de Filippis, D. 1988. *Sin otro profeta que su canta*. Santo Domingo: Editora Taller.

Finlay, B. 1989. *The Women of Azua: work and family in the Dominican Republic*. New York: Praeger.

Franco, F. J. 1979. *Santo Domingo: cultura, política é ideología*. Santo Domingo: Editora Nacional.

Franco, F. J. 1989. *Los negros, los mulatos y la nación dominicana*. Santo Domingo: Editora Valle.

Freyre, G. 1946. *The Masters and the Slaves: a study in the development of Brazilian civilisation*. New York: Knopf.

Galván, M. de J. 1989. *Enriquillo*. Santo Domingo: Editora Taller.

Gamio, M. 1960. *Forjando patria*. Mexico City: Editorial Porrúa.

Gates Jr, H. L. 1987. *Figures in Black: words, signs and the racial self*. Oxford: Oxford University Press.

Gayle Jr, A. (Ed.). 1971. *The Black Aesthetic*. New York: Doubleday.

Geertz, C. 1975. *The Interpretation of Cultures: selected essays*. London: Hutchinson.

Georges, E. 1990. *The Making of a Transnational Community: migration, development and cultural change in the Dominican Republic*. New York: Columbia University Press.

Gilbertson, G. A., and G. T. Gurak. 1992. 'Household transitions in the migrations of Dominicans and Colombians to New York.' *International Migration Review* 26:22-45.

Gilmore, D. D. 1990. *Manhood in the Making: cultural concepts of masculinity*. London: Yale University Press.

Gilroy, P. 1987. *'There Ain't No Black in the Union Jack': the cultural politics of race and nation*. London: Routledge.

Girvan, N. 1975. 'Aspects of the political economy of race in the Caribbean and the Americas.' in *Institute of Social and Economic Studies Working Paper*. Kingston: University of the West Indies.

Goldberg, D. T. 1992. 'The semantics of race.' *Ethnic and Racial Studies* 5:543-

569.

González, N. L. 1970. 'Peasants' progress: Dominicans in New York.' *Caribbean Studies* 10:154-171.

González, N. L. 1973. 'El Carnaval en Santiago de los Caballeros.' *Eme-Eme* 2:80-95.

Grasmuck, S. 1982. 'Migration within the periphery: Haitian labour in the Dominican sugar and coffee industries.' *International Migration Review* 16:365-377.

Grasmuck, S. 1984. 'Immigration, ethnic stratification and native working class discipline: comparison of documented and undocumented Dominicans.' *International Migration Review* 18 (3): 692-713.

Grasmuck, S., and P. R. Pessar. 1991. *Between Two Islands: Dominican international migration*. Berkeley: University of California Press.

Guarnizo, L. E. 1993. 'Going home: class, gender, and household transformation among Dominican return transmigrants.' Washington: Commission for Hemispheric Migration and Refugee Policy.

Guillaumen, C. 1972. 'Caractères spécifiques de l'idéologie raciste.' *Cahiers Internationaux de Sociologie* 52:247-274.

Gurak, D. T. 1987. 'Family formation and marital selectivity among Colombian and Dominican immigrants in New York City.' *International Migration Review* 21:275-298.

Guzmán, D. J. 1974. 'Raza y lenguaje en el Cibao.' *Eme-Eme* 2:3-45.

Hall, S. 1980. 'Race, articulation and societies structured in dominance.' Pp. 305-345 in *Sociological Theories: race and colonialism*, edited by UNESCO. Paris: UNESCO.

Hall, S. 1980. 'Pluralism, race and class in Caribbean society.' Pp. 150-182 in *Sociological Theories: race and colonialism*, edited by UNESCO. Paris: UNESCO.

Hall, S. 1990. 'The whites of their eyes.' Pp. 7-23 in *The Media Reader*, edited by M. Alvarado and J. O. Thompson. London: British Film Institute.

Hall, S. 1992. 'New ethnicities.' Pp. 252-259 in *'Race', Culture and Difference*, edited by J. Donald and A. Rattansi. London: Sage.

Harris, M. 1970. 'Referential ambiguity in the calculus of Brazilian racial identity.' *Southwestern Journal of Anthropology* 26:1-12.

Hartlyn, J. 1993. 'The Dominican Republic: contemporary problems and challenges.' Pp. 150-172 in *Democracy in the Caribbean: political, economic and social perspectives*, edited by J. I. Domínguez, R. A. Pastor, and R. D. Worrell. Baltimore: Johns Hopkins University Press.

Hendricks, G. 1974. *Dominican Diaspora: from the Dominican Republic to New York City—villagers in transition*. New York: Teachers College Press.

Hewstone, M., and R. Brown. 1986. 'Contact is not enough: an intergroup perspective on contact hypothesis.' in *Contact and Conflict in Inter-Group Encounters*, edited by M. Hewstone and R. Brown. Oxford: Blackwell.

Hoetink, H. 1967. *The Two Variants in Caribbean Race Relations*. Oxford: Oxford University Press.

Hoetink, H. 1970. 'The Dominican Republic in the nineteenth century: some notes on stratification, immigration and race.' Pp. 96-121 in *Race and Class in Latin America*, edited by M. Mörner. New York: Columbia University Press.

Hoetink, H. 1982. *The Dominican Republic, 1850-1900*. Baltimore: Johns Hopkins University Press.

Hoetink, H. 1992. 'Ideology, intellectuals and identity: the Dominican Republic, 1880-1980.' Pp. 132-144 in *Intellectuals in the Twentieth-Century Caribbean*, edited by A. Hennessy. London: Macmillan.

Hondagneu Sotelo, P. 1992. 'Overcoming patriarchal constraints: the reconstruction of gender relations among Mexican immigrant women and men.' *Gender and Society* 6:393-415.

hooks, b. 1984. *Feminist Theory: from margin to center*. Boston: South End Press.

Howard, D. J. 1993. '"We're neighbours but..." A study of racial identification in the Dom,inican Republic.' Unpublished M.Phil. Thesis, University of Oxford.

Incháustegui Cabral, H. 1969. *Literatura dominicana del siglo XX*. Santiago: UCMM.

Incháustegui Cabral, H. 1976. 'Los negros y las trigueñas en la poesía dominicana.' *Eme-Eme* 4:3-19.

Inoa, O. 1991. 'Los árabes en Santo Domingo.' *Estudios Sociales* 65:35-58.

Itzigsohn, J., C. Dore Cabral, E. Hernández Medina, and O. Vásquez. 1999. 'Mapping Dominican transnationalism: narrow and broad transnational practices.' *Ethnic and Racial Studies* 22:316-339.

Jackson, R. L. 1976. *Black Image in Latin American Literature*. Alburquerque: University of New Mexico Press.

Jackson, P. 1989. *Maps of Meaning: an introduction to cultural geography*. London: Unwin Hyman.

James, C. L. R. 1994. *The Black Jacobins: Toussaint L'Ouverture and the San Domingo revolution*. London: Allison and Busby.

Jiménes Grullón, J. I. 1965. *La República Dominicana: una ficción*. Mérida: Talleres Graficos Universitarios.

Jiménez, B. R. 1980. *Aquí... otro español*. Santo Domingo: Editora Incoco.

Jiménez, B. R. 1984. *Caribe africano en despertar*. Santo Domingo: Editora Nuevas Rutas.

Jiménez, B. R. 1987. *Exigencias de un cimarrón (en sueños)*. Santo Domingo: Editora Taller.

Kallendorf, H. 1995. 'A myth rejected: the Noble Savage in Dominican dystopia.' *Journal of Latin American Studies* 27:449-470.

Kipnis, L. 1986. '"Refunctioning" reconsidered: towards a left popular culture.' in *High Theory/Low Culture: analysing popular television and film*, edited by C. MacCabe. Manchester: Manchester University Press.

Knight, A. 1990. 'Racism, revolution, and indigenismo: Mexico, 1910-1940.' Pp. 71-113 in *The Idea of Race in Latin America, 1870-1940*, edited by R.

Graham. Austin: University of Texas Press.

Krohn Hansen, C. 1995. 'Magic, money and alterity among Dominicans.' *Social Anthropology* 3:129-146.

Kutzinski, V. M. 1993. *Sugar's Secrets: race and the erotics of Cuban nationalism.* Charlottesville: University Press of Virginia.

Lancaster, R. N. 1992. *Life is Hard: machismo, danger, and the intimacy of power in Nicaragua.* Oxford: University of California Press.

Lantigua, J. R. 1989. 'Notas sobre la poesía de tema negro en Manuel del Cabral.' *Eme-Eme* 15:107-114.

Lartortue, P. R. 1985. 'Neoslavery in the cane fields.' *Caribbean Review* 14:18-20.

Lebrón Saviñón, C. 1985. *Canto iluminado.* Santo Domingo: Editorial Cenapec.

Lemoine, M. 1985. *Bitter Sugar.* London: Zed Books.

Lewis, M. A. (Ed.). 1983. *Afro-Hispanic Poetry, 1940-1980.* Columbia: University of Missouri Press.

Leyburn, J. G. 1941. *The Haitian People.* New Haven: Yale University Press.

Lizardo, F. 1979. *Cultura africana en Santo Domingo.* Santo Domingo: Editora Taller.

Lobb, J. 1940. 'Caste and class in Haiti.' *Journal of American Sociology* 46:23-34.

Logan, R. W. 1968. *Haiti and the Dominican Republic.* London: Oxford University Press.

López, B. Bautista. 1995. *Diversión dominicana.* Santo Domingo: Impresora VM.

Lowenthal, D. 1972. *West Indian Societies.* Oxford: Oxford University Press.

Mejía Ricart, M. A. 1953. *Las clases sociales en Santo Domingo.* Ciudad Trujillo: Librería Dominicana.

Menéndez Alarcón, V. A. 1987. *El universitario dominicano.* Santo Domingo: Instituto Tecnológico de Santo Domingo.

Menéndez Alarcón, V. A. 1994. 'Racial prejudice: a Latin American case.' *Research in Race and Ethnic Relations* 7:299-319.

Miles, R. 1980. 'Class, race and ethnicity: a critique of Cox's theory.' *Ethnic and Racial Studies* 3:169-187.

Miles, R. 1982. *Racism and Migrant Labour.* London: Allen and Unwin.

Miles, R. 1987. 'Recent Marxist theories of nationalism and the issue of racism.' *British Journal of Sociology* 38:24-43.

Minority Rights Group (Ed.). 1996. *Afro-Central Americans: rediscovering the African heritage.* London: Minority Rights Group.

Mir, P. 1993. *Countersong to Walt Whitman and Other Poems.* Washington: Azul Editions.

Montagu, A. 1974. *Man's Most Dangerous Myth: the fallacy of race.* New York: Oxford University Press.

Morales, J. L. 1976. *Poesía afroantillana y negrista: Puerto Rico, la República Dominicana y Cuba.* Río Piedras: Editora Universitaria.

Moya Pons, F. 1981. 'Dominican national identity and return migration.' Gainsville: Center for Latin American Studies, University of Florida.

Moya Pons, F. 1986. *El pasado dominicano*. Santo Domingo: Editora Corripio.

Moya Pons, F. 1995. *The Dominican Republic: a national history*. New Rochelle: Hispaniola Books.

Muschkin, C. G. 1993. 'Consequences of return migrant status for employment in Puerto Rico.' *International Migration Review* 27:79-102.

Muschkin, C. G., and G. C. Myers. 1993. 'Return migrant status and income attainment in Puerto Rico.' *Social and Economic Status* 42:149-170.

Múnoz, M. E. 1995. *Las relaciones domínico-haitianas: geopolítica y migración*. Santo Domingo: Editora Alfa y Omega.

Nicholls, D. 1996. *From Dessalines to Duvalier: race, color and national dependence in Haiti*. London: Macmillan.

Núñez, M. 1990. *El ocaso de la nación dominicana*. Santo Domingo: Editora Alfa y Omega.

Omi, M., and H. Winant. 1994. *Racial Formation in the United States: from the 1960s to the 1990s*. London: Routledge.

Parsons, T. 1975. 'Some theoretical considerations on the nature and trends of change of ethnicity.' Pp. 53-83 in *Ethnicity: theory and experience*, edited by N. Glazer and D. P. Moynihan. London: Harvard University Press.

Pérez, J. J. (Ed.). 1989. *Fantasías indígenas y otros poemas*. Santo Domingo: Editora Corripio.

Pérez, L. J. 1990. *Santo Domingo frente al destino*. Santo Domingo: Editora Taller.

Peréz Cabral, P. A. 1967. *La comunidad mulata*. Santo Domingo: Editora Montaivo.

Pessar, P. R. 1985. 'The role of gender in Dominican settlement in the United States.' Pp. 273-294 in *Women and Change in Latin America*, edited by J. Nash and H. I. Safa. South Hadley: Bergin and Garvey.

Pessar, P. R. 1995. *A Visa for a Dream: Dominicans in the United States*. Boston: Allyn and Bacon.

Pessar, P. R. 1997. 'Dominicans: forging an ethnic community in New York.' Pp. 131-149 in *Beyond Black and White: new faces and voices in U.S. schools*, edited by M. Seller and L. Weir. Albany: SUNY Press.

Pichardo, T. 1992. *... Antes y después del fuego... Avan e apré dife a*. Santo Domingo: Ediciones Ceedee.

Piña Contreras, G. 1995. 'Dominicanos en España: la tragedia de una inmigración.' *Rumbo* :8-22.

Piore, M. J. 1979. *Birds of Passage: migrant labor and industrial societies*. Cambridge: Cambridge University Press.

Plant, R. 1987. *Sugar and Modern Slavery: a tale of two countries*. London: Zed.

Portes, A, and L. E. Guarnizo. 1991. *Capitalistas del trópico: la inmigración en los Estados Unidos y el desarollo de la pequeña empresa en la República Dominicana*. Santo Domingo: Facultdad Latinoamericana de Ciencias Sociales.

Portes, A. (Ed.). 1995. *The Economic Sociology of Immigration*. New York: Russell Sage Foundation.

Post, K. 1978. *Arise Ye Starvelings: the Jamaica labour rebellion of 1938 and its aftermath*. The Hague.

Prestol Castillo, F. 1973. *El masacre se pasa a pie*. Santo Domingo: Editora Taller.

Price-Mars, J. 1973. *Ainsi parla l'oncle*. Montreal: Lemiac.

Profamilia. 1993. *Encuesta demográfica y de salud (Endesa-91)*. Santo Domingo: Profamilia.

Ramón Lopéz, J. R. 1975. *El gran pesimismo dominicano*. Santiago: Universidad Católica Madre y Maestra.

Rex, J. 1973. *Race, Colonialism and the City*. London: Routledge and Kegan Paul.

Reyes, R. 1991. 'Microenterprise and the informal sector in the Dominican Republic: operation and promotion policy.' in *Migration, Remittances, and Small Business Development: Mexico and Caribbean Basin countries*, edited by S. Díaz-Briquets and S. Weintraub. Boulder: Westview Press.

Rhoades, R. 1978. 'Intra-European return migration and rural development: lessons from the Spanish case.' *Human Organization* 37:136-147.

Ringer, B. B., and E. R. Lawless. 1989. *Race-Ethnicity and Society*. New York: Routledge.

Rodríguez Demorizi, E. 1975. *Lengua y folklore de Santo Domingo*. Santiago: Universidad Católica Madre y Maestra.

Roorda, E. P. 1996. 'Genocide next door: the Good Neighbor Policy, the Trujillo regime, and the Haitian massacre of 1937.' *Diplomatic History* 20:301-319.

Ross, E., and R. Rapp. 1981. 'Sex and society: a research note from social history and anthropology.' *Comparative Studies in Society and History* 23:51-72.

Rueda, M. 1985. 'Cultura dominicana y medios de comunicación.' *Ciencia y Sociedad* 10:70-77.

Salmador, V. 1990. *José Francisco Peña Gómez*. Madrid: Editora Gráfica 82.

Salmador, V. 1994. *La isla de Santo Domingo: desde los indios tainos hasta Peña Gómez*. Santo Domingo: Editora de Colores.

Sanderlin, G. (Ed.). 1971. *Bartolmé de Las Casas: a selection of his writings*. New York: Alfred A. Knopf.

Sanjek, R. 1971. 'Brazilian racial terms: some aspects of meaning and learning.' *American Anthropologist* 73:1126-1144.

Sassen-Koob, S. 1979. 'Formal and informal associations: Dominicans and Colombians in New York City.' *International Migration Review* 8:314-332.

Sáez, J. L. 1991. 'El supermercado: punto de encuentro de dos sociedades en cambio.' *Estudios Sociales* 85:59-69.

Sharpe, K. E. 1977. *Peasant Politics: struggle in a Dominican village*. London: Johns Hopkins University Press.

Sherif, M. 1996. *Group Conflict and Cooperation: their social psychology*.

London: Routledge and Kegan Paul.

Silvestre, E. 1986. *Coloquio sobre Hombre y Sociedad: definición de las razas en Santo Domingo.* Santo Domingo: INTEC.

Smith, M. G. 1974. *Corporations and Society.* London: Duckworth.

Smith, M. G. 1984. *Culture, Race and Class in the Commonwealth Caribbean.* Mona: University of California Press.

Smith, A. D. 1986. *The Ethnic Origin of Nations.* Oxford: Blackwell.

Smith, A. D. 1992. *Ethnicity and Nationalism.* Leiden: E. J. Brill.

Solaún, M., and S. Kronus. 1973. *Discrimination Without Violence: miscegenation and racial conflict in Latin America.* New York: John Wiley and Sons.

Sollors, W. (Ed.). 1989. *The Invention of Ethnicity.* Oxford: Oxford University Press.

Solomos, J. 1989. *Race and Racism in Contemporary Britain.* London: Macmillan.

Solomos, J., and L. Black. 1995. *Race, Politics and Social Change.* London: Routledge.

Sommer, D. 1983. *One Master for Another: populism as patriarchal rhetoric in Dominican novels.* Latham: University Press of America.

Sørensen, N. N. 1997. 'National identity across Dominican worlds.' Pp. 241-269 in *Transnationalism from Below,* edited by M. P. Smith and L. E. Guarnizo. New Brunswick: Transaction Publishers.

Spender, D. 1980. *Man Made Language.* London: Routledge.

Sutton, C. R., and E. M. Chaney (Eds.). 1987. *Caribbean Life in New York City: sociocultural dimensions.* New York: Center for Migration Studies.

Tajfel, H. 1978. *Differentiation Between Social Groups: studies in the social psychology of intergroup relations.* London: Academic Press.

Telles, E. R. 1995. 'Race, class and space in Brazilian cities.' *Journal of International Urban and Rural Research* 19:394-406.

Torres, A. 1994. *Arco iris de amor y de fuego.* Santo Domingo: Impresos y Servicios.

Torres-Saillant, S. 1994. 'Dominican literature and its criticism: anatomy of a troubled identity.' Pp. 49-64 in *A History of Caribbean Literature,* edited by A. J. Arnold, J. Rodríguez-Luis, and M. J. Dash. Amsterdam: John Benjamins.

Torres-Saillant, S. 1995. 'The Dominican Republic.' Pp. 109-138 in *No Longer Invisible: Afro-Latino Americans today,* edited by Minority Rights Group. London: Minority Rights Group.

Torres-Saillant, S., and R. Hernández. 1998. *The Dominican Americans.* Westport: Greenwood.

Ugalde, A., F. Bean, and G. Cardenas. 1979. 'International migration from the Dominican Republic: findings from a national survey.' *International Migration Review* 13:235-257.

UNDP. 1997. *Human Development Report 1997.* New York: Oxford University Press.

UNESCO. 1977. *Race and Class in Post-Colonial Society: a study of ethnic group relations in the English-speaking Caribbean, Bolivia, Chile and Mexico.* Paris: UNESCO.

United States Bureau of the Census. 1993. *1990 Census of Population: social and economic characteristics, New York.* Washington: United States Department of Commerce.

Vega, B. 1993. 'Etnicidad y el futuro de las relaciones dominico-haitianos.' *Estudios Sociales* 94.

Velázquez Mainardi, M. A. 1994. *El fraude del fraude: una conjura internacional.* Santo Domingo: Editora Tele-3.

Veloz Maggiolo, M. 1986. *Sobre cultura dominicana... y otros culturas.* Santo Domingo: Editora Alfa y Omega.

Vicioso, S. 1994. 'An oral history.' Pp. 270-275 in *Barrios and Borderlands: cultures of latinos and latinas in the US*, edited by D. L. D. Heyck. London: Routledge.

Wade, P. 1993. *Blackness and Race Mixture: the dynamics of racial identity in Colombia.* London: Johns Hopkins University Press.

Wade, P. 1997. *Race and Ethnicity in Latin America.* London: Pluto Press.

Walby, S. 1990. *Theorizing Patriarchy.* Oxford: Blackwell.

Warner, W. L. 1960. *Social Class in America.* New York: Harper and Row.

Waters, M. C. 1994. 'Ethnic and racial identities of second-generation black immigrants in New York City.' *International Migration Review* 28:795-820.

Watts, D. 1987. *The West Indies: patterns of development, culture and environmental change since 1492.* Cambridge: Cambridge University Press.

Weber, M. 1947. *The Theory of Social and Economic Organization.* London: William Hodge.

Westhoff, W. 1993. 'A psychological study of albinism in a predominantly mulatto Caribbean community.' *Psychological Reports* 73:1007-1010.

Westwood, S., and S. A. Radcliffe. 1993. 'Gender, racism and the politics of identities.' in *'Viva': women and popular protest in Latin America*, edited by S. A. Radcliffe and S. Westwood. London: Routledge.

Wiarda, H. J., and M. J. Kryzanek. 1992. *The Dominican Republic: a Caribbean crucible.* Oxford: Westview Press.

Williams, E. 1944. *Capitalism and Slavery.* Chapel Hill: University of North Carolina.

Williams, R. 1983. *Keywords: a vocabulary of culture and society.* London: Fontana.

Wilson, W. J. 1978. *The Declining Significance and Race.* Chicago: University of Chicago Press.

Winant, H. 1992. 'Rethinking race in Brazil.' *Journal of Latin American Studies* 24:173-192.

Winddance Twine, F. 1997. 'Mapping the terrain of Brazilian racism.' *Race and Class* 38:49-61.

Winship, J. 1980. 'Sexuality for sale.' Pp. 217-223 in *Culture, Media, Language*, edited by S. Hall. London: Hutchinson.

224   *Coloring the Nation*

Wolch, J., and M. Dear (Eds.). 1989. *The Power of Geography: how territory shapes social life*. London: Unwin Hyman.

World Bank. 1999. *World Development Report 1998/99*. New York: Oxford University Press.

Wright, W. A. 1990. *Café con Leche: race, class and national image in Venezuela*. Austin: University of Texas Press.

Yunén, R. E. 1985. *La isla como es: hipótesis para su comprobación*. Santiago: Universidad Católica Madre y Maestra.

Zaiter, J. 1987. 'La identidad como fenómeno psico-social.' *Ciencia y Sociedad* 12:488-499.

Zaiter, R. 1993. *Peña: ¿leal o traidor?* Santo Domingo: Zaiter.

Index